CONTENTS

ANCIENT SECRETS, NEW MEANINGS

- How do the numbers of the gods reveal clues that decipher the secret meanings in divine names?
- What do we now know about the Sumerian understanding of sophisticated genetic knowledge that was passed on to us?
- How could Enoch really write down prophecies of future events, including the secrets of Creation and the cycles of events on Earth, as explained in the *Book of Jubilees*—and how could the Biblical prophets foretell the future?
- Who were the master builders who constructed the platform of the Holy Temple, the Landing Place in Baalbek and the platform on which the Great Pyramid of Giza still stands?

THE COSMIC CODE

Avon Books are available at special quantity discounts for bulk purchases for sales promotions, premiums, fund raising or educational use. Special books, or book excerpts, can also be created to fit specific needs.

For details write or telephone the office of the Director of Special Markets, Avon Books, Inc., Dept. FP, 1350 Avenue of the Americas, New York, New York 10019, 1-800-238-0658.

ZECHARIA SITCHIN

THE
COSMIC CODE

BOOK VI OF THE EARTH CHRONICLES

AVON BOOKS NEW YORK

AVON BOOKS, INC.
1350 Avenue of the Americas
New York, New York 10019

Copyright © 1998 by Zecharia Sitchin
Published by arrangement with the author
Visit our website at **http://www.AvonBooks.com**
Library of Congress Catalog Card Number: 98-93178
ISBN: 0-380-80157-4

First Avon Books Printing: December 1998

AVON TRADEMARK REG. U.S. PAT. OFF. AND IN OTHER COUNTRIES, MARCA
REGISTRADA, HECHO EN U.S.A.

Printed in the U.S.A.

WCD   10 9 8 7 6 5 4 3 2 1

1

STAR STONES

It took a war—a fierce and bloody war—to bring to light, just decades ago, one of the most enigmatic ancient sites in the Near East. If not *the* most enigmatic, it certainly is the most puzzling, and for sure one rooted in great antiquity. It is a structure that has no parallel among the remains of the great civilizations that had flourished in the Near East in past millennia—at least so far as has been uncovered. Its closest parallels are thousands of miles away, across the seas and on other continents; and what it mostly brings to mind is Stonehenge in faraway Britain.

There, on a windswept plain in England about eighty miles southwest of London, circles of imposing megaliths form the most important prehistoric monument in the whole of Britain. There, a semicircle of huge upright stones that have been connected at their tops by lintel stones encompasses within it a semicircle of smaller stone uprights, and is surrounded in turn by two circles of other megaliths. The multitudes that visit the site find that only some of the megaliths still remain standing, while others have collapsed to the ground or are somehow gone from the site. But scholars and researchers have been able to figure out the configuration of the circles-within-circles (Fig. 1, which highlights the still-standing megaliths), and observe the holes indicating where two other circles—of stones or perhaps wooden pegs—had once existed, in earlier phases of Stonehenge.

The horseshoe semicircles, and a fallen large megalith nicknamed the Slaughter Stone, indicate beyond doubt that the structure was oriented on a northeast–southwest axis.

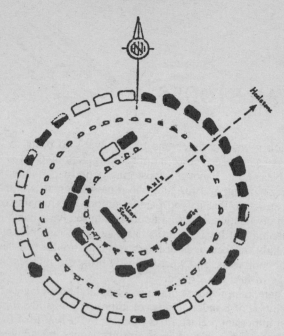

Figure 1

They point to a line of sight that passes between two stone uprights through a long earthworks Avenue, straight to the so-called Heel Stone (Fig. 2). All the studies conclude that the alignments served astronomical purposes; they were first oriented circa 2900 B.C. (give or take a century or so) to sunrise on the summer solstice day; and then realigned circa 2000 B.C. and again circa 1550 B.C. toward sunrise on summer solstice day in those times (Fig. 3).

One of the shortest yet most fierce and ferocious recent wars in the Middle East was the Six Day War of 1967, when the hemmed-in and besieged Israeli army defeated the armies of Egypt, Jordan, and Syria and captured the Sinai peninsula, the West Bank of the Jordan River, and the Golan Heights.

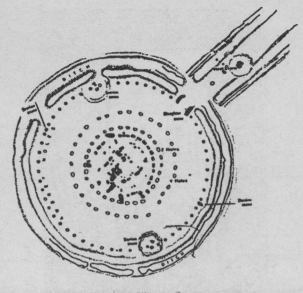

Figure 2

In the years that followed Israeli archaeologists conducted extensive archaeological surveys and excavations in all those areas, bringing to light settlements from early Neolithic times through biblical times to Greek, Roman, and Byzantine periods. Yet nowhere was the surprise greater than on the sparsely inhabited and mostly empty plateau called the Golan Heights. Not only was it discovered that it had been an actively inhabited and cultivated area in the earliest times of human habitation; not only were remains of settlements found from the several millennia preceding the Common Era.

Virtually in the middle of nowhere, on a windswept plain (that had been used by the Israeli army for artillery practice), piles of stones arranged in circles turned out—when viewed from the air—to be a *Near Eastern "Stonehenge"* (Fig. 4).

The unique structure consists of several concentric stone circles, three of them fully circular and two forming only

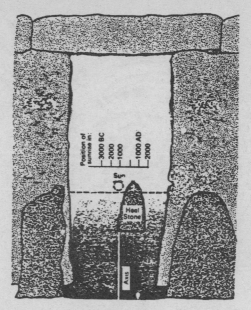

Position of
sunrise in:
—3000 BC
—2000
—1000
—1000 AD
—2000

Sun

Heel
Stone

Axis

Figure 3

semicircles or "horseshoes." The outer circle is almost a third of a mile in circumference, and the other circles get smaller as they get nearer the structure's center. The walls of the three main stone circles rise to eight feet or more, and their width exceeds ten feet. They are constructed of field stones, ranging in size from small to *megalithic ones that weigh five tons and even more*. In several places the circular concentric walls are connected to each other by radial walls, narrower than but about the same height as the circular walls. In the precise center of the complex structure there rises a huge yet well-defined pile of stones, measuring some sixty-five feet across.

Apart from its unique shape, this is by far one of the largest single stone structures in western Asia, so large in

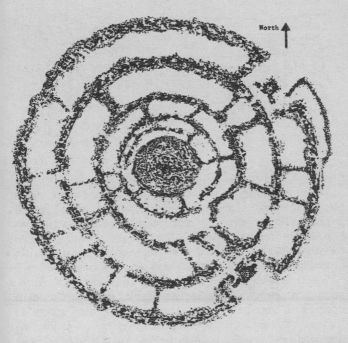

Figure 4

fact that it can be seen from space by Earth-orbiting spacecraft.

Engineers who have studied the site estimated that, even in its present condition, it contains more than 125,000 cubic feet of stones weighing an aggregate of close to 45,000 tons. They estimated that it would have taken one hundred workmen at least six years to create this monument—collect the basalt stones, transport them to the site, place them according to a preconceived architectural plan, and raise the walls (undoubtedly taller than the now-visible remains) to form the cohesive complex structure.

All of which raises the questions, by whom was this structure built, when, and for what?

Figure 5

The easiest question to answer is the last one, for the structure itself seems to indicate its purpose—at least its original purpose. The outermost circle clearly showed that it contained two breaks or openings, one located in the northeast and the other in the southeast—locations that indicate an orientation toward the summer and winter solstices.

Working to clear away fallen rocks and ascertain the original layout, Israeli archaeologists exposed in the northeastern opening a massive square structure with two extended "wings" that protected and hid narrower breaks in the two next concentric walls behind it (Fig. 5); the building thus served as a monumental gate providing (and guarding) an entrance into the heart of the stone complex. It was in the walls of this entryway that the largest basalt boulders, weighing as much as five and a half tons each, were found. The southeastern break in the outer ring also provided access to the inner parts of the structure, but there the entranceway did not possess the monumental building; but piles of fallen stones starting in this entranceway and leading outward from it suggest the outlines of a stone-flanked avenue extending in the southeastern direction—an avenue that might have outlined an astronomical line of sight.

These indications that the place was indeed, as Stonehenge in Britain, built to serve as an astronomical observatory (and primarily to determine the solstices) is reinforced by the existence of such observatories elsewhere—structures that are

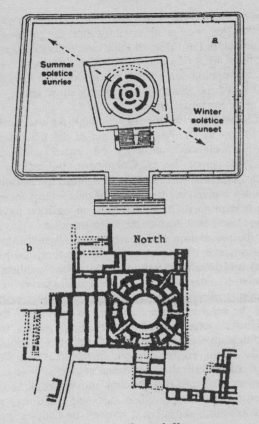

Figures 6a and 6b

even more similar to the one on the Golan, for they feature not only the concentric circles, but also the radial walls connecting the circles. What is amazing is that those similar structures are at ancient sites all the way on the other side of the world, in the Americas.

One is the Mayan site Chichén Itzá in the Yucatán peninsula of Mexico (Fig. 6a), nicknamed the Caracol (''Snail'') on account of the winding stairs inside the observatory's tower. Another is the circular observatory atop the promontory of Sacsahuaman in Peru (Fig. 6b) that overlooks the Inca capital Cuzco; there, as at Chichén Itzá, there was probably a lookout tower; its foundations reveal the layout and astronomical alignments of the structure and clearly show the concentric circles and connecting radials.

Such similarities were reason enough for the Israeli scientists to call in Dr. Anthony Aveni of the USA, an internationally acclaimed authority on ancient astronomies, especially those of the pre-Columbian civilizations of the Americas. His task was not only to confirm the astronomical orientations underlying the design of the Golan site, but also to help determine its age—and thus, in addition to the For What question, also answer the question When.

That the orientation of a structure—if aligned to the solstices—can reveal the time of its construction, has been an accepted tool in archaeoastronomy since the publication of *The Dawn of Astronomy* by Sir Norman Lockyer in 1894. The apparent movement of the Sun from north to south and back as the seasons come and wane is caused by the fact that the Earth's axis (around which the Earth rotates to create the day/night cycle) is inclined to the plane ("ecliptic") in which the Earth orbits the Sun. In this celestial dance—though it is the Earth that moves and not the Sun—it appears to observers on Earth that the Sun, moving back and forth, reaches some distant point, hesitates, stops, and then as if it changed its mind, starts back; crosses the equator, goes all the way to the other extreme, hesitates, and stops there, and goes back. The two crossings a year over the equator (in March and September) are called equinoxes; the two stops, one in the north in June and one in the south in December, are called solstices ("Sun Standstills")—the summer and winter solstices for observers in the Earth's northern hemisphere, as people at Stonehenge and on the Golan had been.

Studying ancient temples, Lockyer divided them into two classes. Some, as the Temple of Solomon in Jerusalem and the temple to Zeus at a place called Baalbek in Lebanon, were built along an east–west axis that oriented them to sunrise on the days of the equinoxes. Others, as pharaonic temples in Egypt, were aligned on an axis inclined southwest–northeast, which meant that they were oriented to the solstices. He was surprised, however, to discover that while in the former the orientation never changed (so he called them Eternal Temples), the latter—such as the great Egyptian temples in Karnak—showed that as successive Pharaohs needed to see the rays of the Sun strike the holy of holies on the day of the solstice, they kept changing the direction of the avenues and corridors toward a slightly different point in the skies. Such realignments were also made at Stonehenge.

What had caused those directional changes? Lockyer's answer was: changes in the Earth's inclination, resulting from its wobble.

Nowadays the inclination of the Earth's axis ("obliquity") to its orbital path ("ecliptic") is 23.5 degrees, and it is this inclination that determines how far northward or southward the Sun would appear to move seasonally. If this angle of inclination were to remain unchanged forever, the solstice points would also remain the same. But astronomers have concluded that the Earth's tilt (caused by its wobble) changes over the centuries and millennia, rising and falling over and over again.

Right now, as in the preceding several millennia, the tilt has been in a narrowing phase. It was over 24 degrees circa 4000 B.C., declined to 23.8 degrees circa 1000 B.C., and continued to fall to its present smidgen under 23.5 degrees. The great innovation of Sir Norman Lockyer was to apply this change in Earth's obliquity to the ancient temples and establish the dates of construction of the various phases of the Great Temple in Karnak (Fig. 7) as well as for the phases of Stonehenge (as indicated by changes in the location of the Heel Stone, Fig. 3).

The same principles have since been used to determine the age of astronomically oriented structures in South America earlier this century, by Arthur Posnansky in respect to the ruins of Tiwanaku on the shores of Lake Titicaca, and by

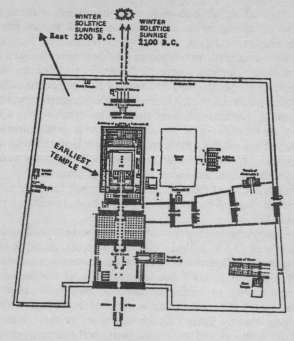

Figure 7

Rolf Müller for the semicircular Torreon in Machu Picchu and the famed Temple of the Sun in Cuzco. Their meticulous researches showed that in order to determine exactly the angle of the Earth's tilt—which indicates, when elevation and geographic position are taken into account, the structure's age—it is essential to determine precisely where north is. It is thus undoubtedly significant that in the case of the Golan site, the researchers there found that the dominant and on clear days visible *peak of Mount Hermon lies precisely north of the structure's center.* Dr. Aveni and his Israeli colleagues, Yonathan Mizrachi and Mattanyah Zohar, were thus able to determine that the site was so oriented as to enable an observer standing in its center and following a sight line through the center of the northeastern gateway, to see the Sun rise there on solstice day on a June dawn at about *3000 B.C.*!

By 2000 B.C., the scientists concluded, the Sun would have appeared to a similar observer noticeably off-center, but probably still within the gateway. Five hundred years later, the structure had lost its value as a precise astronomical observatory. It was, then, sometime between 1500 and 1200 B.C.—as confirmed by carbon dating of small artifacts recovered there—that the central stone heap was enlarged to form a cairn—a stone mound under which a cavity has been dug out, probably to serve as a burial chamber.

Uncannily, these phased dates are virtually identical to the dates assigned to the three phases of Stonehenge.

Because it was protected by the mound of stones above it, the cavity under the cairn—the presumed burial chamber—remained the most intact part of the ancient site. It was located with the aid of sophisticated seismic instruments and ground-penetrating radar. Once a large cavity had been indicated, the excavators (led by Dr. Yonathan Mizrachi) dug a trench that led them into a circular chamber of over six feet in diameter and about five feet high. It led to a larger chamber, oval in shape, about eleven feet long and about four feet wide. The latter's walls were constructed of six courses of basalt stones rising in a corbelled fashion (i.e. slanting inward as the walls rose); the chamber's ceiling was made of two massive basalt slabs, each weighing some five tons.

There was no coffin and no body, nor any other human or animal remains in either the chamber or antechamber. But the archaeologists did find, as a result of meticulous sifting of the soil, a few gold earrings, several beads made of carnelian semiprecious stone, flint blades, bronze arrowheads, and ceramic shards. They therefore concluded that indeed it was a burial chamber, but one that had been looted, probably in antiquity. The fact that some of the stones used to pave the chamber's floor were pried out reinforced the conclusion that the place had been broken into by grave robbers.

The finds have been dated to the period known as Late Bronze Age, which extended from about 1500 to 1200 B.C. That was the time frame of the Exodus of the Children of Israel from Egypt under the leadership of Moses, and the conquest of the Promised Land under the leadership of Joshua. Of the twelve tribes, the tribes of Reuben and Gad and half the tribe of Manasseh were allotted parts of Transjordan, from the River Arnon in the south to the foothills of Mount Hermon in the north. Those domains included the mountain range of Gilad east of the Jordan River and the plateau that is now the Golan. It was therefore perhaps unavoidable that Israeli researchers turned to the Bible for an answer to the question: Who?

According to the books of Numbers and Joshua, the northern part of the Gilead mountains was ruled by a king called Og from his capital of Bashan. The capture of Og's domain is described in Deuteronomy (chapter 3). "Og and all his men took the field against the Children of Israel," the narrative states. Winning the battle, the Israelites captured sixty towns that were "fortified with high walls and gates and barriers, apart from a great number of unwalled towns." The construction of high stone walls and gates—features of the enigmatic Golan site—was thus within the capabilities of the kingdoms in the time of King Og.

Og, according to the Bible, was a big and stout man: "His iron bedstead is nine cubits long and four cubits wide" (equivalent to over thirteen feet and six feet, respectively). This giant size, the Bible hints, was due to his being a descendant of the Repha'im, a giantlike race of demigods who had once dwelt in that land. (Other giantlike descendants of the Repha'im, including Goliath, are mentioned in the Bible as siding with the Philistines at the time of David). Combining the references to the Repha'im with the biblical account of the circular stone structure erected by Joshua after the crossing of the Jordan River, and the naming of the place Gilgal—"The Circular Stone Heap"—some in Israel have nicknamed the Golan site Gilgal Repha'im—"The Circular Stone Heap of the Repha'im."

While the biblical verses alone do not support such a naming, nor do they really link King Og to the burial chambers, the biblical assertions that the area had once been the domain of the Repha'im and that Og was descended of them are quite intriguing, because we find the Repha'im and their offspring mentioned in Canaanite myths and epic tales. The texts, which clearly place the divine and semidivine actions and events in the area we are dealing with here, were written on clay tablets discovered in the 1930s at a coastal site in northern Syria whose ancient name was Ugarit. The texts describe a group of deities whose father was El ("God, the Lofty One") and whose affairs centered on El's son Ba'al ("the Lord") and his sister Anat ("She who answers"). The focus of Ba'al's attention was the mountainous stronghold and sacred place Zaphon (meaning both "the northern place" and "the place of secrets") and the arena of Ba'al and his sister was what nowadays is northern Israel and the Golan. Roaming the area's skies with them was their sister Shepesh (the name's uncertain meaning suggests an association with the Sun); and of her the texts clearly state that "she governs the Repha'im, the divine ones" and rules over demigods and mortals.

Several of the discovered texts deal with such involvement on the part of the trio. One, titled by scholars *The Tale of Aqhat*, pertains to Danel ("Whom God Judges," Daniel in Hebrew), who—although a Rapha-Man (i.e. descended of the Repha'im)—could not have a son. Growing old and despondent about not having a male heir, Danel appeals to Ba'al and Anat, who in turn intercede with El. Granting the Rapha-Man's wish, El instills in him a "quickening lifebreath" and enables him to mate with his wife and have a son whom the gods name Aqhat.

Another tale, *The Legend of King Keret* (Keret, "The Capital, the Metropolis," is used as the name of both the city and its king), concerns the claim to immortality by Keret because of his divine descent. Instead, he falls ill; and his sons wonder aloud: "How could an offspring of El, the Merciful One, die? Shall a divine one die?" Foreseeing the seemingly incredible death of a demigod, the sons envision not only the Peak of Zaphon, but also the Circuit of Broad Span lamenting for Keret:

> *For thee, father,*
> *shall weep Zaphon, the Mount of Ba'al.*
> *The sacred circuit, the mighty circuit,*
> *the circuit of broad span,*
> *[for thee] shall lament.*

There is here, then, a reference to two highly venerated places that shall mourn the death of the demigod: Mount Zaphon, the Mount of Ba'al—and a renowned sacred *circular* structure—"the sacred circuit, the mighty circuit, the circuit of broad span." If Mount Zaphon, the "Mount of the North," was Mount Hermon, which lies precisely north of the Golan site, *was then the Sacred Circuit the enigmatic Golan site?*

Granting appeals for mercy, El at the last moment sent the goddess Shataqat, "a female who removes the illness," to save Keret. "She flies over a hundred towns, she flies over a multitude of villages" on her rescue mission; arriving at Keret's home in the nick of time, she manages to revive him.

But being only a demigod, Keret in the end did die. Was he then the one buried in the tomb within "the sacred circuit, the mighty circuit, the circuit of broad span"? Though the Canaanite texts give no chronological hint, it is evident that they relate events from the Bronze Age—a time frame that could well fit the date of the artifacts discovered in the Golan site's tomb.

Whether or not any of those legendary rulers ended up being buried at the Golan site, we may never know for sure; especially since the archaeologists studying the site raised the possibility of intrusive burials—namely, the entombment of a later-deceased in a burial place from earlier times, involving as often as not the removal of the earlier remains. They are, however, certain (based on structural features and various dating techniques) that the construction of the "henge"—concentric walls of what we might dub Star Stones because of the astronomical function—preceded, by 1,000 to 1,500 years, the addition of the cairn and its burial chambers.

As at Stonehenge and other megalithic sites, so too regarding the Golan site, the enigma of who built them is only intensified by establishing their age and determining that an advanced knowledge of astronomy underlay their orientations. Unless they were indeed the divine beings themselves, who was there capable of the feat—circa 3000 B.C. in the case of the Golan site?

In 3000 B.C. there was in western Asia only one civilization high enough, sophisticated enough, and with an extraordinary astronomical knowledge, capable of planning, orienting astronomically, and carrying out the kind of major structures here considered: the Sumerian civilization. It blossomed out in what is nowadays southern Iraq, "suddenly, unexpectedly, out of nowhere" in the words of all scholars. And within a few centuries—an instant as human evolution goes—accounted for virtually all the firsts of what we deem essential to a high civilization, from the wheel to the kiln and bricks and high-rise buildings, writing and poetry and music, codes of law and courts, judges and contracts, temples and priests, kings and administrators, schools and teachers, doctors and nurses; and amazing knowledge of mathematics, exact sciences, and astronomy. Their calendar, still in use as the Jewish calendar, was inaugurated in a city called Nippur in 3760 B.C.—embracing all the sophisticated knowledge required for the structures we are discussing.

It was a civilization that preceded that of Egypt by some eight hundred years and by a thousand years that of the Indus Valley. The Babylonians, Assyrians, Hittites, Elamites, Canaanites, and Phoenicians followed later, some much later. They all bore the imprint and borrowed the underlying firsts of the Sumerians; so did the civilizations that in time rose in Greece and the Mediterranean islands.

Did the Sumerians venture as far as the Golan Heights? Undoubtedly, for their kings and their merchants went westward toward the Mediterranean Sea (which they called the

Upper Sea), and sailed the waters of the Lower Sea (the Persian Gulf) to other distant lands. When Ur was their capital, its merchants were familiar in all parts of the ancient Near East. And one of Sumer's most famed kings, Gilgamesh—a famed king of Uruk (the biblical Erech)—in all probability passed through the site. The time was circa 2900 B.C., soon after the Golan site was first constructed.

The father of Gilgamesh was the city's High Priest; his mother was the goddess Ninsun. Aiming to be a mighty king and aggrandize his city, Gilgamesh started his reign by challenging the authority of the then-principal city of Sumer, Kish. A clay tablet describing the episode names the king of Kish Agga, and twice describes him as being "stout." Kish was then the capital of a wide domain that might have extended beyond the Euphrates River; and one must wonder whether the stout king Agga might have been a forerunner of the giantlike Og of biblical fame; for the naming of kings after earlier predecessors was a common Near Eastern practice.

Proud, ambitious, and swashbuckling in his youth, Gilgamesh took hard his creeping aging. To sustain his prowess he took to dropping in on newlyweds in his city, claiming the royal right to be the first to have sex with the bride. When the townspeople could not stand it anymore, they appealed to the gods for help; and the gods responded by creating a double for Gilgamesh, who stopped the king's shenanigans. Subdued, Gilgamesh grew gloomy and reflective. He witnessed people his age or even younger dying; and then it occurred to him that there is another way: he was, after all, partly divine—not just a *demi*god, but *two-thirds* divine, for it was not his father but his mother who was a goddess!

Should he, Gilgamesh, then die as a mortal, or be entitled to the everlasting life of the gods? He presented his case to his mother. Yes, she told him, you are right. But in order to attain the divine life span, you must ascend the heavens and reach the gods' abode. And the places from which such ascents are possible, she told him, are under the command of his godfather Utu (later known as Shamash).

Utu/Shamash tried to dissuade Gilgamesh: "Who, Gilgamesh, can scale heaven? Only the gods live forever under the Sun. As for Mankind, numbered are their days.'' Go, be with your family and your townsfolk, enjoy the rest of your days, the god said to him.

The story of Gilgamesh and his quest for immortality is told in the *Epic of Gilgamesh*, a long text written on clay tablets and discovered by archaeologists in both the original Sumerian and various ancient translations. As the tale unfolds, we read that Gilgamesh was not dissuaded, and an object that fell from the skies was deemed by him a sign from heaven that he should not give up. Agreeing to help, Ninsun revealed to him that there is a place in the Cedar Mountains—the Landing Place—from which Gilgamesh could ascend to the divine abode. It would be a journey fraught with dangers, she warned Gilgamesh. But what is the alternative? he asked her. If I fail in my quest, he said, at least future generations will know that I tried.

Giving her blessing to the journey, Ninsun insisted that the artificial man, Enkidu, go in front of Gilgamesh and protect him along the way. The choice was opportune, for the area of their destination was the very area from which Enkidu had come, the hills where he had roamed with the wild beasts. He explained to Gilgamesh how dangerous the undertaking would be; but Gilgamesh insisted on going.

In order to reach the Cedar Mountains in what is now Lebanon from Sumer (which was in what is now southern Iraq), Gilgamesh had to cross the plateau that we now call the Golan. And indeed we find it stated, in the preamble to the epic in which the king's adventures and achievements are enumerated, that it was ''he who opened the mountain passes.'' It was a first that merited recalling, for there are no mountains in the land called Sumer.

On their way Gilgamesh stopped several times to seek divine oracles from the Sun God. When they reached the hill land and the woodlands (the likes of which there were none in Sumer), Gilgamesh had a series of omen-dreams. At a crucial stop, from where they could already see the Cedar Mountains, Gilgamesh sought to induce a dream-omen by

Figure 8

sitting within a circle that was formed for him by Enkidu. Was it Enkidu, possessing superhuman strength, who arranged the field stones for Gilgamesh to form Star Stones?

We can only guess. But physical evidence attesting to the familiarity of those who had lived on the Golan Heights for generations with Gilgamesh and his tale has recently been found on the Heights.

One of the most recounted episodes in the king's adventures has been the incident in which he encountered two ferocious lions, fought them off, and killed them with his bare hands. The heroic deed was a favorite subject of Near Eastern artists in antiquity. Yet it was a totally unexpected discovery to find, at a site near the concentric circles, a stone slab with such a depiction (Fig. 8)! (The artifact is on exhibit at the new and most-interesting Golan Archaeological Museum in Qatzrin).

While the textual references and the depiction on the stone slab do not constitute conclusive evidence that Gilgamesh reached the site on his journey to the Cedar Mountains of Lebanon, there is one more intriguing clue to be considered. After the site was identified from the air, the Israeli archaeologists discovered that it was marked on (captured) Syrian army maps by the name Rugum el-Hiri—a most puzzling name, for it meant in Arabic "Stone heap of the bobcat."

The explanation for the puzzling name, we suggest, may well lie in the *Epic of Gilgamesh*, reflecting a memory of the King Who Fought the Lions.

And, as we shall see, that is just the beginning of intricate and interwound associations.

2

FATE HAS TWELVE STATIONS

Scholars have long recognized that in the lore of diverse nations the same theme, the same basic tale, appears and reappears though under different guises, names, and localities. It is thus perhaps no wonder that the carved basalt stone on which Gilgamesh is depicted fighting with the lions was discovered near a village bearing the name Ein Samsum—"Samson's Spring." For, it will be recalled, Samson also fought and killed a lion with his bare hands. That was some two thousand years after Gilgamesh, and certainly not on the Golan Heights. Is the village's name, then, just a coincidence, or the lingering memory of a visitor called Gilgamesh becoming Samson?

Of greater significance is the association with King Keret. Though the venue of the Canaanite tale is not stated, it is presumed by many (e.g. Cyrus H. Gordon, *Notes on the Legend of Keret*) that the combined name for the king and his capital in fact identified the island of Crete. There, according to Cretan and Greek legends, civilization began when the god Zeus saw Europa, the beautiful daughter of a king of Phoenicia (present-day Lebanon) and, taking the form of a bull, abducted her and swam with her on his back across the Mediterranean Sea to the island of Crete. There he had three sons by her, among them Minos, who in time became the one with whom the beginning of Cretan civilization is associated.

Thwarted in his aspirations to the throne, Minos appealed to Poseidon, god of the seas, to bestow upon him a sign of divine favor. In response, Poseidon made a Divine Bull, pure white, appear from the sea. Minos vowed to offer the beau-

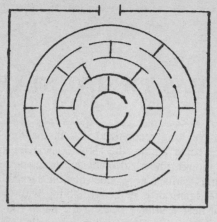

Figure 9

tiful bull as a sacrifice to the god, but was so enthralled by
it that instead he kept it to himself. In punishment, the god
made the king's wife fall in love and mate with the bull; the
offspring was the legendary Minotaur, a half-man, half-bull
creature. Minos then commissioned the divine craftsman
Daedalus to build in the Cretan capital Knossos an underground maze from which the bull-man would be unable to
escape. The maze was called the Labyrinth.

A huge stone sculpture of a bull's horns does greet the
visitor to the excavated remains of Knossos, but not the remains of the Labyrinth. Yet its memory and its circular
shape, as a maze of concentric circular walls with passages
blocked by radials (as in this suggested layout, Fig. 9) have
not been forgotten.

It certainly resembles the layout of the Golan site; and it
calls for going back to the *Epic of Gilgamesh* for the heroes'
encounter with the Bull of Heaven.

As the epic tells it, during the final night before attempting
to enter the Cedar Forest, Gilgamesh envisioned a rocketship
thunderously rising, in a fiery ascent, from the Landing
Place. The next morning they found the hidden entryway into

Figure 10

the forbidden enclosure; but no sooner did they start on their way in than a robotic guardian blocked their way. It was "mighty, its teeth as the teeth of a dragon, its face of a ferocious lion, its advance like the onrushing headwaters." A "radiating beam" emanated from its forehead, "devouring trees and bushes"; "from its killing force, none could escape."

Seeing the predicament of Gilgamesh and Enkidu, Utu/Shamash "down from the skies spoke to the heroes." He advised them not to run, but instead to draw near the monster as soon as the god would blow a swirling wind whose dust would blind the guardian. As soon as that happened, Enkidu struck and killed it. Ancient artists depicted on cylinder seals (Fig. 10) Gilgamesh, Enkidu, and Utu/Shamash together with the menacing robot; its depiction brings to mind the biblical description of the "angels with the whirling sword" that God placed at the entrance to the Garden of Eden to make sure that the expelled Adam and Eve would not reenter it.

The fight was also watched by Inanna (later known as Ishtar), the twin sister of Utu/Shamash. She had quite a record of enticing human males to spend a night with her—a night which they rarely survived. Captivated by the beauty of Gilgamesh as he bathed naked in a nearby river or waterfall, she invited him: "Come, Gilgamesh, be my lover!" But knowing the record, he turned her down.

Enraged by this insulting refusal, Ishtar summoned the

Bull of Heaven to smite Gilgamesh. Running for their lives, the duo rushed back to Uruk; but the Bull of Heaven caught up with them on the banks of the Euphrates River. At the moment of mortal danger it was again Enkidu who managed to strike and kill the Bull of Heaven.

Inanna/Ishtar, enraged, "sent up a wail to Heaven," demanding that the two comrades be put to death. Though temporarily spared, Enkidu died first; then so did Gilgamesh (after a second journey that took him to a spaceport in the Sinai peninsula).

What was the Bull of Heaven—GUD.ANNA in Sumerian? Many students of the *Epic*, such as Giorgio de Santillana and Hertha von Dechend in *Hamlet's Mill*, have come to the conclusion that the *Epic*'s events, taking place on Earth, are but a mirror image of events taking place in Heaven. Utu/Shamash is the Sun, Inanna/Ishtar is what she was later called in Greek and Roman times—Venus. The menacing guardian of the Cedar Mountains with the face of a lion is the *constellation of Leo* (the Lion), and the Bull of Heaven the celestial group of stars that has been called— since Sumerian times!—the *constellation of the Bull* (Taurus).

There are, indeed, Mesopotamian depictions with the Lion/ Bull theme (Fig. 11a and 11b); and as was first remarked upon by Willy Hartner (*The Earliest History of the Constellations in the Near East*), in the fourth millennium B.C. the Sumerians would have observed the two constellations in key zodiacal positions: the constellation of the Bull (Taurus) as the constellation of the spring equinox and the constellation of the Lion (Leo) as that of the summer solstice.

The attributing of zodiacal connotations to epic events on Earth, as told by the Sumerians, implies that they had such celestial knowledge—in the fourth millennium B.C., some three millennia before the usually presumed time of the grouping of stars into constellations and the introduction of the twelve zodiacal ones by the Greeks. In fact, the Greek savants (of Asia Minor) themselves explained that the knowledge came to them from the "Chaldeans" of Mesopotamia;

Figures 11a and 11b

and, as Sumerian astronomical texts and pictorial depictions attest, the credit should go to them. Their names and symbols for the zodiacal constellations remained unchanged to our time.

The Sumerian zodiacal lists began with Taurus, which was indeed the constellation from which the Sun was observed rising at dawn on the day of the spring equinox in the fourth millennium B.C. It was called in Sumerian GUD.ANNA ("Bull of Heaven" or "Heavenly Bull")—the very same term used in the *Epic of Gilgamesh* for the divine creature that Inanna/Ishtar had summoned from the heavens and that the two comrades slew.

Did the slaying represent or symbolize an actual celestial event, circa 2900 B.C.? While the possibility cannot be ruled out, the historical record indicates that major events and changes did occur on Earth at that time; and the "slaying" of the Bull of Heaven represented an omen, a heavenly omen, predicting or even triggering events on Earth.

For the better part of the fourth millennium B.C. the Sumerian civilization was not only the greatest on Earth, but also the only one. But circa 3100 B.C. the Civilization of the Nile (Egypt and Nubia) joined the one on the Euphrates-

Figure 12

Tigris Rivers. Did this split-up on Earth—alluded to by the
biblical tale of the Tower of Babel and the end of the era
when Mankind spoke one tongue—find expression in the description (in the Gilgamesh epic) of the coup de grace dealt
the Bull of Heaven by the tearing off of its foreleg by Enkidu? Egyptian celestial-zodiacal depictions indeed associated
the beginning of their civilization with the cutting off of the
forepart of the constellation of the Bull (Fig. 12).

As we have detailed in *The Wars of Gods and Men*, In-
anna/Ishtar had expected at that time to become mistress of
the new civilization, but it was—literally and symbolically—
torn away from her. She was partly appeased when a third
civilization, that of the Indus Valley, was put under her aegis,
circa 2900 B.C.

As significant as celestial omens had been for the gods,
they were even more consequential to mortals on Earth; witness the fate that befell the two comrades. Enkidu, an artificially created being, died as a mortal. And Gilgamesh,
two-thirds divine, could not escape mortality. Though he
went on a second journey, enduring hardships and dangers,
and though he did find the Plant of Everlasting Youth, he
returned to Uruk empty-handed. According to the Sumerian
King List, "the divine Gilgamesh, whose father was a human, the High Priest of the temple precinct, ruled 126 years;
Urlugal, son of Gilgamesh, ruled after him."

We can almost hear the son of Gilgamesh crying out, as

did the sons of King Keret: "How could an offspring of El, The Merciful One, die? Shall a divine one die?" But Gilgamesh, though more than a demigod, tangled with his Fate. His was the Age of the Bull, and he slew it; and his Fate, a Fate made in Heaven, changed from a chance for immortality to that of a mortal's death.

A thousand years after the probable stay of Gilgamesh at the Golan site, it was visited by another ancient VIP who also saw Fate written in the zodiacal constellations. He was Jacob, the grandson of Abraham; and the time, by our calculations, was about 1900 B.C.

A question that is often ignored regarding the megalithic structures around the globe is, Why have they been constructed where they are? The location obviously had to do with their particular purpose. The great pyramids of Giza, we have suggested in our writings, served as anchors for a Landing Corridor leading to a spaceport in the Sinai peninsula, and were emplaced precisely because of that link on the thirtieth parallel north. Stonehenge, it was suggested by leading astronomers, was erected where it is because it is precisely there that its astronomical functions could combine both solar and lunar observations. Until more might come to light concerning the Golan Circles, the most likely reason for its being where it is was that it lay astride one of the few linkways that connected two major international routes (in antiquity and still now): the King's Highway, which ran along the hills east of the Jordan River, and the Way of the Sea, which ran on the west along the coast of the Mediterranean Sea (Map). The two routes connected Mesopotamia and Egypt, Asia and Africa—be it for peaceful trade or military invasions. The links between the two routes were dictated by geography and topography. At the Golan site, the crossing could be made on either side of the Sea of Galilee (Lake Kinnereth); the preferred one—then and now—is the one on the north, where the bridge has retained its ancient name: The Bridge of the Daughters of Jacob.

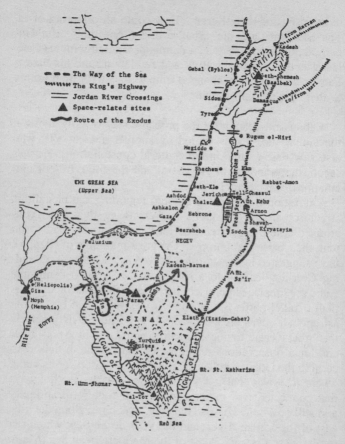

The Golan site was thus located where travelers from different nations and diverse homelands could stop and scan the heavens for omens, to seek out clues regarding their Fates, perhaps to mingle at a neutral site because it was sacred, and there negotiate issues of war or peace.

Based on biblical and Mesopotamian data, we believe that this was what Jacob had used the site for.

The story began two centuries earlier, in Sumer; and it began not with Jacob's grandfather Abraham but with Jacob's great-grandfather, Terah. His name suggests that he was an oracle priest (*Tirhu*); the family's care to be known as *Ibri* (Hebrew) people suggests to us that they considered themselves to be Nippurians—people from the city Nippur that in Sumerian was rendered NI.IBRU—"The Beautiful/ Pleasant Abode of Crossing." The religious and scientific center of Sumer, Nippur was the site of the DUR.AN.KI, the "Bond Heaven-Earth," located in the city's sacred precinct. It was the focal point for the preservation, study, and interpretation of accumulated astronomical, calendrical, and celestial knowledge; and Abraham's father, Terah, was one of its priests.

Circa 2100 B.C. Terah was transferred to Ur. The time was a period known to Sumerologists as Ur III, for it was then that Ur, for the third time, became the capital not only of Sumer, and not only of an enlarged political entity called Sumer and Akkad, but also of a virtual empire that flourished and was held together not by force of arms but by a superior culture, a unified pantheon (what is known as Religion), a capable administration, and—not least of all—a thriving trade. Ur was also the cult-center of the Moon god Nannar (later known by the Semitic people as Sin). Rapidly developing events in Sumer and beyond triggered first the transfer of Terah to Ur and then to a distant city called Harran. Situated on the Upper Euphrates and its tributaries, the city served as a major crossroads and trading post (which its name, meaning the Caravanry, indicated). Founded by Sumerian merchants, Harran also boasted a large temple to the Moon god, so much so that the city was looked upon as an "Ur away from Ur."

On these transfers Terah took with him his family. The move to Harran included Abram (as he was then called), Terah's firstborn; a son called Nahor; the two sons' wives, Sarai (later renamed Sarah) and Milcah; and Terah's grandson Lot, the son of Abram's brother Haran who had died in Ur. They dwelt there, in Harran, "many years" according to the Bible, and it was there that Terah died when he was 205 years old.

It was after that that God said unto Abram: "Get thee out of thy country, and out of thy birthplace, and from thy father's dwelling place, unto the land that I will show thee . . . There I will make thee unto a great nation, and I will bless thee and make great thy name." And Abram took Sarai his wife and Lot his nephew and all the people in their household and all of their belongings, and went to the Land of Canaan; "and Abram was seventy-five years old when he departed from Harran." His brother Nahor stayed behind, with his family, in Harran.

Acting on divine instructions, Abram moved quickly in Canaan to establish a base in the Negev, the arid area of Canaan bordering the Sinai peninsula. On a visit to Egypt he was received in the Pharaoh's court; back in Canaan, he dealt with the local rulers. He then played a role in an international conflict, known in the Bible (Genesis 14) as the War of the Kings. It was after that that God promised Abram that his "seed" should inherit and rule the lands between the Brook of Egypt and the Euphrates River. Doubting the promise, Abram pointed out that he and his wife Sarai had no children. So God told Abram not to worry. "Look now toward the heavens," he told him, "and count the stars if you can . . . so numerous shall be thy seed." But Sarai remained barren even after that.

So, at her suggestion Abram slept with her handmaiden Hagar, who did bear him a son, Ishmael. And then, miraculously—after the upheaval of Sodom and Gomorrah, when the couple's names were changed to Abraham and Sarah— Abraham, then aged one hundred, had a son by his wife Sarah, aged ninety. Though not the firstborn, Sarah's son, Isaac, was the Legitimate Heir under the Sumerian succession rules that the Patriarch followed; for he was a son of his father's half sister: "the daughter of my father but not of my mother," Abraham said of Sarah (Genesis 20:12).

It was after the death of Sarah, his lifelong companion, that Abraham, "old and advanced in years" (137 years, by our calculations) became concerned about his unmarried son Isaac. Fearing that Isaac would end up marrying a Canaanite, he sent the overseer of his household to Harran, to find there a bride for Isaac from among the relatives that had remained there. Arriving at the dwelling village of Nahor, he met at the watering well Rebecca, who turned out to be Nahor's granddaughter and ended up going to Canaan to become Isaac's wife.

Twenty years after they got married Rebecca gave birth to twins, Esau and Jacob. Esau was first to get married, taking two wives right off, both of them Hittite lasses; "they were a source of grief to Isaac and Rebecca." The troubles are not detailed in the Bible, but the situation between mother and daughters-in-law was so bad that Rebecca told Isaac: "I am disgusted with life on account of the Hittite women; should Jacob too marry such a Hittite woman, of the local females, what good would life be to me?" So Isaac called Jacob and instructed him to go to Harran, to his mother's family, to find there a bride. Heeding his father's words, "Jacob left Beersheba and set out for Harran."

Of Jacob's journey from the south of Canaan to distant Harran, the Bible reports only one episode—though a very significant one. It was the nighttime vision by Jacob, "as he came upon a certain place," of a stairway to heaven on which Angels of the Lord were ascending and descending. Awakened, Jacob realized that he had come upon "a place of the *Elohim* and a gateway to heaven." He marked the place by setting up there a commemorative stone, and named the site Beth-El—"The House of El," the Lord. And then, by a route that is not stated, he continued to Harran.

On the city's outskirts he saw shepherds gathering with their flocks at a well in the field. Addressing them, Jacob inquired whether they knew Laban, his mother's brother. Indeed we know him, the shepherds said, and here comes his daughter Rachel, shepherding his flocks. Bursting into tears, Jacob introduced himself as the son of Rebecca, her aunt. No sooner did Laban hear the news than he, too, came running, hugging and kissing his nephew, inviting him to stay with him and meet his other daughter, the older Leah. Marriage was clearly in the father's mind; but Jacob fell in love with Rachel, and offered to work for Laban seven years in lieu of a dowry. But on the night of the wedding, after the banquet, Laban substituted Leah for Rachel in the bridal bed . . .

When Jacob discovered the bride's identity in the morning, Laban was nonplussed. Here, he said, we do not marry off the younger daughter before her elder sister; why don't you work for me another seven years, and then marry Rachel, too? Still in love with Rachel, Jacob agreed. After seven years, he married Rachel; but the wily Laban held on to the hard worker and capable shepherd that Jacob was, and would not let him go. To keep Jacob from leaving, he let him start raising his own flocks; but the more Jacob succeeded, the more were Laban's sons grumbling with envy.

And so it was, when Laban and his sons were away to shear their flocks of sheep, that Jacob gathered his wives and children and flocks and fled Harran. "And he crossed the river"—the Euphrates—"and set his course toward the mount of Gile'ad."

"On the third day it was told to Laban that Jacob had escaped; so he took his kinfolk with him and pursued after Jacob; and after seven days he caught up with him at the mount of Gilead."

Gilad—"The Everlasting Stone Heap" in Hebrew—the site of the circular observatory in the Golan!

The encounter started with bitter exchanges and reciprocal accusations. It ended with a peace treaty. In the manner of boundary treaties of the time, Jacob selected a stone and erected it to be a Witnessing Pillar, to mark the boundary beyond which Laban would not cross into Jacob's domains nor would Jacob cross to Laban's domains. Such boundary stones, called *Kudurru* in Akkadian because of their rounded tops, have been discovered at various Near Eastern sites. As a rule, they were inscribed with details of the treaty and included the invoking of each side's gods as witnesses and guarantors. Adhering to the custom, Laban called for "the God of Abraham and the gods of Nahor'' to guarantee the treaty. Apprehensive, Jacob ''swore by the fear of his father Isaac.'' Then he added his own touch to the occasion and the place:

> *And Jacob said to his sons:*
> *Gather stones;*
> *And they gathered stones*
> *and arranged them in a heap . . .*
> *And Jacob called the stone heap*
> *Gal'ed.*

By a mere change of pronunciation, from *Gilad* to *Gal-Ed*, Jacob changed the meaning of the name from its long-standing ''The Everlasting Stone Heap'' to ''The Stone Heap of Witnessing.''

How certain can we be that the place was that of the Golan circles' site? Here, we believe, is the convincing final clue: In his oath of treaty, Jacob also described the site as *Ha-Mitzpeh—the Observatory*!

The *Book of Jubilees*, an extrabiblical book that recounted the biblical tales from varied early sources, added a postscript to the recorded event: ''And Jacob made there a heap for a witness, wherefore the name of the place is called 'The Heap of Witness'; but before they used to call the land of Gilead the Land of the Repha'im.''

And thus we are back to the enigmatic Golan site and its nickname Gilgal Repha'im.

The *Kudurru* boundary stones that have been found in the Near East bore, as a rule, not just the terms of the agreement and the names of the gods invoked as its guarantors, but also the gods' celestial symbols—sometimes of the Sun and Moon and planets, sometimes of the zodiacal constellations (as in Fig. 13)—all twelve of them. For that, since the earliest Sumerian times, was the count—twelve—of the zodiacal constellations, as evidenced by their names:

Figure 13

GUD.ANNA—Heavenly Bull (*Taurus*)
MASH.TAB.BA—Twins (*Gemini*)
DUB—Pincers, Tongs (*Cancer*)
UR.GULA—Lion (*Leo*)
AB.SIN—Whose Father Was Sin ("the Maiden" = *Virgo*)
ZI.BA.AN.NA—Heavenly Fate ("the Scales" = *Libra*)
GIR.TAB—Which Claws and Cuts (*Scorpio*)
PA.BIL—the Defender ("the Archer" = *Sagittarius*)
SUHUR.MASH—Goat-Fish (*Capricorn*)
GU—Lord of the Waters (*Aquarius*)
SIM.MAH—Fishes (*Pisces*)
KU.MAL—Field Dweller (the Ram = *Aries*)

1. Aries. 2. Taurus. 3. Gemini. 4. Cancer. 5. Leo. 6. Virgo. 7. Libra. 8. Scorpio. 9. Sagittarius. 10. Capricorn 11. Aquarius. 12. Pisces.

Figure 14

While not all the symbols depicting the twelve zodiacal constellations have survived from Sumerian times, or even Babylonian times, they have been found on Egyptian monuments, in identical depictions and names (Fig. 14).

Should anyone doubt that Abraham, a son of the astronomer-priest Terah, was aware of the twelve zodiacal houses when God told him to observe the skies and see therein the future? As the stars you observe in the heavens, so shall thy offspring be, God told Abraham; and when his

first son was born by the handmaiden Hagar, God blessed
the boy, Ishmael ("By God Heard"), by this prophecy:

> *As for Ishmael:*
> *Indeed I have heard him.*
> *By this do I bless him:*
> *I will make him fruitful*
> *and I will multiply him exceedingly;*
> *Of him twelve chieftains will be born,*
> *his shall be a great nation.*
>
> *Genesis 17:20*

With that prophetic blessing, linked to the starry heavens
as observed by Abraham, does the Bible for the first time
record the number twelve and its significance. It then relates
(Genesis 25) that Ishmael's sons—each a chief of a tribal
state—indeed numbered twelve. Listing them by their names,
the Bible emphasizes: "Those were the sons of Ishmael according to their courts and strongholds—twelve chieftains,
each to his own nation." Their domains encompassed Arabia
and the desertland to its north.

The next time the Bible employs the number twelve is in
listing Jacob's twelve sons at the time when he was back at
his father's estate in Hebron. "And the number of the sons
of Jacob was twelve," the Bible states in Genesis 35, listing
them by the names that later became familiar as names of
the Twelve Tribes of Israel:

Six by Leah:
Reuben, Simeon, Levi, Judah, Issachar, Zebulun.
Two by Rachel:
Joseph, Benjamin.
Two by Bilhah, *Rachel's handmaiden:*
Dan, Naphtali.
And two by Zilpah, *Leah's handmaiden:*
Gad and Asher.

There is, however, sleight of hand in this list: This was not the original count of the twelve children who came back with Jacob to Canaan: Benjamin, the youngest, was born by Rachel when the family was already back in Canaan, in Bethlehem, where she died while giving birth. Yet the number of Jacob's children was twelve before that: The last child born by Leah was a *daughter*, Dinah. The list—perhaps by more than a coincidence—was thus made up of eleven males and one female, matching the list of zodiacal constellations that is made up of one female (Virgo, the Virgin) and eleven "male" ones.

The zodiacal implications of the twelve children of Jacob (renamed *Israel* after he had wrestled with a divine being when crossing the Jordan River) can be discerned twice in the continuing biblical narrative. Once, when Joseph—a master of having and solving dream-omens—boasted to his brothers that he had dreamed that the Sun and the Moon (the elder Jacob and Leah) and eleven *Kokhavim* were bowing to him. The word is usually translated "stars," but the term (stemming from the Akkadian) served equally to denote constellations. With Joseph's, the total added up to twelve. The implication, that his was a superior constellation, annoyed greatly his brothers.

The next time was when Jacob, old and dying, called his twelve sons to bless them and foretell their future. Known as the *Prophecy of Jacob*, the last words of the Patriarch begin by associating the eldest son, Reuben, with Az—the zodiacal constellation of Aries (which, by then, was the constellation of the spring equinox instead of Taurus). Simeon and Levi were lumped together as the Twins, Gemini; because they had killed many men when they revenged the rape of their sister, Jacob prophesied, they would be dispersed among the other tribes and forfeit their own domains. Judah was compared to a Lion (Leo) and foreseen as the holder of the royal scepter—a prediction of Judea's kingship. Zebulun was envisioned as a Dweller of the Seas (Aquarius), which he indeed became. The predictions of the twelve tribal sons' future continued, linked by name and symbol to the zodiacal

constellations. Last were Rachel's sons: Joseph was depicted
as the Bowman (Sagittarius); and the last one, Benjamin—
having substituted for his sister Dinah (Virgo)—was described as a predator that feeds off others.

The strict adherence to the number twelve, emulating the
twelve houses of the zodiac, involved another sleight of hand
that usually escapes notice. After the Exodus and the division
of the Promised Land among the Twelve Tribes, they again
included some rearrangement. Suddenly the account of the
Twelve Tribes who shared territories lists the two sons of
Joseph (who were born to him in Egypt)—Manasseh and
Ephra'im. The list, nevertheless, stayed at twelve; for, as
prophesied by Jacob, the tribes of Simeon and Levi did not
share in the territorial distributions and, as foretold, were
dispersed among the other tribes. The requirement—the
sanctity—of the Celestial Twelve was again preserved.

Archaeologists excavating the remains of Jewish synagogues in the Holy Land are sometimes puzzled to find the
floors of such synagogues decorated with the zodiacal circle
of twelve constellations, depicted by their traditional symbols
(Fig. 15). They tend to view the finds as aberrations resulting
from Greek and Roman influences in the centuries before
Christianity. Such an attitude, stemming from the belief that
the practice was prohibited by the Old Testament, ignores
the historical record—the Hebrews' familiarity with the zodiacal constellations and their association with predictions of
the future—with Fate.

For generations and to this day, one can hear cries of
Mazal-tov! Mazal-tov! at Jewish weddings or when a boy is
circumcised. Ask anyone what it means, and the answer will
be: It means ''Good Luck,'' let the couple or boy have good
luck with them.

Few realize, however, that though that is what is intended,
that is not what the phrase means. *Mazal-tov* literally means
''a good/favorable *zodiacal constellation.*'' The term comes
from the Akkadian (the first or Mother Semitic language), in
which *Manzalu* meant ''station''—the zodiacal station in

Figure 15

which the Sun was seen to "station" itself on the day of wedding or birth.

Such an association of one's zodiacal house with one's Fate is in vogue through horoscopic astrology, which starts by establishing (through the date of birth) what sign one is—a Pisces, a Cancer, or any other of the twelve zodiacal constellations. Going back, we could say that according to the Prophecy of Jacob, Judah was a Leo, Gad a Scorpio, and Naphtali a Capricorn.

The observation of the heavens for fateful indications, a task performed by a corps of astronomer-priests, assumed a key role in royal decisions during Babylonian times. The fate of the king, the fate of the land and of nations were divined from the position of the planets in a particular zodiacal constellation. Royal decisions awaited the word of astronomer-priests. Was the Moon, expected in Sagittarius, obscured by clouds? Had the comet seen in Taurus moved on to another constellation? What was the meaning for the king or the land of the observation that, on the same evening, Jupiter rose in Sagittarius, Mercury in Gemini, and Saturn in Scorpio? Records literally requiring hundreds of tablets reveal that those heavenly phenomena were interpreted to foretell invasions, famines, floodings, civil unrest—or, on the other hand, long life for the king, a stable dynasty, victory in war, prosperity. Most of the records of such observations were written down as straight prose on clay tablets; sometimes, the astrological almanacs, as horoscopical handbooks, were illustrated with the symbols of the relevant zodiacal constellations. In all instances, Fate was deemed to be indicated by the heavens.

Today's horoscopic astrology's roots go back well beyond the Babylonians, the ''Chaldeans'' of Greek reports. Coupled with the twelve-month calendar, the notion that Fate and the Zodiac are two aspects of the same course of events undoubtedly began at least when the calendar began—in Nippur, in 3760 B.C. (which is when the count of the Jewish calendar began). That such an association is really that old can be gleaned, in our opinion, from one of the Sumerian constellation names, that of ZI.BA.AN.NA. The term, understood to mean ''Heavenly Fate,'' literally means ''Life-Decision in the heavens'' as well as ''The Heavenly Scales of Life.'' This was a concept that was recorded in Egypt in the *Book of the Dead*; it was a belief that one's hope for an eternal afterlife depends on the weighing of his heart on the Day of Judgment. The scene was magnificently depicted on the Papyrus of Ani, where the god Anubis is shown weighing the heart in a balance and the god Thoth, the Divine Scribe, recording the result on a pallet (Fig. 16).

An unsolved puzzle in Jewish traditions is why the biblical Lord had chosen the *seventh* month, Tishrei, as the month in which the Hebrew New Year was to begin, rather than starting it in the month counted in Mesopotamia as the first month, Nissan. If it was, as has been suggested by way of

Figure 16

an explanation, a desire to enforce a clear break from the Mesopotamian veneration of stars and planets, why still call it the seventh month and not renumber it the first month?

It seems to us that the opposite is true, and that the answer lies in the very name of the constellation ZI.BA.AN.NA and its connotation of the Scales of Fate. We believe that the crucial clue is the calendrical link with the zodiac. At the time of the Exodus (mid–second millennium B.C.) the first constellation, that of the spring equinox, was Aries, not Taurus anymore. *And starting with Aries, the constellation of the Heavenly Scales of Life was indeed the seventh*. The month in which the Jewish New Year was to begin, the month in which it would be decided in heaven who is to live and who is to die, who is to be healthy or to be sick, to be richer or poorer, happy or unhappy—was the month that paralleled the zodiacal month of the Celestial Scales.

And in the heavens, Fate had twelve stations.

3

DIVINE GENERATIONS

The twelve-part zodiac and its antiquity stir up two puzzles: Who originated it and why was the celestial circle divided into *twelve* parts?

The answers require the crossing of a threshold—to a realization that underlying the seemingly astrological significance of dividing the heavens into twelve parts is a highly sophisticated astronomy—an astronomy, in fact, so advanced that Man, by himself, could not have possessed it when this division of the celestial circle began.

In its annual orbit around the Sun, the Sun appears to be rising each month—a twelfth part of the year—in a different station. But the one that counts most, the one that was deemed crucial in antiquity and which determines the transition from Age to Age (from Taurus to Aries to Pisces and soon to Aquarius), is the one in which the Sun is seen rising on the day of the spring equinox (Fig. 17). As it happens, the Earth in its annual orbit around the Sun does not return to the exact same spot. Owing to a phenomenon called Precession, there is a slight retardation; it accumulates to one degree every 72 years. The retardation (assuming each of the twelve segments to be equal, 30 degrees each) thus requires 2,160 years (72 × 30) to execute a shift from sunrise on equinox day against the starry background of one zodiacal constellation (e.g. Taurus) to the one *before* it (i.e. Aries)—while the Earth orbits the Sun in a counterclockwise direction, the retardation causes the Day of the Equinox to shift backwards.

Now, even with the longer longevity in Sumerian/biblical

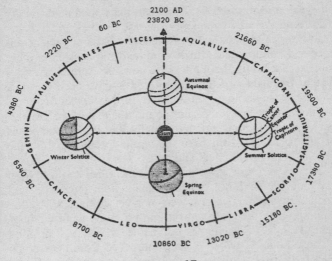

Figure 17

times (Terah 205, Abraham 175) it would have taken a life-
time to notice a retardation of one (72 years) or two (144
years) degrees—a highly unlikely achievement without the
advanced astronomical equipment that would be needed.
So much more the ability to realize and verify a complete
Zodiacal Age shift of 2,160 years. Even the pre-Diluvial Patriarchs with what scholars consider "fantastic" longevities—
969 years for the record holder Methuselah and 930 for
Adam—did not live long enough to observe a full zodiacal
period. Noah, the hero of the Deluge, lived a mere 950 years;
yet Sumerian recollections of the event named the zodiacal
constellation—Leo—in which it had happened.

This was only part of the impossible knowledge possessed
by the Sumerians. How could they have known all that they
did? They themselves provided the answer: All that we know
was taught to us by the Anunnaki—"Those Who From
Heaven to Earth Came." And they, coming from another
planet with a vast orbital period and a longevity in which

one year encompassed 3,600 of Earthlings', had no difficulty discerning Precession and devising the twelve-part Zodiac.

In a series of texts which formed the basis of ancient science and religion, and which were rendered later on in other tongues, including the biblical Hebrew, the Sumerians' tales of the Anunnaki—of the ancient gods—have been the stuff of which "mythology" was made. In the Western cultures the mythology that jumps first to mind is that of the Greeks; but it, as all the ancient mythologies and divine pantheons of all the nations—all over the world—stemmed from the original Sumerian beliefs and texts.

There was a time, the Sumerians told, when civilized Man was not yet on Earth, when animals were only wild and undomesticated and crops were not yet cultivated. At that long-ago time there arrived on Earth a group of fifty Anunnaki. Led by a leader whose name was E.A. (meaning "whose home is water"), they journeyed from their home planet NIBIRU ("planet of crossing") and, reaching Earth, splashed down in the waters of the Persian Gulf. A text known to scholars as the "myth" of *Ea and the Earth* describes how that first group waded ashore, finding themselves in a marshland. Their first task was to drain the marshes, clear river channels, check out food sources (found to be fish and fowl). They then began to make bricks from the clay of the soil and established the first-ever settlement on Earth by extraterrestrials. They named the habitat ERIDU, which meant "Home in the Faraway" or "Home away from home." That name is the origin of the name "Earth" in some of the oldest languages. The time: 445,000 years ago.

The astronauts' mission was to obtain gold by extracting it from the waters of the gulf—gold needed for survival on Nibiru; for there the planet was losing its atmosphere and thus also its internal heat, slowly endangering continued life on Nibiru. But the plan proved unworkable, and the leaders back home decided that gold could be obtained only the hard way—by mining it where it was in abundance, in southeastern Africa.

The new plan called for a substantial increase in the number of Anunnaki on Earth, and in time they numbered six hundred. There was also a need for an elaborate operation of shipping out from Earth the refined gold and bringing in varied supplies. For that three hundred additional Nibiruans were employed as IGI.GI ("Those Who Observe and See"), operating orbiting platforms and shuttlecraft. Nibiru's ruler, AN ("The Heavenly One"—Anu in Akkadian) came to Earth to supervise the expanded presence and operations. He brought along with him two of his children: his son EN.LIL ("Lord of the Command"), a strict disciplinarian, to serve as Chief of Operations; and a daughter, NIN.MAH ("Mighty Lady"), Chief Medical Officer.

The division of duties between the pioneer Ea and the newly arrived Enlil proved tricky, and at a certain moment of impasse Anu was willing to stay on earth and let one of his sons act as viceroy on Nibiru. In the end the three drew lots. Anu returned to reign on Nibiru; Enlil's lot was to stay in the area of the original landing and expand it to an E.DIN ("Home of the Righteous Ones"). His task was to establish additional settlements, each with a specific function (a spaceport, a Mission Control Center, a metallurgical center, a medical center, or as landing beacons). And Ea's lot was to organize the mining operations in southeastern Africa—a task for which he, as an outstanding scientist, was not unsuited.

That the task was within his competence did not mean that Ea liked the assignment away from the Edin. So to compensate him for the transfer he was given the title-name EN.KI—"Lord of Earth."

Enlil might have thought that it was just a gesture; Ea/Enki, however, took the title more seriously. Though both were sons of An, they were only half brothers. Ea/Enki was the Firstborn Son, and normally would have followed his father on the throne. But Enlil was a son born to Anu by a half sister of his; and according to the succession rules on Nibiru, that made Enlil the Legal Heir, even if not firstborn. Now the two half brothers found themselves on another planet, facing a potential conflict: If the mission to Earth would become an extended affair—perhaps even a permanent colonization of another planet—who would be in supreme authority, the Lord of Earth or the Lord of the Command?

The matter became an acute problem for Enki in view of the presence on Earth of his son Marduk as well as Enlil's son Ninurta; for while the former was born to Enki by his official consort, the latter was born to Enlil (on Nibiru) by the half sister Ninmah (when both were unmarried; Enlil married Ninlil on Earth, Ninmah never married). And that gave Ninurta precedence over Marduk in the line of succession.

Unabashed philanderer that he was, Enki decided to remedy the situation by having sex with his half sister, too, hoping also to have a son by her. The lovemaking produced a daughter instead. Unrelenting, Enki lost no time in sleeping with the daughter as soon as she matured; but she, too, bore a daughter. Ninmah had to temporarily immobilize Enki to put an end to his conjugal attempts.

Though he could not attain a son by a half sister, Enki was not lacking other male offspring. In addition to MAR.DUK ("Son of the Pure Mound"), who had also come from Nibiru, there were the brothers NER.GAL ("Great Watcher"), GIBIL ("He of the Fire"), NIN.A.GAL ("Prince of the Great Waters"), and DUMU.ZI ("Son Who Is Life"). It is not certain that all of them were in fact mothered by Enki's official spouse, NIN.KI ("Lady Earth"); it is virtually certain that the sixth son, NIN.GISH.ZID.DA ("Lord of the Artifact/Tree of Life") was the result of a liaison between Enki and Enlil's granddaughter Ereshkigal when she was a passenger on his ship, on the way from the Edin to Africa. A Sumerian cylinder seal depicted Enki and his sons (Fig. 18).

Once Enlil had married his official consort, a young nurse who was given the epithet-name NIN.LIL ("Lady of the Command"), he never wavered in his fidelity to her. They had together two sons—the Moon god NANNAR ("The Bright One"), who was later known as *Sin* by the Semitic-

Figure 18

speaking peoples; and a younger son, ISH.KUR ("He of the Mountains"), who was better known by the name *Adad*—"The Beloved" son. This paucity of offspring, compared to Enki's clan, might explain why the three children of Nannar/Sin and his spouse, NIN.GAL ("Great Lady"), were quickly included in the leadership of the Anunnaki, in spite of their being three generations removed from Anu. They were the above-mentioned ERESH.KI.GAL ("Mistress of the Great Land") and the twins UTU ("The Shiny One") and IN.ANNA ("An's Beloved")—the *Shamash* ("Sun god") and *Ishtar* (Astarte/Venus) of later pantheons.

At the peak of their presence on Earth the Anunnaki numbered six hundred, and the texts named quite a number of them—as often as not indicating their roles or functions. The very first text dealing with Enki's initial splashdown names some of his lieutenants and the tasks assigned to them. The governors of each of the settlements established by the Anunnaki were named, as were all ten ante-Diluvial rulers in the Edin. The female offspring born as a result of Enki's shenanigans were identified, as were their assigned husbands. Recalled by name were chamberlains and emissaries of the principal gods, as were male and female deities in charge of specific activities (e.g. Ninkashi, in charge of beer making).

Contrary to the total absence of a genealogy for Yahweh, the biblical God, the Anunnaki "gods" were fully cognizant of genealogies and the changing generations. There existed as part of the secret knowledge kept in temples God Lists, in which the Anunnaki "gods" were listed in genealogical/ generational succession. Some such discovered lists named no fewer than twenty-three Divine Couples who were the precursors of Anu (and thus of Enlil and Enki) on Nibiru. Some lists just named the Anunnaki gods in chronological succession; others carefully noted the name of the divine mother alongside the divine father's name, for who the mother was determined the offspring's status under the Rules of Succession.

Towering above them all was always a circle of twelve Great Gods, the forerunner of the Twelve Olympians of the Greek pantheon. Beginning with the Olden Gods, then changing with the times and the generations, the composition of the Circle of Twelve varied—but always remained twelve; as someone dropped off, another was added instead; as someone had to be elevated in rank, someone else had to be demoted.

The Sumerians depicted their gods wearing distinctive horned caps (Fig. 19), and we have suggested that the number of pairs of such horns reflected the numerical rank of the deities. The ranking in the original Sumerian pantheon began with 60 (the base number in Sumerian mathematics) for Anu, and continued with 50 for the legal successor Enlil, 40 for Enki, 30 for Nannar/Sin, 20 for Utu/Shamash, and 10 for Ishkur/Adad. The female component was given the ranks 55, 45, 35, and 25 for the spouses Antu, Ninlil, Ninki, and Ningal, then 15 for the unmarried Ninmah and 5 for the single Inanna/Ishtar; reflecting the generational changes, the latter in time attained the rank "15" and Ninmah dropped to 5.

It is noteworthy that the two contenders for the Succession on Earth, Ninurta and Marduk, were kept off the initial "Olympian" list. But when the contest heated up, the Council of the Gods recognized Ninurta as the legal successor and assigned to him the rank of 50—the same as that of his father Enlil. Marduk, on the other hand, was given the low rank 10.

These rankings were considered divine secrets, revealed

Figure 19

only to selected priestly "initiates." The tablets on which the "secret numbers of the gods" were inscribed (such as tablet K.170 from the temple of Nineveh) contained a strict prohibition against showing it to the *la mudu'u*—the "uninitiated." Frequently, information about the gods was recorded without naming them by their names; instead, their secret numbers were used, e.g. "the god 30" for Nannar/Sin.

The table in Fig. 20 identifies the Great Gods by parentage and rank, highlighting the twelve Great Gods.

But why *twelve*?

The answer, we believe, lies in another major problem that the Anunnaki faced once they changed their mission from a one-time mineral-extracting expedition to a long-term settlement with almost a thousand of them involved. From their viewpoint, they had come from a planet with a "normal" orbit to one that crazily runs around the Sun, orbiting the Sun 3,600 times in one (Nibiru) year (one orbital period). Besides the physical adjustments, there was a need somehow

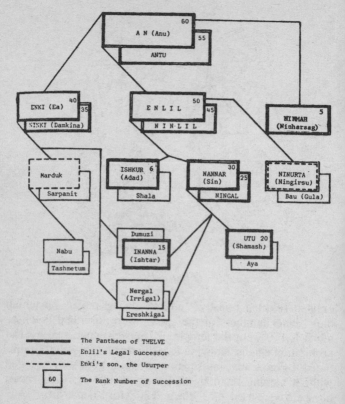

Figure 20

to relate Earthtime to Nibirutime. Establishing their sophisticated equipment at Mission Control Center in Nippur (a facility called DUR.AN.KI—"Bond Heaven-Earth"), they certainly became aware of the gradual retardation that we call precession, and realized that the Earth, besides the orbital fast year, also had another longer cycle—the 25,920 years it took the Earth to return to the same heavenly spot, a cycle that came to be known as the Great Year.

As depictions on cylinder seals (Fig. 21) show, the An-

Figure 21

unnaki considered the "family of the Sun" to consist of twelve members: the Sun (in the center), the Moon (for reasons which were given), the nine planets we know of at present, and one more—their own planet, Nibiru. To them this number, twelve, was a basic number to be applied in all celestial matters affecting the Bond Heaven-Earth, including the division of the starry circle around the Sun. Using their detailed sky charts, they grouped the stars in each sky segment into constellations. What shall they name them? Why not after their very own leaders?

Here was Ea, "Whose Home Is Water," who had splashed down to Earth in the waters of the Persian Gulf, who loved to sail the marshes in a boat, who filled the lakes with fish. They honored him by naming accordingly two constellations, those of the Waterman (Aquarius) and the Fishes (Pisces); in Sumerian times, he was so depicted on cylinder seals (Fig. 22a) and the priests that oversaw his worship were dressed as Fishmen (Fig. 22b). Enlil—forceful, strong-headed, and

Figures 22a, 22b, and 22c

frequently compared to a bull, was honored with naming his constellation as that of the Bull (Taurus). Ninmah, desired but never married, had the constellation Virgo named for her. Ninurta, often called Enlil's Foremost Warrior, was honored with the Bow—Sagittarius; Ea's firstborn, stubborn and hardheaded, was likened to a roaming Ram (Aries). And when the twins Utu/Shamash and Inanna/Ishtar were born, it was only befitting that a constellation, Gemini (the Twins), be named in their honor. (In recognition of Enlil's and Utu's roles in the Anunnaki's space activities, the Enlilite priests dressed as Eaglemen, Fig. 22c). As the hierarchial ranks changed and as second- and third-generation Anunnaki joined the scene on Earth, all the twelve zodiacal constellations were assigned to Anunnaki counterparts.

Not men, but the gods, devised the zodiac.

And the number, no matter what the changes, always had to add up to twelve.

After forty "Repetitions" (orbits) of Nibiru since the first arrival, the Anunnaki assigned to the gold mines mutinied. A text called *Atra Hasis* describes the events that preceded the mutiny, the mutiny itself, and its consequences. The most important consequence was the creation of The Adam: the text tells how Mankind was brought about. Encouraged by Enki, the mutiny was directed primarily against Enlil and his son NIN.UR.TA ("Lord Who Completes the Foundation"). Enlil demanded that the mutineers be given the maximum punishment; Enki described the impossibility of continuing the harsh toil; Anu sided with Enki. But the gold was still needed for survival; so how would it be obtained?

At the moment of impasse, Enki sprang on the Anunnaki leadership his astounding suggestion: Let us, he said, create a Primitive Worker who shall be capable of doing the work! When the amazed Council of the Gods asked how a new being could be created, Enki explained that the being he had in mind "already exists"—a hominid that had evolved on Earth, but had not yet reached the evolutionary stage of the Anunnaki. All we have to do, he said, is to "put the mark of the gods" on them—to alter them genetically to resemble the Anunnaki.

The discussion and the suggested solution are echoed in the Bible:

> *And* Elohim *said:*
> *"Let us make Man in our image*
> *and after our likeness"*

—a being that would resemble the Anunnaki both physically and mentally. This being, Enki promised, "will be charged with the service of the gods, that they might have their ease." Enticed by the prospect of relief from the hard toil, the gods agreed.

Several Sumerian texts describe how, with the help of Nin-

Figure 23

mah and after much trial and error, a *Lullu*—a "Mixed One"—was created. Satisfied that a "perfect model" had been attained, Ninmah raised him and shouted: "My hands have made it!"

She considered the moment to mark a momentous event. So should we—for, in the depiction of the moment by a Sumerian artist on a cylinder seal (Fig. 23), we are shown the most momentous event in the annals of Mankind: the moment when we, *Homo sapiens*, emerged on Earth.

Using the successful genetic combination, the slow process of making duplicates—a process we now call cloning—was started. The reproduction, involving the need for Anunnaki females to serve as Birth Goddesses, cloned the Primitive Worker in sets of seven males, seven females. The Bible (Genesis chapters 1 and 5) tells it thus:

> *On the day that* Elohim *created the Adam,*
> *in the likeness of* Elohim *he made him;*
> *Male and female created he them.*

Cloning was a slow process, requiring the service of the Birth Goddesses because the new being, as a hybrid, could not procreate on its own. So to speed it up Enki performed a second feat of genetic engineering—but this time on his own initiative. Tinkering with what are now called chromosomes X and Y, he gave the human race the ability to procreate on its own. The Bible recorded the event in the tale of Adam and Eve in the Garden of Eden (the Sumerian E.DIN), in which Enki plays the role of the *Nachash*—a term translated ''serpent'' but which also means ''He who knows/possesses secrets.''

Though he had voted for the genetic experiment, Enlil did so reluctantly. Unlike the great scientist Enki, he was not carried away by the scientific challenge. Whimsically we might even imagine him saying, ''We did not come to another planet to play God'' . . . He was infuriated when Enki performed the second (unauthorized) genetic manipulation. ''You have made the Adam to be like one of us,'' able to procreate, he shouted; one more step, and he would also partake of the fruit of the Tree of Life!

So Mankind was banished from the Garden of Eden, to fend for itself; but instead of withering, it proliferated and filled the Earth. Enlil's displeasure grew when young Anunnaki began to fraternize with the Daughters of Man, even had children with them. In the Bible (Genesis chapter 6) the story of the *Nefilim* (''Those Who Came Down''), the ''sons of the *Elohim*'' who intermarried with human females, serves as a preamble to the story of the Deluge, the explanation for the decision to wipe Mankind off the face of the Earth.

Enlil put his plan before the Council of the Gods. A great calamity, he said, is about to happen. On its next passage Nibiru will cause a huge tidal wave that will engulf the Earth. Let us not warn Mankind—let all flesh perish! The gods agreed and swore to secrecy. So did Enki; but he found a way to warn his faithful worshiper Ziusudra (''Noah'' in the Bible) and instructed him to build the Ark to save his family and friends, as well as to preserve the ''seed'' of living animals.

The story of the Great Flood is one of the longest in the Bible; yet as long as it is, it is but a short version of much longer and more detailed Sumerian and Akkadian texts that deal with this watershed event. In its aftermath even Enlil relented. Realizing that after everything that the Anunnaki had built on Earth had been destroyed, they needed Mankind as a partner to make Earth habitable again. With Enlil's consent, the Anunnaki began to advance Mankind culturally and technologically, in intervals that lasted 3,600 years (matching the orbital period of Nibiru). The culmination of the process was the great Sumerian civilization.

On the eve of the Deluge, the Anunnaki took to their craft to escape the calamity, watching the havoc and total destruction from Earth's skies. Not only Mankind perished: All that the Anunnaki had built in the past 432,000 years was wiped off the face of the Earth or buried under miles-thick layers of mud; and that included the spaceport they had in the E.DIN.

As soon as the tidal wave began to recede, they could bring their Earth-orbiting craft down on the Near East's highest peaks, the peaks of Ararat. As more of the dry land appeared, they could use the Landing Place—a vast stone platform that had been erected before the Flood in the Cedar Mountains of what is now Lebanon. But to resume the space operations they needed a spaceport; and the decision was made to erect it in the Sinai peninsula. The Landing Corridor, as before the Flood, was anchored on the conspicuous twin peaks of Mount Ararat; the Landing Place was incorporated; a new Mission Control Center (to replace the one that had been in pre-Diluvial Nippur) was selected; and two artificial twin peaks, to anchor the Landing Corridor's terminus, were erected—the two still-standing great pyramids at Giza in Egypt.

Concerned by the simmering rivalries between what has come to look like two distinct clans on Earth, the location of the spaceport and its auxiliary facilities assumed major importance. To minimize frictions, the de facto division of domains between Enlil in the Edin and Enki in the Abzu was formalized, the former and his descendants granted dominion over Asia and nearby parts of Europe, the latter the whole

African continent. That meant that the pre-Diluvial Landing Place and the new Mission Control Center were in Enlilite territory, and the great pyramids with their intricate guidance systems in Enki'ite hands. It was therefore resolved to place the area of the spaceport, the Sinai peninsula, in the neutral hands of Ninmah. To mark the event, she was given the title-epithet NIN.HAR.SAG—"Lady of the Mountainpeaks."

Our suggestion that the gods of Egypt were none other than Enki and his clan may seem far-fetched at first glance. Weren't their names, to start with, entirely different? The great Olden God of the Egyptians, for example, was called PTAH, "The Developer"; but that was also the meaning of Enki's Sumerian epithet NUDIMMUD, "The Maker of Artful Things." He was the Knower of Secrets, the Divine Serpent, in both pantheons; and (recalling his epithet "whose home is water") was depicted in both as the Divine Waterman (Figs. 14, 22), our Aquarius. In the Egyptian pantheon the Mistress of the Sinai was HATHOR, nicknamed "The Cow" in her old age; so too was Ninharsag nicknamed in Sumer as she grew old.

Enki's principal son and successor in Egypt was RA, "The Pure One," paralleling Marduk, "Son of the Pure Mound," in Mesopotamia. The many other similarities between the two have been expounded in *The Wars of Gods and Men*. So were the reasons for identifying the Egyptian god THOTH, a son of Ptah and keeper of divine secret knowledge, as the god Ningishzidda of the Sumerian texts.

In time Ptah/Enki handed over the reign over Egypt to his son Marduk/Ra; but the latter was not appeased. Reign over the *whole* Earth was his birthright, he kept asserting; and that led to conflicts with the Enlilites that we described as the Pyramid Wars. At one time—circa 8700 B.C. by our calculations—he was forced to leave Egypt; according to Manetho (an Egyptian priest who wrote down the history and prehistory of Egypt in Greek times) the reign was then assigned to Marduk's brother Thoth. Where did Marduk/Ra go? The possibility that he was sent back to Nibiru (the Egyptians called it Planet of Millions of Years) cannot be ruled out. An ancient Egyptian text recorded in pharaonic tombs, called *The Assignment of Functions to Thoth*, has Ra transferring powers to Thoth and designating Thoth as "Thoth, the Place Taker." "Thou shalt be in my place," Ra announces, "a Place Taker." Explaining where he is, Ra tells Thoth: "I am here in the sky, in my proper place." The fact that one segment of the absence, that of demigods, lasted 3,650 years—almost exactly the average 3,600 years of Nibiru's orbit—strongly suggests that that is where Ra/Marduk spent his absence from Earth. Texts, both Egyptian and Mesopotamian, that describe a tough space journey that became especially perilous near Saturn, may well have dealt with Ra/Marduk's return voyage to Earth.

The returning Ra/Marduk found an Earth that he could hardly recognize. In the intervening period, the Sumerian civilization had burst into full bloom. There, in addition to the expansion of the headquarters of Enlil and Enki into sacred precincts surrounded by teeming cities (Nippur and Eridu, respectively), Cities Of Man had been established. The newly created institution of Kingship was inaugurated in a new city, Kish, under the aegis of Ninurta. Nannar/Sin was given mastery over a new urban center called Ur. A sacred precinct built for a visit of Anu and Antu was expanded to become the city of Uruk (the biblical Erech) and was given as a gift to Inanna/Ishtar. The functions of the Priesthood were formalized; a calendar—the famed Calendar of Nippur—was introduced, based on sophisticated astronomical knowledge and official festivals. Started in 3760 B.C., it is still in use as the Hebrew calendar.

The returning Marduk must have cried out to his father and the Council of the Gods: And what about me?

He set his sights on a place not far from where the pre-Diluvial spaceport had been, and determined to make it into a *Bab-Ili*—"Gateway of the Gods" (hence its lasting name *Babylon*). It was to be a symbolic and actual expression of his supremacy.

What ensued is recalled in the Bible as the incident of the Tower of Babel; it took place in Shine'ar (the biblical name

Figures 24a, 24b, and 24c

for Sumer). There the followers of the god of Babylon began to build "a tower whose head can reach the heavens"—a launch tower, we would say nowadays. "Let us make us a *Shem*," they said—not a "name" as is commonly translated, but the original meaning of the Sumerian source of the word *MU*—a rocketlike object. The time, by our calculations, was 3450 B.C.

Descending from the skies, the leader of the *Elohim* ordered the tower destroyed. Both the biblical version and the Mesopotamian texts report that it was in the aftermath of this incident that the *Elohim* decided to "confuse Mankind's language," to prevent Mankind from acting in unison. Until then "there was one language and one kind of words upon the whole Earth" (Genesis 11:1). Until then there was indeed one civilization, that of Sumer, with a single language and form of writing (Fig. 24a). In the aftermath of the incident at Babylon, a second civilization, the Nile Civilization (Egypt and Nubia), was established, with its own language and script (Fig. 24b); and several centuries later, the third civilization, that of the Indus Valley, was begun with its own language and script (Fig. 24c), a script that is still undeciphered. Thus was Mankind alloted three Regions; the Fourth Region was retained by the gods: the Sinai peninsula, where the spaceport was.

Defied in Mesopotamia, Ra/Marduk returned to Egypt to reassert his supremacy there, as the Great God of the new civilization. The time was 3100 B.C. There was, of course, the small problem of what to do with Thoth, who had been the reigning deity in Egypt and Nubia while Ra/Marduk was gone. Unceremoniously, he was sent away . . . In *The Lost Realms* we have suggested that, taking along a group of his African followers, he went all the way to the New World, to become Quetzalcoatl, the Winged Serpent god. The first calendar instituted by him in Mesoamerica (the Long Count calendar) began in the year 3113 B.C.; it was, we believe, the precise date of the arrival in the New World of Thoth/Quetzalcoatl.

Still seething from his failure in Mesopotamia, the bitter Marduk turned to settling other scores. During his absence a divine "Romeo and Juliet"—his brother Dumuzi and Inanna/Ishtar, the granddaughter of Enlil—fell in love and were to be betrothed. The union was anathema to Ra/Marduk; he was especially alarmed by Inanna's hopes to become Mistress of Egypt through the marriage. When Marduk's emissaries tried to seize Dumuzi, he accidentally died as he tried to escape. His death was blamed on Marduk.

Texts that have been discovered in several copies and versions provide details of the trial of Marduk and his punishment: to be buried alive in the Great Pyramid, which was sealed tight to create a divine prison. With only air to breathe but no food or water, Marduk was sentenced to die in that colossal tomb. But his spouse and mother successfully appealed to Anu to commute the death sentence into one of exile. Using the original construction plans, an escape shaft was dug and blasted into the passages above the massive plugs. The return of Marduk from certain death, his emergence from his tomb, were aspects of the view that the texts—titled by early translators "The Death and Resurrection of the Lord"—were precursors of the New Testament tale of the death, entombment, and resurrection of Jesus.

Sentenced to exile, Ra/Marduk became *Amen-Ra*, the unseen god. This time, however, he roamed the Earth. In an autobiographical text in which his return was prophesied, Marduk described his wanderings thus:

> *I am the divine Marduk, a great god.*
> *I was cast off for my sins.*
> *To the mountains I have gone,*
> *in many lands I have been a wanderer.*
> *From where the sun rises*
> *to where it sets I went.*

And wherever he roamed, he kept asking the Gods of Fate: "Until when?"

The answer regarding his Fate, he realized, came from the heavens. The Age of the Bull, the age zodiacally belonging to Enlil and his clan, was ending. The dawn was nearing when the Sun would rise on the first day of spring, the day of the New Year in Mesopotamia, in the zodiacal constellation of the Ram (Aries)—*his* constellation. The celestial cycle of Fates augurs his, Marduk's, supremacy!

Not everyone agreed. Was it just so because of time calculations, or an observable celestial phenomenon? Marduk could not care less; he launched a march on Mesopotamia while his son, Nabu, organized followers to invade the Sinai and seize the spaceport. The escalating conflict is described in a text known as the *Erra Epos*; it tells how, seeing no other choice, the gods opposing Marduk used nuclear weapons to obliterate the spaceport (and, as a sideshow, the unfaithful cities of Sodom and Gomorrah).

But Fate intervened on the side of Marduk. The prevailing western winds carried the deathly nuclear cloud eastward, toward Sumer. Babylon, farther north, was spared. But in southern Mesopotamia the Evil Wind caused sudden death and lasting desolation. Sumer's great capital, Ur, was a place where wild dogs roamed.

And so, in spite of the extraordinary efforts of Marduk's opponents, the Age of the Ram indeed ushered in the rise of Babylon.

4

BETWEEN FATE
AND DESTINY

Was it Fate, or was it Destiny, that led Marduk by an unseen hand through all his troubles and tribulations over many millennia to his final goal: supremacy on Earth?

Not many languages have such a choice of words for that "something" that predetermines the outcome of events before they happen, and even in the English language many would be hard put to explain the difference. The best dictionaries (such as *Webster's*) explain the one term by the other, regarding as synonyms for both "doom," "lot," and "fortune." But in the Sumerian language, and thus in Sumerian philosophy and religion, there was a clear distinction between the two. *Destiny*, NAM, was the predetermined course of events that was *unalterable*. *Fate* was NAM.TAR—a predetermined course of events that *could be altered*; literally, TAR, to cut, break, disturb, change.

The distinction was not a matter of mere semantics; it went to the core of things, affecting and dominating the affairs of gods and men, lands and cities. Was something that was about to happen, even something that had happened—a Destiny, the outcome (and, if you will, the destination to which it leads) unalterable; or was it a combination of chance events, or willed decisions, or temporary ups or downs that might or might not be fatal, that another chance event or a prayer or a change in a lifestyle might lead to a different end result? And if the latter, what might have been different?

The fine line distinguishing between the two may be blurred today, but it was a difference well-defined in Sumerian and biblical times. For the Sumerians, Destiny began

61

in the heavens, starting with the preordained orbital paths of the planets. Once the Solar System begot its shape and composition after the Celestial Battle, the planetary orbits became everlasting Destinies; the term and concept could then be applied to the future course of events on Earth, starting with the gods who had celestial counterparts.

In the biblical realm, it was Yahweh who controlled both Destinies and Fates, but while the former was predetermined and unalterable, the latter (Fate) could be affected by human decisions. Because of the former powers, the course of future events could be foretold years, centuries, and even millennia earlier, as when Yahweh revealed to Abraham the future of his descendants, including the sojourn of four hundred years in Egypt (Genesis 15:13–16). How that sojourn would come about (it began with a search for food during a great famine) was a matter of Fate; that the sojourn would begin with an unexpected welcome (because Joseph, through a series of consecutive occurrences, became Overseer over all of Egypt) was a matter of Fate; but that the sojourn (after a period of enslavement) would end with a liberating Exodus at a predetermined time was a Destiny, preordained by Yahweh.

Because they were called to prophecy by God, the biblical prophets could foretell the future of kingdoms and countries, of cities and kings and individuals. But they made it clear that their prophecies were merely expressions of divine decisions. "Thus sayeth Yahweh, Lord of Hosts," was a frequent way in which the Prophet Jeremiah began as the future of kingdoms and rulers was foretold. "So sayeth the Lord Yahweh," the Prophet Amos announced.

But when it came to Fates, the free will and free choice of people and nations could come and did come into play. Unlike Destinies, Fates could be changed and punishments could be averted if righteousness replaced sin, if piety replaced profanity, if justice prevailed over injustice. "It is not the death of the evildoer that I seek, but that the wicked shall turn from his ways and live," the Lord God told the Prophet Ezekiel (33:11).

The distinction made by the Sumerians between Fate and

Destiny, and how they can both play a role even in the life of a single individual, becomes apparent in the life story of Gilgamesh. He was, as we have mentioned, the son of Uruk's high priest and the goddess Ninsun. As he grew older and began to contemplate issues of life and death, he posed the question to his godfather, the god Utu/Shamash:

> In my city man dies; oppressed is my heart.
> Man perishes, heavy is my heart . . .
> Man, the tallest, cannot stretch to heaven;
> Man, the widest, cannot cover the Earth.
> Will I too 'peer over the wall'?
> Will I too be fated thus?

The answer of Utu/Shamash was not encouraging. "When the gods created Mankind," he said, "death to Mankind they allotted; Life they retained in their own keeping." This is your Destiny; so, while you are alive and what you do in the meantime is a Fate that you can change or affect, enjoy it and make the most of it—

> Let full be thy belly, Gilgamesh;
> Make thou merry by day and night!
> Of each day, make a feast of rejoicing;
> Day and night, dance thou and play!
> Let thy garments be sparkling fresh,
> Bathe in water, let thy head be washed.
> Pay heed to the little one who holds thy hand,
> Let thy spouse delight in your bosom.
> This is the fate of Mankind.

Receiving this answer, Gilgamesh realized that what he must do is take some drastic action to change his Destiny, not merely his Fate; otherwise, he would meet the same end as any mortal. With his mother's reluctant blessing, he embarked on the journey to the Landing Place in the Cedar Mountains, there to join the gods. But Fate intervened, again and again. First it was in the shape of Huwawa, the robotic guardian of the Cedar Forest, then through the lusting of Inanna/Ishtar for the king and the rebuff that led to the slaying of the Bull of Heaven. The role of Fate—*Namtar*—was recognized and considered by Gilgamesh and his companion Enkidu right then, even right after the slaying of Huwawa. The epic text relates how the two comrades sit and contemplate the expected punishment. As the actual slayer, Enkidu ponders what his fate will be. Gilgamesh comforts him: Worry not, he says; the "Adjurer" Namtar indeed can devour—but he also "lets the caught bird go back to its place, lets the caught man return to the bosom of his mother." Falling into the hands of Namtar is not an unalterable occurrence; as often as not, Fate reverses itself.

Refusing to give up, Gilgamesh embarked on a second journey, this time to the spaceport in the Sinai peninsula. His troubles and tribulations on the way were countless, yet he persevered. At last he managed to obtain the fruit that would have given him eternal youth; but in the end a serpent snatched it from him as the weary Gilgamesh fell asleep, and he returned to Uruk empty-handed, there to die.

A series of *What if?* questions naturally come to mind. What if things had gone differently in the Cedar Mountains—would Gilgamesh have succeeded to ascend heavenward and join the gods on their planet? What if he had not fallen asleep and kept the Plant of Everlasting Youth?

A Sumerian text titled by scholars *The Death of Gilgamesh* provides an answer. The end, it explains, was preordained; there was no way that Gilgamesh, taking his Fate into his own hands over and over again, could have changed his Destiny. The text provides this conclusion by reporting an omendream of Gilgamesh that contained a prediction of his end. Here is what Gilgamesh is told:

> *O Gilgamesh,*
> *this is the meaning of the dream:*
> *The great god Enlil, father of the gods,*
> *had decreed thy destiny.*

> *Thy fate for kingship he determined;*
> *For eternal life he has not destined thee.*

The Fate of Gilgamesh, he is told, has been overridden by Destiny. He was fated to be a king; he was not destined to avoid death. And so destined, Gilgamesh is described dying. "He who was firm of muscle, lies unable to rise . . . He who had ascended mountains, lies, rises not." "On the bed of Namtar he lies, rises not."

The text lists all the good happenings that Gilgamesh had experienced—kingship, victories in battle, a blessed family, faithful servants, beautiful garments; but recognizing the interplay of Fate and Destiny, concludes by explaining to Gilgamesh: Both "the light and the darkness of Mankind were granted to thee." But in the end, because Destiny has overridden Fate, "Gilgamesh, the son of Ninsun, lies dead."

The *What if?* question can be expanded from one individual to Mankind as a whole.

What would have been the course of events on Earth (and elsewhere in the Solar System) were Ea's original plan to obtain gold from the waters of the Persian Gulf to succeed? At a crucial turn of events, Anu, Enlil, and Ea drew lots to see who would rule Nibiru, who would go to the mines in southeast Africa, who would be in charge of the expanded Edin. Ea/Enki went to Africa and, encountering there the evolving hominids, could tell the gathered gods: The Being that we need, *it exists*—all that we have to do is put on it our genetic mark!

The *Atra Hasis* text, brought together from several renditions and many fragments by W. G. Lambert and A. R. Millard, described the fateful moment thus:

> *The gods had clasped hands together,*
> *had cast lots and had divided.*

Would the feat of genetic engineering have taken place had either Anu or Enlil been the one to go to southeastern Africa?

Would we have shown up on our planet anyway, through evolution alone? Probably—for that is how the Anunnaki (from the same seed of life!) had evolved on Nibiru, but far ahead of us. But on Earth we came about through genetic engineering, when Enki and Nimah jumped the gun on evolution and made Adam the first "test tube baby."

The lesson of the *Epic of Gilgamesh* is that Fate cannot change Destiny. The emergence of *Homo sapiens* on Earth, we believe, was a matter of Destiny, a final outcome that might have been delayed or reached otherwise, but undoubtedly reached. Indeed, we believe that even though the Anunnaki deemed their coming to Earth their own decision for their own needs, that too, we believe, was preordained, destined by a cosmic plan. And equally so, we believe, will be Mankind's Destiny: to repeat what the Anunnaki had done to us by going to another planet to start the process all over again.

One who understood the connection between Fate and the twelve zodiacal constellations was Marduk himself. They constituted what we have termed Celestial Time, the link between Divine Time (the orbital period of Nibiru) and Earthly Time (the Year, months, seasons, days, and nights resulting from the Earth's orbit, tilt, and revolution about its own axis). The heavenly signs that Marduk had invoked— the arrival of the Zodiacal Age of the Ram—were signs in the realm of Fate. What he needed to solidify his supremacy, to eliminate from it the notion that, as Fate, it could be changed or revised or reversed, was a Celestial Destiny. And to that aim he ordered what can be considered the most audacious falsification ever.

We are talking about the most sacred and basic text of the ancient peoples: the *Epic of Creation*, the core and bedrock of their faith, religion, science. Sometimes called by its opening lines *Enuma elish (When in the Heights of Heaven)*, it was a tale of events in the heavens that involved celestial gods and a Celestial Battle, the favorable outcome of which made possible all the good things on Earth, including the

Figure 25

coming into being of Mankind. Without exception the text was viewed by the scholars who began to piece it together from many fragments as a celestial myth, an allegory of the eternal fight between good and evil. The fact that wall sculptures discovered in Mesopotamia depicted a winged (i.e. celestial) god fighting a winged (i.e. celestial) monster (Fig. 25) solidified the notion that here was an ancient forerunner of the tale of St. George and the Dragon. Indeed, some of the early translations of the partial text titled it *Bel and the Dragon*. In those texts, the Dragon was called Tiamat and Bel (''the Lord'') was none other than Marduk.

It was only in 1876 that George Smith, working in the British Museum on piecing together fragments of inscribed clay tablets from Mesopotamia, published the master work *The Chaldean Genesis* that suggested the existence of a Babylonian story that paralleled the creation parts of Genesis in the Bible; and then the Museum's Keeper of Babylonian Antiquities, L. W. King, followed with the authoritative work *The Seven Tablets of Creation* to establish conclusively the correlation between the biblical seven days of creation and the earlier Mesopotamian sources.

But if that was the case, how could the Babylonian text still be called an allegory? For doing so would also categorize the tale in Genesis as an allegory and not an unalterable Divine Act that has been a bedrock of monotheism and Judeo-Christian beliefs.

In our 1976 book *The Twelfth Planet* we have suggested that neither the Mesopotamian text nor its condensed biblical version was myth or allegory. They were based, we suggested, on a most sophisticated cosmogony that, based on advanced science, described the creation of *our* Solar System stage by stage; and then the appearance of a stray planet from outer space that was gradually drawn into our Solar System, resulting in a collision between it and an olden member of the Sun's family. The ensuing Celestial Battle between the invader—"Marduk"—and the olden planet—Tiamat—led to the destruction of Tiamat. Half of it broke up into bits and pieces that became a Hammered Bracelet; the other half, shunted to a new orbit, became the planet Earth, carrying with it Tiamat's largest satellite that we call the Moon. And the invader, attracted into the center of our Solar System and slowed down by the collision, became permanently the twelfth member of our Solar System.

In the subsequent companion book *Genesis Revisited* (1990), we showed that all the advances in our celestial knowledge corroborated the Sumerian tale—a tale which explained satisfactorily the history of our Solar System, the enigma of Earth's continents starting only on one side with an immense gap (the Pacific basin) on the other side, the origin of the Asteroid Belt and the Moon, the reason for Uranus lying on its side and Pluto having an odd orbit, and on and on. The extra knowledge we have gained through the study of comets, the use of the Hubble telescope, and the probes of the Moon (manned) and other planets in our Solar System (by unmanned spacecraft) continue to corroborate the Sumerian data as we have understood it.

By calling the cosmogony underlying the *Epic of Creation* Sumerian, rather than Babylonian, we provide a clue to the true source and nature of the text. The discovery of fragments of an earlier *Sumerian* version of *Enuma elish* convinced scholars that the *Epic of Creation* was originally a Sumerian text, in which the invading planet was called NIBIRU, not "Marduk." They are now convinced that the extant Babylonian version was a deliberate forgery, intended to equate the Marduk who was on Earth with the celestial/planetary "god" who changed the makeup of our heavens, gave our Solar System its present shape, and—in a manner of speaking—created the Earth and all that was on it. That included Mankind, for according to the Sumerian original version it was Nibiru, coming from some other part of the universe, that brought with it and *imparted to Earth during the collision* the "Seed of Life."

(For that matter, it should be realized that the illustration so long deemed to represent Marduk battling the Dragon is also all wrong. It is a depiction from Assyria, where the supreme god was Ashur, and not Babylon; the deity is depicted as an Eagleman, which indicates an Enlilite being; the divine cap he wears has three pairs of horns, indicating the rank of 30, which was not Marduk's rank; and his weapon is the forked lightning, which was the divine weapon of Ishkur/Adad, Enlil's—not Enki's—son.)

No sooner did Marduk seize the sovereignty in Babylon, than the pivotal New Year rites were changed, to require the public reading (on the festival's fourth evening) of *Enuma elish* in its new, Babylonian, version; in it the supremacy of Marduk on Earth only paralleled his supremacy in the heavens, as the planet with the greatest orbital path, the one that embraces all the others in its loop.

The key to this distinction was the term "Destiny." That was the term used to describe the orbital paths. The everlasting, unchanging orbit was a planet's Destiny; and that is what Marduk was granted according to *Enuma elish*.

Once one realizes that this is the meaning and significance of the ancient term for "orbits," one can follow the steps by which the Destiny was attained by Marduk. The term is used, for the first time in the text, in connection with the principal satellite of Tiamat (which the text calls Kingu). At first it is only one of Tiamat's eleven satellites (moons); but as it "grows in stature," it becomes the "leader of her host."

Once the only large planet and a consort of Apsu (the Sun), Tiamat "grew haughty" and was not too pleased to see other celestial gods appear in pairs: Lahmu and Lahamu (Mars and Venus) between her and the Sun (where there had been before only the Sun's messenger Mummu/Mercury), and the pairs Kishar and Anshar (Jupiter and Saturn, the latter with his messenger Gaga/Pluto); then Anu and Nudimmud (Uranus and Neptune). Tiamat and her group of moons on the one hand and the new planets on the other hand, in a still unstable Solar System, begin to encroach on each other's domains. The others get especially concerned when Tiamat "unlawfully" extends to Kingu, her largest satellite, the privileged status of having an orbit of his own—of becoming a full-fledged planet:

> *She has set up an Assembly . . .*
> *She has borne monster-gods;*
> *Withal eleven of this kind she has brought forth.*
>
> *From among the gods who formed her Assembly*
> *she has elevated Kingu, her firstborn,*
> *made him chief among the gods;*
> *She exalted Kingu, in their midst made him great . . .*
>
> *She gave him a Tablet of Destinies,*
> *she fastened it upon his chest, [saying:]*
> *"Now the command shall never be altered,*
> *the decree shall be unchangeable!"*

Unable to withstand the "raging host" of Tiamat by themselves, the celestial gods see salvation coming from outside the Solar Syatem. As was the case when The Adam was created when an impasse was faced, so was it in the primordial heavens: It was Ea ("Nudimmud," the "Artful Creator" in Sumerian) who brought off the saving creature. As the outermost planet, facing the "Deep"—outer space—he attracts a stranger, a new planet. Passing in the vicinity of our Solar System as a result of a catastrophe, a cosmic accident far out, the new planet is the result of Fate, and does not yet orbit our Sun—he has no Destiny as yet:

> *In the Chamber of Fates,*
> *the Hall of Designs,*
> *Bel, most wise, wisest of the gods,*
> *was engendered;*
> *In the heart of the Deep was the god created.*

It is noteworthy that the newly arrived planet, a celestial god, is called even in the Babylonian rendition *Bel*, "The Lord," and in the Assyrian version the word "Bel" is replaced by the word "Ashur." The Babylonian version—the most commonly used nowadays—repeats however the last line, and in this second time renders it: "In the heart of the pure Deep was *Marduk* created," the addition of the word *pure* intended no doubt to explain the origin of the name MAR.DUK, "Son of the Pure Place." (This double rendition is one of the clues exposing the falsification).

Beyond Ea (Neptune), Anu (Uranus) welcomed the invader. The increasing gravitational pull made the invader sprout four moons, as well as pull him more to the Solar System's midst. By the time it reached Anshar (Saturn), and sprouted three more moons, the invader was already inexorably caught in the Sun's gravitational pull. His course curved inward (Fig. 26), starting to form an orbital path around the Sun. *The invader, in other words, was envisioning a Destiny for himself!*

Once he was "kissed" by Anshar/Saturn,

> *The gods, his forebears,*
> *the destiny of Bel then determined;*
> *They set him on the path,*
> *the way to success and attainment.*

The path thus ordained for him, Bel found out, was set on a collision course with Tiamat. He was willing to accept the

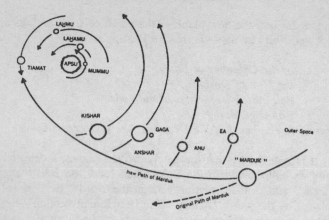

Figure 26

challenge but on a condition. Becoming now Marduk (both celestial and on Earth), he said to Anshar:

> *Lord of the gods,*
> *determiner of the great gods' destinies:*
> *If I am indeed to be your Avenger,*
> *to vanquish Tiamat and save your lives,*
> *convene the divine Assembly,*
> *proclaim supreme my Destiny!*

The celestial gods accepted Marduk's conditions. "For Marduk, their Avenger, they decreed a destiny;" and that Destiny, that orbit, "shall be unequaled." Now then, they said—go and slay Tiamat!

The ensuing Celestial Battle is described in the fourth tablet of *Enuma elish*. Unavoidably set on a collision course, Marduk and Tiamat cast lightnings, blazing flames, and gravitational nets against each other, "shaking with fury." As they neared each other—Tiamat moving like all planets in a counterclockwise direction, Marduk onrushing in a clockwise path—it was one of Marduk's satellite moons that struck

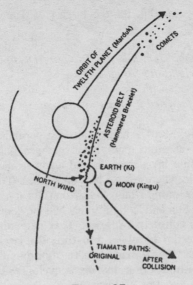

Figure 27

Tiamat first; then another and another of his moons struck Tiamat—"tearing into her insides, splitting her up." A "divine lightning," an immense electrical bolt, then shot out from Marduk into the fissure, and "the life-breath of Tiamat extinguished."

The intact Marduk swept by, made an orbital round, and returned to the site of the battle. This time he himself struck Tiamat with far-reaching consequences. One half of her he smashed into bits and pieces to become the Great Band (the Asteroid Belt); the other half, struck by Marduk's moon named North Wind, was shunted to a new place in the heavens, to become Earth in a new orbital path. Its Sumerian name, KI (from which the Akkadian/Hebrew "Gei" and the Greek "Gaea" come) meant "the cleaved one" (Fig. 27).

As Tiamat's own moons were dispersed—many changing direction to clockwise (retrograde) orbits—a special fate was determined by Marduk for the largest of Tiamat's moons, Kingu:

> *He took from him the Tablet of Destinies,*
> *not rightfully Kingu's,*
> *sealed it with a seal*
> *and fastened it to his own breast.*

Now, finally, Marduk had obtained a permanent, unalterable Destiny—an orbital path that, ever since, has kept bringing the erstwhile invader again and again to the site of the Celestial Battle where Kingu had once been. Together with Marduk, and counting Kingu (our Moon) for it had possessed a Destiny, the Sun and its family reached the count of twelve.

It was this count, we suggest, that determined twelve to be the celestial number, and thus the twelve stations ("houses") of the zodiac, twelve months of the year, twelve double-hours in a day-night cycle, twelve tribes of Israel, twelve apostles of Jesus.

The Sumerians considered the abode (called "cult center" by most scholars) of Enlil as the Navel of the Earth, the place from which other key locations were equidistant, the epicenter of concentric divinely ordained sites. Best known by its later Akkadian/Semitic name Nippur, its Sumerian name was NIBRU.KI—"The Place of the Crossing," representing on Earth the Celestial Place of Crossing, the site of the Celestial Battle to which Nibiru keeps returning every 3,600 years.

Functioning as a Mission Control Center, Nippur was the site of the DUR.AN.KI, the "Bond Heaven-Earth" from which the space operations of the Anunnaki were controlled, and at which the sky-maps, and all the formulas concerning the celestial motions of the members of our Solar System and the tracking of Divine Time, Celestial Time, and Earthly Time and their interrelationships, were maintained and calculated.

This tracking of what was deemed to be unalterable orbital

paths was conducted with the aid of the Tablets of Destinies. We can glimpse their functions and the sacred chamber where they whirred and hummed by reading what happened when their operation had come to a sudden halt. The Sumerian text describing that, named by translators *The Myth of Zu*, deals with the scheming of the god Zu (his full name, later discoveries revealed, was AN.ZU—"The Knower of Heavens") to usurp the Bond Heaven-Earth by seizing and carrying off the Tablets of Destinies. Everything came to a standstill; "the lighted brightness petered out; silence prevailed"; and in the heavens those who manned the shuttlecraft and spacecraft, "the Igigi, in space, were confounded." (The epic tale ends with the overpowering of Zu by Enlil's son Ninurta, the reinstallation of the Tablets of Destinies in the Duranki, and the execution of Zu).

The distinction between an unalterable Destiny and a Fate that could be altered or averted was expressed in a two-part *Hymn to Enlil*, that described both his powers as a decreer of Fates and as a pronouncer of Destinies:

> *Enlil:*
> *In the heavens he is the Prince,*
> *On Earth he is the Chief.*
> *His command is far-reaching,*
> *His utterance is lofty and holy;*
> *The shepherd Enlil decrees the Fates.*

> *Enlil:*
> *His command in the heights made the heavens tremble,*
> *down below he made the Earth quake.*
> *He pronounces destinies unto the distant future,*
> *His decrees are unchangeable.*
> *He is the Lord who knows the destiny of the Land.*

Destinies, the Sumerians believed, were of a celestial nature. As high-ranking as Enlil was, his pronouncements of unalterable Destinies were not the result of his own decisions or plans. The information was made known to him; he was a "lord who knows the Destiny of the land," he was a "trustworthy called-one"—not a human prophet but a divine prophet.

That was quite different from the instances when—in consultation with other gods—he decreed Fates. Sometimes he consulted just his trusted vizier, Nusku:

> When in his awesomeness he decrees the fates—
> his command, the word that is in his own heart—
> to his exalted vizier, the chamberlain Nusku,
> does he make known, him he consults.

Not only Nusku, Enlil's chamberlain, but also his spouse Ninlil is depicted in this hymn as participating in deciding Fates:

> Mother Ninlil, the holy wife,
> whose words are gracious . . .
> The eloquent one whose speech is elegant,
> has seated herself by your side . . .
> She speaks eloquently with you,
> whispers words at your side,
> decrees the fates.

Fates, the Sumerians believed, were made, decreed and altered on Earth; and in spite of the hymnal words of adoration or minimal consultation, it appears that the determination of Fates—including that of Enlil himself—was achieved by a process that was more democratic, more akin to that of a constitutional monarchy. The powers of Enlil seemed to stem not only from above, from Anu and Nibiru, but also from below, from an Assembly of the Gods (a kind of parliament or congress). The most crucial decisions—fateful decisions—were made at a Council of the Great Gods, a kind of Cabinet of Ministers where discussions sometimes became debates and as often as not turned into heated exchanges . . .

The references to the Council and the Assembly of the

Anunnaki gods are numerous. The creation of The Adam was a subject so discussed; so was the decision to wipe Mankind off the face of the Earth at the time of the Deluge. The latter clearly states that "Enlil opened his mouth to speak and addressed the Assembly of the gods." The suggestion to annihilate Mankind was opposed by Enki, who, having failed to sway the assembly, "got fed up with the sitting in the Assembly of the Gods." We read that later on, as the gods were orbiting the Earth in their spacecraft, observing the havoc down below, Ishtar bewailed what she saw and wondered how she could have voted for the annihilation of Mankind: "How could I, in the Assembly of the Gods, I myself give evil counsel?"

And after the Deluge, when the remnants of Mankind began to fill the Earth again and the Anunnaki started to give Mankind civilization and institute Kingship as a way to deal with the growing human masses,

> *The great Anunnaki who decree Fates*
> *sat exchanging their counsels regarding the land.*

This manner of determining Fates was not limited to the affairs of Man; it also applied to the affairs of the gods themselves. Thus, when Enlil, in the early times of arrival on Earth, took a liking to a young Anunnaki female and had sex with her over her objections, Enlil was sentenced into banishment first by "the fifty Senior Gods sitting in assembly," and then by the "Fate-decreeing gods, the seven of them."

Such was the manner, according to the Babylonian version of *Enuma elish*, that the Destiny of Marduk, to be supreme on Earth (and in the celestial counterpart), was confirmed. In that text the Assembly of the Gods is described as a gathering of Senior Gods, coming from various places (and perhaps not only from Earth, for in addition to Anunnaki the delegates also included Igigi). The number of those gathered was fifty—a number matching the numerical rank of Enlil. In the Akkadian texts they were designated as *Ilani rabuti sha mu-*

shimu shimati—"Senior/Great Gods who determine Fates."

Describing how such Senior Gods gathered to proclaim Marduk's supremacy, *Enuma elish* paints a scene of camaraderie, of friends who had not seen each other for quite some time. They arrived at a special Place of Assembly; "they kissed one another . . . There was conversation; they sat down to banquet; they ate festive bread, they drank choice wine." And then the camaraderie turned solemn as the "Seven Gods of Destiny" entered the Assembly Hall and sat down to start the business at hand.

For unexplained reasons, Marduk was tested for his magical powers. Show us, the gathered Anunnaki said, how you "can command to destroy as well as command to create!"

They formed a circle and "placed in it the images of the constellations." The term, *Lamashu*, undoubtedly means the images/symbols of the zodiac. "Open thy mouth," they said, "let the images vanish! Speak again, and let the constellations reappear!"

Obliging, Marduk performed the miracle:

> *He spoke, and the constellations vanished;*
> *He spoke again, and the images were restored.*
>
> *When the gods, his elders,*
> *saw the power of his utterance,*
> *they rejoiced, they proclaimed:*
> *"Marduk is supreme!"*

"They bestowed on him the scepter, the throne and the royal robe"—a most resplendent robe, as Babylonian depictions showed (Fig. 28). "From this day," they announced, "thy decree shall be unrivaled, thy command as that of Anu . . . No one among the gods shall transgress thy boundaries."

While the Babylonian text suggests that the supremacy of Marduk was tested, confirmed, and pronounced in one session, other texts that concern the decision-making process suggest that the Assembly stage at which fifty Senior Gods participated was followed by a separate stage of a meeting

Figure 28

of the Seven Great Gods Who Judge; and then the actual pronouncement of the decision, of the Fate or the Destiny, was made by Enlil in consultation with or after approval by Anu. Indeed, the need for this stage-by-stage procedure and the final pronouncement by Enlil in behalf of Anu was recognized even by the followers of Marduk. The renowned Babylonian king Hammurabi, in the preamble to his famous law code, exalted the supremacy of his god Marduk with these words:

> *Lofty Anu,*
> *Lord of the gods who from heaven to Earth came,*
> *and Enlil, Lord of heaven and Earth*
> *who determines the destinies of the land,*
> *Determined for Marduk, the firstborn of Enki,*
> *the Enlil-functions over all mankind.*

Such a transfer of Enlil's authority to Marduk, the Babylonian texts asserted, was executed and symbolized by the bestowal on Marduk of the fifty names. The last and most important of the power-names bestowed on him was that of *Nibiru*—the very name of the planet whom the Babylonians renamed Marduk.

Assemblies of the gods were sometimes called not to proclaim new Fates, but to ascertain what had been determined at an earlier time, on the Tablets of Destinies.

Biblical statements reflect not only the royal custom of writing things down on a scroll or tablet and then sealing the document as preserved evidence; the custom was attributed to (and undoubtedly learned from) the gods. The culmination of those references is found in the Song of Moses, his testament and prophecy before he died. Extolling the almighty Yahweh, and his capacity to proclaim and foresee Destinies, Moses quotes the Lord as saying of the future:

> *Lo and behold:*
> *It is a secret with me hidden,*
> *stored and sealed within my treasures.*

Hittite texts discovered in the royal library of their capital Hattushas contained tales of conflict between the gods that had certainly served as a proximate source of Greek myths. In those texts the names of the Olden Gods are given as had been known from Sumerian times (such as Anu, Enlil, and Enki); or in Hittite for gods known from the Sumerian pantheon (such as *Teshub*, "The Wind Blower," for Ishkur/ Adad); or sometimes for deities whose identity remains obscure. Two epic songs pertain to gods called Kumarbis and Illuyankas. In the first instance, Teshub demanded that the *Tablets of Fate*—"the old tablets with the words of Fate"— be recovered from Enki's abode in southeastern Africa, and brought to the Assembly of the Gods. In the other, after conflict and competition, the gods met in the Assembly to have their order and ranks established—an order and ranks that were pictorially depicted on the rock walls of the sacred sanctuary now known as Yazilikaya (Fig. 29).

Figure 29

But without doubt one of the most crucial, longest, bitterest, and literally fateful was the Assembly of the Gods where it was determined to approve the use of nuclear weapons to vaporize the spaceport in the Sinai peninsula. Using primarily the long and detailed record known as the *Erra Epos*, we have reconstructed the unfolding events, identified the protagonists and antagonists, and rendered almost verbatim (in *The Wars of Gods and Men*) the proceedings of the Assembly. The unintended result, as has already been mentioned, was the demise of Sumer and the end of life in its cities.

The occurrence is also one of the clearest if tragic examples of how Fate and Destiny could be interwoven.

Hardest hit in Sumer was its glorious capital, Ur, seat and center of its people's beloved god Nannar/Sin (the Moon god) and his spouse, Ningal. The lamentation texts (*Lamentation Over the Destruction of Sumer and Ur, Lamentation Over the Destruction of Ur*) describe how, when it was realized that the Evil Wind bearing the cloud of death was wafting toward Sumer, Nannar/Sin rushed to his father Enlil with a plea for help, some divine miracle to avert the calamity from Ur. Was it not, he asked his father, unthinkable to see this pride of Ur, a city throughout renowned, perish? He appealed to Anu: "Utter, 'It is enough!' " He appealed to Enlil: "Pronounce a favorable Fate!" But Enlil saw no way to change the onrushing end.

In desperation Nannar/Sin insisted that the gods meet in Assembly. As the senior Anunnaki seated themselves, Nannar/Sin cried his eyes out to Anu, to Enlil made supplications. "Let not my city be destroyed, verily I said to them," Nannar/Sin later recorded. "Let not the people perish!"

But the response, coming from Enlil, was harsh and decisive:

> *Ur was granted Kingship;*
> *Eternal reign it was not granted.*

5

OF DEATH AND RESURRECTION

The lesson of the destruction of Sumer and Ur was that chance and alterable Fate cannot supersede unalterable Destiny. But what about the other way—can a Fate, no matter by whom decreed, be superseded by Destiny?

The issue had certainly been pondered in antiquity, for otherwise what was the reason for prayers and supplications that had begun then, of the admonitions by the Prophets for righteousness and repentance? The biblical Book of Job raises the question whether Fate—to be afflicted to the point of hopelessness—shall prevail even if Job's righteousness and piety had destined him to long life.

It was a theme whose origins can be found in the Sumerian poem that scholars titled *Man and His God*, whose subject is the righteous sufferer, a victim of cruel fate and undeserved misfortune. "Fate grasped me in its hand, carries away my breath of life," the unnamed sufferer lamented; but he sees the Gates of Mercy opening up for him "now that you, my god, have shown me my sins." Confession and repentance make his god "turn aside the Demon of Fate," and the supplicant lives a long and happy life.

Just as the tale of Gilgamesh demonstrated that Fate could not override his ultimate Destiny (to die as a mortal), so did other tales convey the moral that neither can Fate bring about death if it was not yet so destined. A paramount example was none other than Marduk himself, who of all the gods of antiquity set a record in suffering and setbacks, of disappearances and reappearances, of exiles and returns, of apparent death and unexpected resurrection; so much so, in fact, that when the full scope of the events concerning Marduk became known after the discovery of ancient inscriptions, scholars seriously debated at the turn of this century whether his story was a prototype of the story of Christ. (The notion was abetted by the close affinity between Marduk with his father Enki on the one hand and with his son Nabu on the other hand, creating the impression of an early Trinity).

The impact of Marduk's ordeals and its moral for humanity was evidenced by a Mystery Play in which his apparent death and return from the dead were played out by actors. The Mystery Play was acted out in Babylon as part of the New Year ceremonies, and various ancient records suggest that it served a darker purpose as well—to point an accusing finger at his enemies and judges who were responsible for his death sentence and entombment. As variant renditions indicate, the identity of those responsible changed from time to time to suit the changing political-religious scene.

One of the original accusees was Inanna/Ishtar; and it is ironic that while she truly had died and resurrected, her miraculous experience was neither reenacted (as was Marduk's) nor recalled in the calendar (as was the death of her beloved Dumuzi after whom the month Tammuz was named). This is doubly ironic because it was as a result of the death of Dumuzi that Inanna/Ishtar ended up dead.

Not even a Shakespeare could conceive the tragic irony of the events that followed the entombment and resurrection of Marduk as a result of Inanna's outcry. For as things turned out, while he had not truly died or really come back from the dead, his accuser Inanna did meet actual death and attained true resurrection. And while the death of Dumuzi was the underlying cause of both occurrences, the cause of Inanna's death and resurrection was her own fateful decision.

We use the term ''fateful'' judiciously, for it was her Fate, not her Destiny, to meet her death; and it was because of that distinction that she could be resurrected. And the account of those events illuminates the issues of Life, Death, and Resurrection not, as the *Epic of Gilgamesh*, among mortals or demigods, but among the gods themselves. In her tale of

Fate versus Destiny, there are clues to the resolution of enigmas that have been calling out for solutions.

The suspenseful story of Inanna/Ishtar's death and resurrection reveals, from the very beginning, that she met her death—real death, not just entombment—as a result of her own decisions. She created her own Fate; but since her death (at least at that time) was not her Destiny—in the end she was revived and resurrected.

The tale is recorded in texts written first in the original Sumerian language, with later renderings in Akkadian. Scholars refer to the various renditions as the tale of *Inanna's Descent to the Lower World*, although some prefer the term Netherworld instead of Lower World, implying a hellish domain of the dead. But in fact Inanna set her course to the Lower World, which was the geographic term denoting the southernmost part of Africa. It was the domain of her sister Ereshkigal and Nergal, her spouse; and it appears that as a brother of Dumuzi it was his task to arrange the funeral. And although Inanna was warned not to go there, she decided to make the trip anyway.

Attending the funeral rites of her beloved Dumuzi was the reason Inanna gave for her journey; but it is evident that no one believed her . . . It has been our guess that according to a custom (that later guided biblical laws), Inanna intended to demand that Nergal, as an older brother of Dumuzi, sleep with her so that a son be born as a pseudo-son of Dumuzi (who had died sonless). And that intention infuriated Ereshkigal.

Other texts described the seven objects that Inanna put on for her use during her travels in her Boat of Heaven—a helmet, ear "pendants," a "measuring rod" among them—all held firmly in place by straps. Sculptures (Fig. 30) depicted her similarly attired. As she reached the gates of her sister's abode—seven of them—the gatekeeper stripped her of all those protective devices, one by one. When she finally entered the throne room, Ereshkigal broke into a rage. There was a shouting match. According to the Sumerian text, Ereshkigal ordered that Inanna be subjected to the "Eyes of

Figure 30

Death''—some kind of death rays—that turned the body of Inanna into a corpse; and the corpse was hung on a stake. According to the later Akkadian version, Ereshkigal ordered her chamberlain Namtar to ''release against Ishtar the sixty miseries''—afflictions of the eyes, the heart, the head, the feet, ''of all parts of her, against her whole body''—putting Ishtar to death.

Anticipating trouble, Inanna/Ishtar had instructed her own chamberlain, Ninshubur, to raise an outcry in the event she did not return in three days. When she failed to return, Ninshubur came before Enlil to beg that Inanna be saved from death, but Enlil could not help. Ninshubur appealed to Nannar, Inanna's father, but he, too, was helpless. Then Ninshubur appealed to Enki, and he *was* able to help. He fashioned two artificial beings who could not be harmed by the Eyes of Death, and sent them on the rescue mission. To one android he gave the Food of Life, to the other the Water of

Figure 31

Life; and so provided, they descended to the abode of Ereshkigal to reclaim Inanna's lifeless body. Then,

> *Upon the corpse, hung from the stake,*
> *they directed the Pulser and the Emitter.*
> *Upon the flesh that had been smitten,*
> *sixty times the Food of Life,*
> *sixty times the Water of Life,*
> *they sprinkled upon it;*
> *And Inanna arose.*

The use of radiation—a Pulser, and Emitter—to revive the
dead was depicted on a cylinder seal (Fig. 31) in which we
see a patient whose face is covered with a mask being treated
with radiation. The patient who was being revived (whether
man or god is unclear), lying on a slab, was surrounded by
Fishmen—representatives of Enki. It is a clue to be borne in
mind together with the detail in the tale that while neither
Enlil nor Nannar could help Inanna, Enki could. The androids whom Enki had fashioned to return Inanna from the
dead, however, were not the Fishmen-doctor/priests shown
in the above depiction. Requiring neither food nor water,
sexless and bloodless, they may have looked more like the
figurines of divine android messengers (Fig. 32). It was as

Figure 32

androids that they were not affected by Ereshkigal's death rays.

Having resurrected Inanna/Ishtar, they accompanied her on her safe return to the Upper World. Awaiting her was her faithful chamberlain Ninshubur. She had many words of gratitude for him. Then she went to Eridu, the abode of Enki, "he who had brought her back to life."

Were *Inanna's Descent to the Lower World* made into a Passion Play, as the tale of Marduk was, it would certainly have kept the audience at the edge of their seats; for whereas Marduk's "death" was really only an entombment under a death sentence, and his "resurrection" in reality a rescue before the point of death, Inanna/Ishtar was truly dead and her resurrection a true return from the dead. But were someone in the audience familiar with the nuances of Sumerian terminology, he would have known from the midpoint of the tale that it would turn out all right . . . For the one whom Ereshkigal had ordered to put Inanna to death was her chamberlain *Namtar*—not NAM, "Destiny" that was unalterable, but NAM.TAR, "Fate" that could be altered.

It was Namtar who put Ishtar to death by "releasing against her the sixty miseries," and the one who, after she was revived and resurrected, took her through the seven gates and returned to her, at each gate, her special attire and adornments and her attributes of power.

The notion of the realm of Namtar as a Netherworld, an abode of the dead but at the same time a place from which one could escape and be back among the living, formed the basis for an Assyrian text dealing with the near-death experience of a prince named Kumma.

As in an episode of the TV series *The Twilight Zone*, the prince sees himself arriving in the Netherworld. Right off he sees a man standing before Namtar: "In his left hand he held the hair of his head, in his right he held a sword." Namtaru, Namtar's concubine, stood nearby. Monstrous beasts surrounded them: a serpent-dragon with human hands and feet, a beast with the head of a lion and four human hands. There was *Mukil* ("Smiter"), birdlike with human hands and feet, and *Nedu* ("Who casts down"), who had the head of a lion, the hands of a man, and the feet of a bird. Other monsters had mixed limbs of humans, birds, oxen, lions.

Moving on, the prince comes upon a judgment scene. The man being judged has a pitch-black body and wears a red cloak. In one hand he carries a bow, in the other a sword; with his left foot he treads on a snake. But his judge is not Namtar, who is only the "vizier of the Netherworld"; the judge is Nergal, lord of the Lower World. The prince sees him "seated on a majestic throne, wearing a divine crown." From his arms lightnings flashed, and "the Netherworld was filled with terror."

Trembling, the prince bowed down. When he stood up, Nergal shrieked at him: "Why did you offend my beloved wife, Queen of the Netherworld?!" The prince was dumbfounded and speechless. Was this his end?

But no, no longer in the court of Namtar, that was not the bitter end. It was all, in turns out, a case of mistaken identity. The Queen of the Netherworld herself ordered his release and return to the realm of Shamash, the Upper World of sunlight. But Nergal intervened; the life of the prince might be spared, but he cannot return from the dead unharmed. He must suffer from this near-death experience, and become afflicted with aches, pains, and insomnia . . . He has to suffer from nightmares.

The return of the dead Dumuzi from the Lower World was quite different.

Revived and freed to go back to the Upper World, Inanna did not forget her dead beloved. On her orders, the two divine messengers also took back with them the lifeless body of Dumuzi. They took the body to Bad-Tibira in the Edin; there the body was embalmed at Inanna's request:

> As for Dumuzi, the lover of my youth:
> Wash him with pure water,
> anoint him with sweet oil,
> clothe him in a red garment,
> lay him on a slab of lapis-stone.

Inanna ordered that the preserved body be put upon a stone slab of lapis lazuli to be kept in a special shrine. It should be preserved, she said, so that one day, on the Final Day, Dumuzi could return from the dead and "come up to me." For that, she asserted, would be the day when

> The dead one will arise
> and smell the sweet incense.

This, one should note, is the first mention of a belief in a Final Day when the dead shall arise. It was such a belief that caused the annual wailing for Tammuz (the Semitic rendering of Dumuzi) that continued for millennia even unto the time of the Prophet Ezekiel.

The death and mummification of Dumuzi, though so briefly told here, provide important insights. When he and Inanna/Ishtar fell in love—he an Enkiite, she an Enlilite—

in the midst of conflicts between the two divine clans, the betrothal received the blessing of Inanna's parents, Nannar/Sin and his spouse Ningal/Nikkal. One of the texts in the series of *Dumuzi and Inanna* love songs has Ningal, "speaking with authority," saying to Dumuzi:

> *Dumuzi, the desire and love of Inanna:*
> *I will give you life unto distant days;*
> *I will preserve it for you,*
> *I will watch over your House of Life.*

But in fact Ningal had no such authority, for all matters of Destiny and Fate were in the hands of Anu and Enlil. And, as all later knew, a tragic and untimely death did befall Dumuzi.

The failure of a divine promise in a matter of life and death is not the only disturbing aspect of the tragic fate of Dumuzi. It raises the issue of the gods' immortality; we have explained in our writings that it was only a relative longevity, a life span resulting from the fact that one year on Nibiru equaled 3,600 Earth years. But to those who in antiquity considered the Anunnaki to be gods, the tale of Dumuzi's death had to come as a shock. Was it because she had indeed expected Dumuzi to come back to life on the Final Day that Inanna ordered his embalmment and his placement on a stone slab rather than burial—or in order to preserve the illusion of divine immortality for the masses? Yes, she might have been saying, the god had died, but that is only a temporary, transitional phase, for in due time he shall be resurrected, he will arise and enjoy the sweet incense smells.

The Canaanite tales concerning Ba'al, "the Lord," seem to take the position that one had to distinguish between the good guys and the bad guys. Seeking to assert his supremacy and to establish it on the peak of Zaphon (the Secret Place of the North), Ba'al fought to the death his brother-adversaries. But in a fierce battle with the "godly *Mot*" ("Death"), Ba'al is killed.

Anat, the sister-lover of Ba'al, and their sister Shepesh,

bring the terrible news to Ba'al's father, *El*: "Puissant Ba'al is dead, the Prince, Lord of Earth, is perished!" they tell the shocked father; in the fields of Dabrland "we came upon Ba'al, fallen on the ground." Hearing the news, El steps off his throne and sits down on a stool, as mourner's custom is (among the Jews) to this day. "He pours dust of mourning on his head, puts on sackcloth." With a stone knife he gashes himself; "he lifts up his voice and cries: Ba'al is dead!"

The grieving Anat returns to the field where Ba'al had fallen and, like El, puts on sackcloth, gashes herself, then "weeps her fill of weeping." Then she calls her sister Shepesh to come and help her carry the lifeless body to the Fastness of Zaphon, there to bury the dead god:

> *Hearkening, Shepesh, the gods' maiden,*
> *picks up Puissant Baal,*
> *sets him on Anat's shoulder.*
> *Up to Zaphon's fastness she brings him,*
> *bewails him and buries him;*
> *She lays him in a hollow,*
> *to be with the earth-ghosts.*

Completing the requisites of mourning, Anat returns to El's abode. Bitterly she tells those gathered: Now you can go and rejoice, for Ba'al is dead, and his throne is free! The goddess Elath and her kinsmen, ignoring Anat's irony, merrily go about discussing succession. As one of the other of El's sons is recommended, El says no, he is a weakling. Another candidate is permitted to go to Zaphon, to try out Ba'al's throne; "but his feet reach not down to the footstool," and he, too, is eliminated. No one, it appears, can replace Ba'al.

This gives Anat hope: resurrection. Enlisting again the help of Shepesh, she penetrates Mot's abode. Using subterfuge, she "draws near to him, like a ewe for her lamb . . . She seizes the godly Mot and with a sword she cleaves him." Then she burns the dead Mot's body, grinds the remains, spreads the ashes over the fields.

And the killing of Mot, who had killed Ba'al, triggers a miracle: *the dead Ba'al comes back to life!*

> *Indeed did Puissant Baal die;*
> *Indeed did the Lord of Earth perish.*
> *But lo and behold:*
> *Alive is Puissant Baal!*
> *Behold, existent is the princely Lord of Earth!*

Getting the news, El wonders whether it is all a dream, "a vision." But it is true! Casting off the sackcloth and ways of mourning, El rejoices:

> *Now will I sit up and find rest,*
> *and my heart shall be at ease;*
> *For alive is Puissant Baal,*
> *Existent is the prince, Lord of Earth.*

In spite of El's evident uncertainty whether the resurrection is an illusory vision, a mere dream, the Canaanite storyteller chose to assure the people that in the end even El accepts the miracle. The assurance is echoed in the tale of Keret, who is only a demigod; yet his sons, seeing him in the throes of death, cannot believe that "a son of El shall die."

It is perhaps in light of the unacceptability of a god's death that the notion of resurrection has been brought into play. And whether or not Inanna herself believed that her beloved would return from the dead, the elaborate preservation of Dumuzi's body and her accompanying words also preserved, among the human masses, the illusion of the immortality of the gods.

The procedure that she personally outlined for the preservation, so that on the Final Day Dumuzi could arise and rejoin her, is undoubtedly the procedure known as mummification. This might come as a shock to Egyptologists, who have held that mummification began *in Egypt* at the time of the Third Dynasty, circa 2800 B.C. There the procedure en-

Figure 33

tailed washing the body of the departed Pharaoh, rubbing it with oils, and wrapping it in a woven cloth—preserving the body so that the Pharaoh could undertake a Journey to the Afterlife.

Yet here we have a *Sumerian* text recording mummification centuries earlier!

The procedure's step-by-step details in this text are identical to what was later practiced in Egypt, down to the color of the enshrouding cloth.

Inanna ordered that the preserved body be put to rest upon a stone slab of lapis lazuli, to be kept in a special shrine. She named the shrine E.MASH—''House/Temple of the Serpent.'' It was perhaps more than a symbolic gesture of placing the dead son of Enki in his father's hands. For Enki was not only the *Nachash*—Serpent, as well as Knower of Secrets—of the Bible. In Egypt, too, his symbol was the serpent and the hieroglyph of his name PTAH represented the double helix of DNA (Fig. 33), for that was the key to all matters of life and death.

Though venerated in Sumer and Akkad as Inanna's betrothed and mourned in Mesopotamia and beyond as Ishtar's departed Tammuz, Dumuzi was an African god. It was thus perhaps inevitable that his death and embalmment would be compared by scholars to the tragic tale of the great Egyptian god *Osiris*.

The story of Osiris is akin to the biblical tale of Cain and

Figure 34

Abel in which a rivalry ended in a brother killing a brother. It begins with two divine couples, two half brothers (*Osiris* and *Seth*) marrying two sisters (*Isis* and *Nepthys*). To avoid recriminations, the Kingdom of the Nile was divided between the two brothers: Lower Egypt (the northern part) was allotted to Osiris and the southern part (Upper Egypt) to Seth. But the complex divine rules of succession, giving preference to the Legitimate Heir over the Firstborn Son, inflamed the rivalry to the point where Seth, using a ruse, trapped Osiris inside a chest which was then cast into the Mediterranean Sea, and Osiris was drowned.

Isis, the spouse of Osiris, found the chest when it was washed ashore in what is now Lebanon. She took the body of her husband Osiris back to Egypt, seeking the help of the god Thoth to resurrect Osiris. But Seth found out what was going on, seized the corpse, cut it up into fourteen pieces, and dispersed the pieces all over Egypt.

Unyielding, Isis searched for the pieces and found them all, except (so the tale says) the phallus of Osiris. She put the pieces back together, binding them with a woven purple cloth to reconstitute Osiris's body—thus starting mummification in Egypt. All the depictions of Osiris from pharaonic times show him tightly wrapped in the shroud (Fig. 34).

Like Inanna before her, so did Isis enshroud and mummify her deceased spouse, thereby giving rise in Egypt (as Inanna's deed had done in Sumer and Akkad) to the notion of

Figure 35

the resurrected god. While in Inanna's case the deed by the goddess might have been intended to satisfy a personal denial of the loss as well as to affirm the *gods'* immortality, in Egypt the act became a pillar of the pharaonic belief that the *human king* could also undergo the transfiguration and, by emulating Osiris, attain immortality in an afterlife with the gods. In the words of E. A. Wallis Budge in the preface to his masterwork *Osiris & The Egyptian Resurrection*, "The central figure of the ancient Egyptian Religion was Osiris, and the chief fundamentals of his cult were the belief in his divinity, death, resurrection and absolute control of the destinies of the bodies and souls of men." The principal shrines to Osiris in Abydos and Denderah depicted the steps in the god's resurrection (Fig. 35). Wallis Budge and other scholars believed that these depictions were drawn from a Passion or Mystery Play that had been acted out annually at those places—a religious ritual that, in Mesopotamia, was accorded to Marduk.

The *Pyramid Texts* and other funerary quotes from the

Figure 36

Egyptian *Book of the Dead* related how the dead Pharaoh, embalmed and mummified, was prepared to exit his tomb (deemed only a temporary restplace) through a false door on the east and begin a Journey to the Afterlife. It was presumed to be a journey simulating the journey of the resurrected Osiris to his heavenly throne in the Eternal Abode; and though it was a journey that made the Pharaoh soar heavenward as a divine falcon, it began by passing through a series of underground chambers and subterranean corridors filled with miraculous beings and sights. In *The Stairway to Heaven* we have analyzed the geography and topography of the ancient texts and concluded that it was a simulation of a journey to an underground launch silo in the Sinai peninsula—not unlike the actual depiction of an actual site in the peninsula in the tomb of Hui, a pharaonic governor of the Sinai peninsula (Fig. 36).

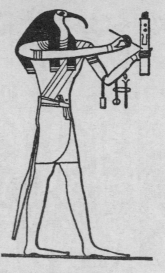

Figure 37

The resurrection of Osiris was coupled with another miraculous feat, that of bringing about the birth of his son, *Horus*, well after Osiris himself was dead and dismembered. In both events, which the Egyptians rightly considered to be magical, a god called *Thoth* (always shown in Egyptian art as Ibis-headed, Fig. 37) played the decisive role. It was he who aided Isis in putting the dismembered Osiris together, and then instructed her how to extract the "essence" of Osiris from his dismembered and dead body, and then impregnate herself artificially. Doing that, she managed to become pregnant and give birth to a son, Horus.

Even those who take the tale to be a recollection of some actual events and not just a "myth" assume that what Isis did was to extract from the dead Osiris his semen, and thus his "essence." But this was impossible, since the one part that Isis could not find and recombine was his male organ. The magical feat of Thoth had to go beyond artificial insemination, now quite common. What he had to do was to obtain for her the *genetic* "essence" of Osiris. The texts as well as depictions coming to us from ancient Egypt confirm that Thoth indeed possessed the "secret knowledge" needed for such feats.

The biomedical—"magical" in human eyes—capabilities of Thoth were called upon once more for the sake of Horus. In order to protect the boy from the ruthless Seth, Isis kept the birth of Horus a secret, hiding him in a swampy area. Unaware of the existence of a son of Osiris, Seth—just as Enki had tried to obtain a son by his half sister Ninmah— tried to force Isis, his half-sister, to have intercourse with him so that he might have a son by a half sister, and thus an uncontested heir. Luring Isis to his abode, he held her captive for a while; but Isis managed to escape and returned to the swamps where Horus was hidden. To her grief she found Horus dead from a sting of a poisonous scorpion. She lost no time in calling for help from Thoth:

> Then Isis sent forth a cry to heaven
> and addressed her appeal to the
> Boat of Millions of Years . . .
> And Thoth came down;
> He was provided with magical powers,
> and possessed the great power which made
> the word turn into deed . . .

> And he said to Isis:
> I have come this day in the Boat of the Celestial
> Disc from the place where it was yesterday.
> When the night cometh,
> this Light [beam] shall drive away [the poison]
> for the healing of Horus . . .
> I have come from the skies to save the child
> for his mother.

Thus revived and resurrected from death (and perhaps forever immunized) by the magical powers of Thoth, Horus grew up to become *Netch-Atef*, the "Avenger" of his father.

The biomedical powers of Thoth in matters of life and death were also recorded in a series of ancient Egyptian texts known as *Tales of the Magicians*. In one of them (Cairo Papyrus 30646) a long tale deals with a couple of royal descent who unlawfully took possession of the *Book of the Secrets of Thoth*. In punishment Thoth buried them in a subterranean chamber in a state of suspended animation—mummified as the dead but able to see, hear, and speak. In another tale, written on the *Westcar Papyrus*, a son of the Pharaoh Khufu (Cheops) told his father of an old man who "was acquainted with the mysteries of Thoth." Among them was the ability to restore life to the dead. Wishing to see this with his own eyes, the king ordered that a prisoner's head be cut off, then challenged the sage to reconnect the severed head and return the man to life. The sage refused to perform this "magic of Thoth" on a human being; so the head of a goose was severed. The sage "spoke certain words of power" from the *Book of Thoth*; and lo and behold, the severed head joined itself back to the body of the goose, the goose stood up, waddled, then began to honk—alive as before.

That Thoth had indeed possessed the ability to resurrect a dead person who had been beheaded, reattach the head, and return the victim to life, was known in ancient Egypt because of an incident that had occurred when Horus finally took up arms against his uncle Seth. After battles that raged on land, water, and in the air, Horus succeeded in capturing Seth and his lieutenants. Bringing them before Ra for judgment, Ra put the captives' fate in the hands of Horus and Isis. Thereupon Horus started to slay the captives by cutting off their heads; but when it came to Seth, Isis could not see this done to her brother and stopped Horus from executing Seth. Enraged, Horus turned on his own mother and beheaded her! She survived only because Thoth rushed to the scene, reattached her head, and resurrected her.

To appreciate Thoth's ability to achieve all that, let us

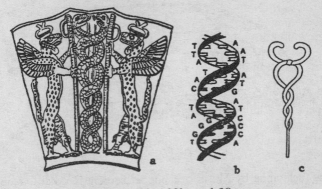

Figures 38a, 38b, and 38c

recall that we have identified this son of Ptah as Ningishzidda (son of Enki in Sumerian lore), whose Sumerian name meant "Lord of the Tree/Artifact of Life." He was the Keeper of [the] Divine Secrets of the exact sciences, not the least of which were the secrets of genetics and biomedicine that had served well his father Enki at the time of the Creation of Man. Sumerian texts, in fact, attest that at one time Marduk complained to his father Enki that he was not taught all the knowledge that Enki possessed.

"My son," responded Enki, "what is it that you do not know? What more could I give to you?" The withheld knowledge, Marduk pointed out, was the secret of resurrecting the dead; that secret knowledge was imparted by Enki to Marduk's brother, Ningishzidda/Thoth, but not to Marduk/Ra.

That secret knowledge, those powers granted to Thoth/ Ningishzidda, found expression in Mesopotamian art and worship by depicting him by or with the symbol of the En-twined Serpents (Fig. 38a)—a symbol that we have identified as a representation of the double helix DNA (Fig. 38b)—a symbol that has survived to our time as the emblem of medicine and healing (Fig. 38c).

There was undoubtedly a connection between all that and

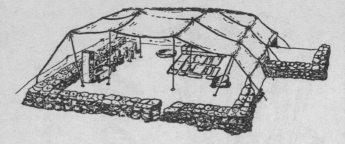

Figure 39

the fashioning by Moses of a copper serpent in order to stop a pestilence that felled countless Israelites during the Exodus. Raised in the Pharaoh's court and trained by Egypt's magicians, Moses, on the Lord's instructions, "made a copper serpent, and placed it atop a Miracle Pole," and when those who were afflicted by the plague looked up to the copper serpent, they remained alive (Numbers 21:8–10).

It is perhaps more than a coincidence that one of the leading international authorities on ancient copper mining and metallurgy, Professor Benno Rothenberg (*Midianite Timna* and other publications), discovered in the Sinai peninsula a shrine dating back to the time of the Midianite period—the time when Moses, having escaped to the Sinai wilderness for his life—dwelt with the Midianites and even married the daughter of the Midianite high priest. Located in the area where some of the earliest copper mining had taken place, Professor Rothenberg found in the shrine's remains a small copper serpent; it was the sole votive object there. (The shrine has been reconstructed as an exhibit in the Nechushtan Pavilion of the Eretz Israel Museum in Tel Aviv, Fig. 39, where the copper serpent can also be seen.)

The biblical record and the finds in the Sinai peninsula have a direct bearing on the depiction of Enki as a *Nachash*. The term has not just the two meanings that we have already mentioned ("Serpent," "Knower of Secrets") but also a third one—"He of Copper," for the Hebrew word for copper, *Nechoshet*, stems from the same root. One of Enki's epithets in Sumerian, BUZUR, also has the double meaning "He who knows/solves secrets" and "He of the copper mines."

These various interconnections may offer an explanation of the otherwise puzzling choice by Inanna of a resting place for Dumuzi: Bad-Tibira. Nowhere in the relevant texts is there any indication of a connection between Dumuzi (and, for that matter, Inanna) and that City of the Gods. The only possible connection is the fact that Bad-Tibira was established as the metallurgical center of the Anunnaki. Did Inanna, then, place the embalmed Dumuzi near where not only gold but also copper was refined?

Another possibly relevant tidbit concerns the construction of the Tabernacle and Tent of Appointment in the desert of the Exodus, in accordance with very detailed and explicit instructions by Yahweh to Moses: where gold or silver were to be used and how, what kinds of woods or timbers and in what sizes, what manner of cloth or skins, how sewn, how decorated. Great care is also taken in these instructions regarding the rites to be performed by the priests (only Aaron and his sons at that time): their clothing, the sacred objects they would wear, the very explicit combination of ingredients that would make the unique incense that would result in the proper cloud to shield them from the deathly radiation by the Ark of the Covenant. And then one more requirement: the fashioning of a washbasin in which they had to wash their hands and feet, "so that they die not when they enter the Ark of the Covenant." And the washbasin, Exodus 30: 17 specified, must be made of copper.

All these dispersed but seemingly connected facts and tidbits suggest that copper somehow played a role in human biogenetics—a role which modern science is only beginning to uncover (a recent example is a study, published in the journal *Science* of 8 March 1996, about the disruption of copper metabolism in the brain associated with Alzheimer's disease).

Such a role, if not part of the first genetic endeavor by

Enki and Ninmah to produce The Adam, seems to have certainly entered the human genome when Enki, as the Nachash, engaged in the second manipulation when Mankind was endowed with the ability to procreate.

Copper, in other words, was apparently a component of our Destiny, and a studious and expert analysis of the Sumerian creation texts might well lead to medical breakthroughs that could affect our own daily lives.

As for the gods, Inanna, for one, believed that copper might assist her beloved's resurrection.

6

THE COSMIC CONNECTION: DNA

Even before television, courtroom dramas have titillated many and trials made history. We have come a long way from the biblical rule, "by two witnesses shall the verdict be." From eyewitnesses court evidence has moved to documentary evidence, to forensic evidence, and—what seems at the moment as the epitome—to DNA evidence.

Having discovered that all life is determined by the tiny bits of nucleic acids that spell out heredity and individuality on chains called chromosomes, modern science has attained the capability of reading those entwined DNA letters to distinguish their unique, individually spelled "words." Using DNA readings to prove guilt or innocence has become the highlight of courtroom dramas.

An unmatched feat of twentieth-century sophistication? No, a feat of 100th-century sophistication *in the past*—a court drama from 10,000 B.C.

The ancient celebrated case took place in Egypt, at a time when gods and not yet men reigned over the land; and it concerned not men but the gods themselves. It concerned the adversaries Seth and Horus and had its roots in the rivalry between the half brothers Seth and Osiris. Seth, it will be recalled, resorted to foul play to get rid of Osiris and take over his domains. The first time he tricked Osiris into a chest that Seth quickly sealed and sank in the Mediterranean Sea; but Isis found the chest and, with the help of Thoth, revived Osiris. The next time the frustrated Seth seized and cut up Osiris into fourteen pieces. Isis located the dispersed pieces and put them together, and mummified Osiris to start the

Afterlife legend. She missed, however, the god's phallus, which she could not find, for Seth had disposed of it so that Osiris would have no heir.

Determined to have one so that he would avenge his father, Isis appealed to Thoth, the Keeper of Divine Secrets, to help her. Extracting the "essence" of Osiris from the dead god's available parts, Thoth helped Isis impregnate herself and give birth to a son, Horus.

The "essence" (not "seed"!), we now know, was what we nowadays call DNA—the genetic nucleic acids that form chains on the chromosomes, chains that are arranged in base pairs in a double helix (see Fig. 38b). At conception, when the male sperm enters the female egg, the entwined double helixes separate, and one strand from the male combines with one strand from the female to form a new double-helixed DNA for their offspring. It is thus essential not only to bring together the two double-helixed DNAs, but also to attain a separation—an unwinding—of the double strands, and then a recombining of only one strand from each source into the new entwined double-helixed DNA.

Pictorial depictions from ancient Egypt indicate that Thoth—the son of Ptah/Enki—was well aware of these biological-genetic processes and employed them in his genetic feats. In Abydos, a wall painting (Fig. 40), in which the Pharaoh Seti I acted out the role of Osiris, showed Thoth giving Life (the *Ankh* symbol) back to the dead god while obtaining from him the two distinct strands of DNA. In a depiction from the *Book of the Dead* dealing with the subsequent birth of Horus, we see (Fig. 41) how the two Birth Goddesses assisting Thoth hold *one strand each* of DNA, the DNA's double helix having been separated so that only one strand recombines with that of Isis (shown holding the newborn Horus).

Isis raised the boy in secret. When he came of age, his mother decided that it was time to claim for him his father's inheritance. So one day, to Seth's utter surprise, Horus appeared before the Council of the Great Gods and announced that he was the son and heir of Osiris. It was an incredible

Figure 40

claim, yet one that could not be dismissed out of hand. Was the young god really the son of the dead Osiris?

As recorded in a text known as the *Chester Beatty Papyrus No. 1*, the appearance of Horus astounded the assembled gods, and of course Seth more than any other. As the council began to deliberate the sudden claim, Seth had a conciliatory suggestion: Let the deliberations be recessed, so as to give him a chance to get acquainted with Horus and see if the matter could be settled amicably. He invited Horus to "come, let us pass a happy day in my house," and Horus agreed. But Seth, who had once tricked Osiris to his death, had new treachery in mind:

> *When it was eventide,*
> *the bed was spread for them,*
> *and the twain lay thereon.*

Figure 41

And in the night
Seth caused his member to become stiff,
and he made it go between the loins of Horus.

When the deliberations were resumed, Seth made an astounding announcement. Whether or not Horus is the son of Osiris, he said, matters no more. For now his, Seth's, seed is in Horus, and that makes Horus a successor of Seth rather than a front-runner for the succession!

Then Horus made an even more surprising announcement. On the contrary, he said, it is not I who have been disqualified—it is Seth! And he went on to tell that he was not really asleep when Seth poured his semen. It did not enter my body, he said, because "I caught the seed between my hands." In the morning he took the semen to show it to his mother Isis, and the report gave her an idea. She made Horus erect his member and ejaculate his semen into a cup; then she spread the semen of Horus on lettuce in Seth's garden—a favorite breakfast food of Seth. Unknowingly, he ended up ingesting the semen of Horus. So, Horus said, it is my semen that is in Seth, and now he can succeed me but not precede me on the divine throne . . .

Totally baffled, the Council of the Gods turned to Thoth to resolve the issue. Using his powers of genetic knowledge, he checked the semen that Isis had kept in a pot, and found it to indeed be that of Seth. He examined Horus and found no traces of Seth's DNA in him. Then he examined Seth, and found that he had indeed ingested the DNA of Horus.

Acting as a forensic expert in a modern court, but evidently armed with technical abilities which we are yet to attain, he submitted the DNA analysis results to the Council of the Gods. They voted unanimously to grant the dominion over Egypt to Horus.

(Seth's refusal to yield the dominion led to what we have termed the First Pyramid War, in which Horus enlisted, for the first time, humans in a war between the gods. We have detailed those events in *The Wars of Gods and Men*).

Recent discoveries in genetics throw light on a persistent and seemingly odd custom of the gods, and at the same time highlight their biogenetic sophistication.

The importance of the wife-sister in the succession rules of the gods of Mesopotamia and Egypt, evident from all that we have reported thus far, was echoed also in the Greek myths regarding their gods. The Greeks named the first divine couple, emerging out of Chaos, *Gaea* ("Earth") and *Uranus* ("Sky" or "Heaven"). Of them twelve *Titans* were brought forth, six males and six females. Their intermarriages and varied offspring laid the groundwork for later struggles for supremacy. Of the earliest struggles the one who emerged on top was *Cronus*, the youngest male Titan, whose spouse was his sister *Rhea*; their children were the three sons *Hades, Poseidon* and *Zeus*, and the three daughters *Hestia, Demeter* and *Hera*. Though Zeus fought his way up to the supremacy, he had to share dominion with his brothers. The three divided the domains among them—some versions say by drawing lots—very much as Anu, Enlil, and Enki had: Zeus was the heavenly god (yet residing on Earth, on Mount Olympus); Hades was accorded the Lower World; and Poseidon the seas.

The three brothers and three sisters, offspring of Cronus and Rhea, constituted the first half of the Olympian Circle of twelve. The other six were offspring of Zeus, born when Zeus consorted with a variety of goddesses. Of one of them, Leto, he had his Firstborn Son, the great Greek and Roman god *Apollo*. When it was time, however, to obtain a male heir in accordance with the succession rules of the gods, Zeus turned to his own sisters. Hestia, the oldest, was by all accounts a recluse, too old or too sick to be the object of matrimony and childbearing. Zeus thus sought a son by his middle sister, Demeter; but instead of a son she bore him a daughter, Persephone. This paved the way for Zeus to marry Hera, the youngest sister; and she did bear to Zeus a son, *Ares*, and two daughters (Ilithyia and Hebe). When the Greeks and Romans, who lost the knowledge of the planets beyond Saturn, named the known planets, they assigned one—Mars—to Ares; though not the Firstborn Son, he was Zeus's Foremost Son. Apollo, as great a god as he was, had no planet named after him by the Greeks and Romans.

All this reinforces the importance of the wife-sister in the annals of the gods. In matters of succession, the issue arose again and again: Who will the successor to the throne be— the Firstborn Son or the Foremost Son, if the latter was born by a half sister and the former not? That issue appears to have dominated and dictated the course of events on Earth from the moment Enlil joined Enki on this planet, and the rivalry was continued by their sons (Ninurta and Marduk, respectively). In Egyptian tales of the gods, a conflict for similar reasons reared its head between Ra's descendants, Seth and Osiris.

The rivalry, which from time to time flared into actual warfare (Horus in the end fought Seth in single combat in the skies of the Sinai peninsula), by all accounts did not begin on Earth. There were similar conflicts of succession on Nibiru, and Anu did not come by his rulership without fights and battles.

Like the custom that a widow left without a son could demand the husband's brother to "know" her as a surrogate husband and give her a son, so did the Anunnnaki's rules of succession, giving priority to a son by a half sister, find their way into the customs of Abraham and his descendants. In his case, his first son was Ishmael, born by the handmaiden Hagar. But when, at an incredible old age and after divine intervention, Sarah bore Isaac—it was Isaac who was the Legitimate Heir. Why? Because Sarah was Abraham's half sister. "She is my sister, the daughter of my father but not of my mother," Abraham explained (Genesis 20:12).

The marrying of a half sister as a wife was prevalent among the Pharaohs of Egypt, as a means both to legitimize the king's reign and the succession. The custom was even found among the Inca kings of Peru, so much so that the occurrence of calamities during a certain king's reign was attributed to his marrying a woman who was not his half sister. The Inca custom had its roots in the Legends of Beginnings of the Andean peoples, whereby the god Viracocha created four brothers and four sisters who intermarried and were guided to various lands. One such brother-sister couple, which was given a golden wand with which to find the Navel of the Earth in South America, began kingship in Cuzco (the erstwhile Inca capital). That was why Inca kings—providing they had been born of a succession of brother-sister royal couples—could claim direct lineage to the Creator God Viracocha.

(Viracocha, according to Andean legends, was a great God of Heaven who had come to Earth in antiquity and chose the Andean mountains as his arena. In *The Lost Realms* we have identified him as the Mesopotamian god Adad = the Hittite god Teshub, and pointed to many other similarities, besides the brother-sister customs, between the Andean cultures and those of the ancient Near East).

The persistence of the brother-sister intermarriage and the seemingly totally out of proportion significance attached to it, among gods and mortals alike, is puzzling. The custom on the face of it appears to be more than a localized "let's keep the throne in the family" attitude, and at worst the courting of genetic degradation. Why, then, the lengths to which the Anunnaki (example: Enki's repeated efforts to have a son by Ninmah) went to attain a son by such a union? What was so special about the genes of a half sister—the daughter, let us keep in mind, of the male's *mother* but definitely not of the father?

As we search for the answer, it will help to note other biblical practices affecting the mother/father issues. It is customary to refer to the period of Abraham, Isaac, Jacob, and Joseph as the Patriarchal Age, and when asked most people would say that the history related in the Old Testament has been presented from a male-oriented viewpoint. Yet the fact is that it was the *mothers*, not the fathers, who controlled the act that, in the ancients' view, gave the subject of the tale its status of "being"—the *naming* of the child. Indeed, not only a person but a place, a city, a land, were not deemed to have come into being until they were given a name.

This notion, in fact, goes back to the beginning of time, for the very opening lines of the *Epic of Creation*, wishing to impress on the listener that the story begins before the Solar System had been fully fashioned, declare that the story of Tiamat and the other planets begins

> Enuma elish la nabu shamamu
> *When in the heights heaven had not been named*
> Shapiltu ammatum shuma la zakrat
> *And below, firm ground (Earth) had not been called*

And in the important matter of naming a son, it was either the gods themselves or the mother whose privilege it was. We thus find that when the *Elohim* created *Homo sapiens*, it was they who named the new being "Adam" (Genesis 5:2). But when Man was given the ability to procreate on his own, it was Eve—not Adam—who had the right and privilege of naming their first male child Cain (Genesis 4:1) as well as Seth who replaced the slain Abel (Genesis 4:25).

At the start of the "Patriarchal (!) Age" we find that the privilege of naming the two sons of Abraham was taken over by divine beings. His firstborn by Hagar, his wife's handmaiden, was called Ishma'el by an Angel of Yahweh (Genesis 16:11); and the Legitimate Heir Isaac (*Itzhak*, "Who causes laughter") was so named by one of the three divine beings who visited Abraham before the destruction of Sodom and Gomorrah (because when Sarah had heard God saying that she would have a son, she laughed; Genesis 17:19; 18:12). No specific information is provided in the Bible regarding the two sons of Isaac by Rebecca, Esau and Jacob (it is simply stated that this is how they were called). But then it is clearly stated that it was Leah who named Jacob's sons by her and by her handmaiden, as did Rachel (Genesis chapters 29 and 30). Centuries later, after the Israelites had settled in Canaan, it was Samson's mother who so named him (Judges 13:24); so did the mother of the Man of God, Samuel (1 Samuel 1:20).

The Sumerian texts do not provide this kind of information. We do not know, for example, who named Gilgamesh—his mother the goddess or his father the High Priest. But the tale of Gilgamesh provides an important clue to the solution of the puzzle at hand: the importance of the mother in determining the son's hierarchical standing.

His search for attaining the longevity of the gods, it will be recalled, led him first to the Landing Place in the Cedar Mountains; but he and his companion Enkidu were prevented from entering by its robotic guardian and the Bull of Heaven. Gilgamesh then journeyed to the spaceport in the Sinai peninsula. The access to it was guarded by awesome Rocketmen who trained on him "the dreaded spotlight that sweeps the mountains" whose "glance was death" (Fig. 42); but Gilgamesh was not affected; whereupon one Rocketman shouted to his comrade:

> *He who comes,*
> *of the flesh of the gods*
> *is his body!*

Figure 42

Permitted to approach, Gilgamesh confirmed the guard's conclusion: Indeed he was immune to the death rays because his body was of the "flesh of the gods." He was, he explained, not just a *demi*god—he was *"two-thirds* divine," because it was not his father but his *mother* who was a goddess, one of the female Anunnaki.

Here, we believe, is the key to the puzzle of the succession rules and other emphasis on the mother. It is through her that an extra "qualifying dose" was given to the hero or the heir (be it Anunnaki or patriarchal).

This seemed to make no sense even after the discovery, in 1953, of the double-helix structure of DNA and the understanding how the two strands unwind and separate so that only one strand from the female egg and one strand from the male sperm recombine, making the offspring a fifty-fifty image of its parents. Indeed, this understanding, while explaining the demigod claims, defied the inexplicable claim of Gilgamesh to be two-thirds divine.

It was not until the 1980s that the ancient claims began to make sense. This came with the discovery that in addition to the DNA stored in the cells of both males and females in the double-helix structures on the chromosome stems, forming the cell's nucelus, there was another kind of DNA that floats in the cell outside the nucelus. Given the designation Mito-chondrial DNA (mtDNA), it was found to be transmitted *only from the mother* as is, i.e. without splitting and recom-bining with any DNA from the male.

In other words, if the mother of Gilgamesh was a goddess, then he had indeed inherited both her half of the regular DNA *plus* her mtDNA, making him, as he had claimed, two-thirds divine.

It was this discovery of the existence and transmittal as is of mtDNA that has enabled scientists, from 1986 on, to trace the mtDNA in modern humans to an "Eve" who had lived in Africa some 250,000 years ago.

At first scientists believed that the sole function of mtDNA was to act as the cell's power plant, providing the energy required for the cell's myriad chemical and biological reac-tions. But then it was ascertained that the mtDNA was made of "mitochondrions" containing 37 genes arranged in a closed circle, like a bracelet; and that such a genetic "brace-let" contains over 16,000 base pairs of the genetic alphabet (by comparison, each of the chromosomes making up the cell's core that are inherited half from each parent contains upward of 100,000 genes and an aggregate of more than three billion base pairs).

It took another decade to realize that impairments in the makeup or functions of mtDNA can cause debilitating dis-orders in the human body, especially of the nervous system, of heart and skeletal muscles, and of the kidneys. In the 1990s researchers found that defects ("mutations") in mtDNA also disrupt the production of 13 important body proteins, resulting in various severe ailments. A list published in 1997 in *Scientific American* starts with Alzheimer's dis-ease and goes on to include a variety of vision, hearing, blood, muscle, bone marrow, heart, kidney, and brain mal-functions.

These genetic ailments join a much longer list of bodily malfunctions and dysfunctions that defects in the nuclear DNA can cause. As scientists unravel and understand the "genome"—the complete genetic code—of humans (a feat

Figures 43a and 43b

recently achieved for a single lowly bacterium), the function
that each gene performs (and as the other side of the coin,
the ailments if it is absent or malfunctions) is steadily becoming known. By not producing a certain protein or enzyme
or other key bodily compound, the gene regulating that has
been found to cause breast cancer, or hinder bone formation,
deafness, loss of eyesight, heart disorders, the excessive gain
of weight or the opposite thereof, and so on and on.

What is interesting in this regard is that we come across
a list of similar genetic defects as we read the Sumerian texts
about the creation of the Primitive Worker by Enki with the
assistance of Ninmah. The attempt to recombine the strands
of hominid DNA with strands of Anunnaki DNA to create
the new hybrid being was a process of trial and error, and
the beings initially brought about sometimes lacked organs
or limbs—or had too many of them. The Babylonian priest
Berossus, who in the third century B.C. compiled for the
Greeks the history and knowledge of the earlier Sumerians,
described the failed results of Man's creators by reporting
that some of the trial-and-error beings had two heads on one
body. Such ''monsters'' have indeed been depicted by the
Sumerians (Fig. 43a), as well as another anomaly—a being

with one head but two faces called Usmu (Fig. 43b). Specifically mentioned in the texts was a being who could not hold its urine, and a variety of malfunctions including eye and eyesight diseases, trembling hands, an improper liver, a failing heart, and "sicknesses of old age." The text called *Enki and Ninmah: The Creation of Mankind*, besides listing more dysfunctions (rigid hands, paralyzed feet, dripping semen) also depicted Enki as a caring god who, rather than destroying such deformed beings, found some useful life for them. Thus, when one outcome was a man with faulty eyesight, Enki taught him an art that did not require seeing—the art of singing and the playing of a lyre.

To all those, the text states, Enki decreed this or that Fate. He then challenged Ninmah to try the genetic engineering on her own. The results were terrible: the beings she brought about had the mouth in the wrong place, a sick head, sore eyes, aching neck, shaky ribs, malfunctioning lungs, a heart ailment, inability to move the bowels, hands that were too short to reach the mouth, and so on and on. But as the trial and error continued, Ninmah was able to correct the various defects. Indeed, she reached a point that she became so knowledgeable of the Anunnaki/hominid genomes that she boasted that she could make the new being as perfect or imperfect as she wished:

> How good or bad is man's body?
> As my heart prompts me,
> I can make its fate good or bad.

We, too, have now reached the stage where we can insert or replace a certain gene whose role we have uncovered, and try to prevent or cure a specific disease or shortcoming. Indeed, a new industry, the biotechnology industry, has sprung up, with a seemingly limitless potential in medicine (and the stock market). We have even learned to perform what is called transgenic engineering—the transfer of genes between different species, a feat that is achievable because *all* the genetic material on this planet, from the lowest bacterium to the most complex being (Man), of all living organisms that roam or fly or swim or grow, is made up of the same genetic ABC—the same nucleic acids that formed the ''seed'' brought into our Solar System by Nibiru.

Our genes are, in fact, our cosmic connection.

Modern advances in genetics move along two parallel yet interconnected routes. One is to ascertain the human genome, the total genetic makeup of the human being; this involves the reading of a code that although written with just four letters (A-G-C-T, short for the initials of the names given to the four nucleic acids that make up all DNA) is made up of countless combinations of those letters that then form ''words'' that combine into ''sentences'' and ''paragraphs'' and finally a complete ''book of life.'' The other research route is to determine the function of each gene; that is an even more daunting task, facilitated by the fact that if that very same gene (''genetic word'') can be found in a simpler creature (such as a lowly bacterium, or a laboratory mouse) and its function could be experimentally determined, it is virtually certain that the same gene in humans would have the same functions (or its absence the same malfunctions). The discovery of genes related to obesity, for example, has been achieved that way.

The ultimate goal of this search for the cause, and thus the cure, of human ailments and deficiencies is twofold: to find the genes that control the body's physiology and those that control the brain's neurological functions. To find the genes that control the process of aging, the cell's internal clock of the span of life—the genes of longevity—and the genes that control memory, reasoning, intelligence. Experiments on laboratory mice on the one hand and on human twins on the other hand, and extensive researches in between, indicate the existence of genes and groups of genes that account for both. How tedious and elusive these research targets are can be illustrated by the conclusion of a search for an ''intelligence gene'' by comparing twins: the researchers concluded that there might be as many as 10,000 ''gene sites" or "genetic words" responsible for intelligence and cognitive diseases, each playing a tiny part by itself.

In view of such complexities, one wishes that modern scientists would avail themselves of a road map provided by—yes!—the Sumerians. The remarkable advances in astronomy keep corroborating the Sumerian cosmogony and the scientific data provided in the *Epic of Creation*: the existence of other solar systems, highly elliptic orbital paths, retrograde orbits, catastrophism, water on the outer planets— as well as explanations for why Uranus lies on its side, the origin of the Asteroid Belt and of the Moon, the Earth's cavity on one side and the continents on the other side. All is explained by the scientifically sophisticated tale of Nibiru and the Celestial Battle.

Why not then take seriously, as a scientific road map, the other part of the Sumerian creation tales—that of the creation of The Adam?

The Sumerian texts inform us, first of all, that the "seed of life"—the genetic alphabet—was imparted to Earth by Nibiru during the Celestial Battle, some four billion years ago. If the evolutionary processes on Nibiru began a mere one percent before they were launched on Earth, evolution there had begun forty million years before it started on Earth. It is thus quite plausible that the advanced superhumans, Anunnaki, were capable of space travel half a million years ago. It is also plausible that when they came here, they found on Earth the parallel intelligent beings still at the hominid stage.

But coming from the same "seed," transgenic manipulation was possible, as Enki had discovered and then suggested. "The being we need already exists!" he explained. "All we need to do is put our [genetic] mark on it."

One must presume that by then the Anunnaki were aware of the complete genome of the Nibiruans, and capable of determining no less of the hominids' genome as we are by now of ours. What traits, specifically, did Enki and Ninmah choose to transfer from the Anunnaki to the hominids? Both Sumerian texts and biblical verses indicate that while the first humans possessed some (but not all) of the longevity of the

Anunnaki, the creator couple deliberately withheld from The Adam the genes of immortality (i.e. the immense longevity of the Anunnaki that paralleled Nibiru's orbital period). What defects, on the other hand, remained hidden in the depths of the recombined genome of The Adam?

We strongly believe that were qualified scientists to study in detail the data recorded in the Sumerian texts, valuable biogenetic and medical information could be obtained. An amazing case in point is the deficiency known as Williams Syndrome. Afflicting roughly one in 20,000 births, its victims have a very low IQ verging on retardation; but at the same time they excel in some artistic field. Recent research has discovered that the syndrome resulting in such "idiot savants" (as they are sometimes described) is caused by a minute gap in Chromosome 7, depriving the person of some fifteen genes. One of the frequent impairments is the inability of the brain to recognize what the eyes see—*impaired eyesight*; one of the most common talents is *musical*. **But that is exactly the instance recorded in the Sumerian text of the man with impaired eyesight whom Enki taught to sing and play music!**

Because The Adam could not, at first, procreate (requiring the Anunnaki to engage in cloning), we must conclude that at that stage the hybrid being possessed only the basic twenty-two chromosomes. The types of ailments, deficiencies (and cures) that modern biomedicine should expect to find on those chromosomes are the types and range listed in the Enki and Ninmah texts.

The next genetic manipulation (echoed in the Bible in the tale of Adam and Eve in the Garden of Eden) was the granting of the ability to procreate—the addition of the X (female) and Y (male) chromosomes to the basic 22 (Fig. 44). Contrary to long-held beliefs that these two chromosomes have no other function besides determining the offspring's sex, recent research has revealed that the chromosomes play wider and more diverse roles. For some reason this astonished the scientists in particular regarding the Y (male) chromosome. Studies published at the end of 1997 under

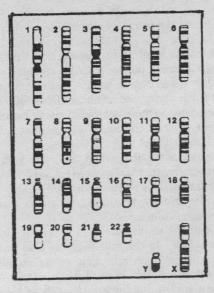

Figure 44

scientific headings as "Functional Coherence of the Human Y Chromosome" received bold headlines in the press such as "Male Chromosome Is Not a Genetic Wasteland, After All" (the *New York Times*, October 28, 1997). (These discoveries confirmed, as an unexpected bonus, that "Adam," too, like Eve, had come out of southeastern Africa).

Where did Enki—the *Nachash*—obtain the X and Y chromosomes? And what about the source of the mtDNA? Hints scattered in the Sumerian texts suggest that Ninki, Enki's spouse, played some crucial role in the final stage of human creation. It was she, Enki decided, who would give the humans the final touch, one more genetic heritage:

> *The newborn's fate,*
> *thou shalt pronounce;*

Ninki would fix upon it
the image of the gods.

The words echo the biblical statement that "in their *image* and after their *likeness* did the *Elohim* create The Adam." And if indeed it was Ninki, Enki's spouse and mother of Marduk, who was the source of the mtDNA of "Eve," the importance attached to the sister-wife lineage begins to make sense; for it constituted one more link to Man's cosmic origins.

Sumerian texts assert that while the gods kept "Eternal Life" to themselves, they did give Mankind *"Wisdom,"* an extra dose of intelligence genes. That additional genetic contribution, we believe, is the subject of a text that scholars call *The Legend of Adapa.*

Clearly identified in the text as a "Son of Eridu," Ea/ Enki's "cult center" in the Edin, he was also called in the text "the son of Ea"—an offspring, as far as other pieces of data suggest, of Ea/Enki himself by a woman other than his spouse. By dint of this lineage, as well as by deliberate action, Adapa was recalled for generations as the Wisest of Men, and was nicknamed the Sage of Eridu:

> *In those days, in those years,*
> *Ea created the Sage of Eridu*
> *as a model of men.*
> *Wide understanding he perfected for him,*
> *disclosing the designs of the Earth.*
> *To him he had given Widsom;*
> *Eternal Life he had not given him.*

This clash between Fate and Destiny takes us to the moment when *Homo sapiens-sapiens* appeared; Adapa, too, being the son of a god, asked for immortality. That, as we know from the *Epic of Gilgamesh*, could be obtained by ascending heavenward to the abode of the Anunnaki; and that was what Ea/Enki told Adapa. Undaunted, Adapa asked for and received Enki's "road map" for reaching the place: "He made

Adapa take the way to heaven, and to heaven he ascended.''
Enki provided him with correct instructions of how to gain
admittance to the throne room of Anu; but also gave him
completely wrong instructions on how to behave when he
would be offered the Bread of Life and the Water of Life.
If you accept them and partake of them, Enki warned Adapa,
surely you shall die! And, so misled by his own father,
Adapa refused the food and the waters of the gods and ended
up subject to his mortal's Destiny.

But Adapa did accept a garment that was brought to him
and wrapped himself in it, and did take the oil that was offered to him, and anointed himself with it. Therefore, Anu
declared, Adapa would be *initiated into the secret knowledge
of the gods*. He showed him the celestial expanse, "from the
horizon of heaven to heaven's zenith." He would be allowed
to return to Eridu safe and sound, and there would be initiated by the goddess Ninkarrak into the secrets of "the ills
that were allotted to Mankind, the diseases that were wrought
upon the bodies of mortals," and taught by her how to heal
such ailments.

It would be relevant here to recall the biblical assurances
by Yahweh to the Israelites in the wilderness in Sinai. Wan-
dering three days without any water, they reached a watering
hole whose water was unpotable. So God pointed out to
Moses a certain tree and told him to throw it into the water,
and the water became potable. And Yahweh said to the Israelites: If you shall give ear to my commandments, I shall
not impose on thee the illnesses of Egypt; "I Yahweh shall
be thine healer" (Exodus 15:26). The promise by Yahweh
to act as the healer of his chosen people is repeated in Exodus
23:25, where a specific reference is made to enabling a
woman who is barren to bear children. (That particular promise was kept in regard to Sarah and other female heroines of
the biblical narrative).

Since we are dealing here with a divine entity, it is safe
to assume that we are dealing here also with *genetic healing*.
The incident with the *Nefilim*, who had found on the eve of
the Deluge that the "Daughters of The Adam" were com-

patible, and sufficiently so to be able to have children together, also involves genetics.

Was such knowledge of genetics, for healing purposes, imparted to Adapa or other demigods or initiates? And if so—how? How could the complex genetic code be taught to Earthlings in those "primitive" times?

For the answer, we believe, we have to search in letters and in numbers.

7

SECRET KNOWLEDGE, SACRED TEXTS

Science—the understanding of the workings of the heavens and the Earth—was the gods' possession; so did the ancient peoples unequivocally believe. It was a "secret of the gods," to be hidden from Mankind or revealed, from time to time and only partly, to selected individuals—initiates into the divine secrets.

"Everything that we know was taught to us by the gods," the Sumerians stated in their writings; and therein lies the foundation, throughout the millennia and unto our own times, of Science and Religion, of the discovered and the occult.

First there was the Secret Knowledge; what was revealed when Mankind was granted Understanding became Sacred Wisdom, the foundation of human civilizations and advancement. As to the secrets that the gods had kept to themselves—those, in the end, proved the most devastating to Mankind. And one must begin to wonder whether the unending search for That Which Is Hidden, sometimes in the guise of mysticism, stems not from the wish to attain the divine but from a fear of what Fate the gods—in their secret conclaves or in hidden codes—have destined for Mankind.

Some of the knowledge that was, or could be, imparted to Mankind when Wisdom and Understanding were granted can be gleaned from God's challenge to Job regarding what he does not know (but God does). "Say if thou knowest science," the biblical Lord stated to the suffering Job:

> *Who has measured the Earth,*
> *that it be known?*

125

Who has stretched a cord upon it?
By what were its platforms wrought?
Who has cast its stone of corners?

Wherefrom cometh Wisdom,
and where is Understanding located?
Mortals know not its arraignment,
in the Land of the Living it is not found.

The ways thereof to Elohim *are known,*
God knows the place thereof;
For he sees to the ends of the Earth
and all that is under the Heavens he views.

With such words did the biblical Lord challenge Job (in chapter 28) to stop questioning the reasons for his Fate, or its ultimate purpose; for Man's knowledge—Wisdom and Understanding—fall so far short of God's, that it serves no purpose to question or try to fathom divine will.

That ancient treatment of Wisdom and Understanding of the secrets of the heavens and the Earth—of science—as a divine domain to which only a few selected mortals can be given access, found expression not only in canonical writings but also in such Jewish mysticism as the *Kaballah*, according to which the Divine Presence symbolized by God's Crown rests on the penultimate supports designated Wisdom (*Hokhmah*) and Understanding (*Binah*) (Fig. 45). They are the same two components of scientific knowledge regarding which Job had been challenged.

The references to *Hokhmah* ("Wisdom") in the Old Testament reveal that it was considered to have been a gift from God, because it was the Lord of the Universe who possessed the Wisdom required for creating the heavens and the Earth. "How great are thy deeds, Oh Lord; with Wisdom hast thou wrought them all," Psalm 104 states as it describes and extols, phase by phase, the Creator's handiwork. When the Lord granted Wisdom to selected humans, the Bible held, He

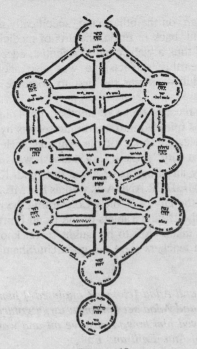

Figure 45

in fact shared with them secret knowledge concerning the heavens and the Earth and all that is upon the Earth. The Book of Job described such knowledge as "Wisdom's Secrets," which had not been revealed to him.

Revelation, the sharing of secret knowledge with humanity through chosen initiates, began before the Deluge. Adapa, the offspring of Enki to whom Wisdom and Understanding (but not Eternal Life) were granted, was shown by Anu the expanse of the heavens not merely as a sightseeing thrill. Post-Diluvial references to him attributed to him the authorship of a work known by its English title *Writings Regarding Time, [from] Divine Anu and Divine Enlil*—a treatise that dealt with time reckoning and the calendar. The

Tale of Adapa, on the other hand, specifically mentions that he was taught, back in Eridu, the arts of medicine and healing. He was thus a well-rounded scientist, adept in both celestial and earthly subjects; he was also anointed as the Priest of Eridu—perhaps the first to combine Science and Religion.

Sumerian records spoke of another, pre-Diluvial Chosen One who was initiated into the divine secrets by being taken up to the celestial abode of the Anunnaki. He came from Sippar (''Bird City'') where Utu/Shamash was in charge, and was probably an offspring of his, a demigod. Known in the texts as EN.ME.DUR.ANNA as well as EN.ME.DUR.AN.KI (''Master of the Divine Tablets Concerning the Heavens'' or ''Master of the Divine Tablets of the Bond Heaven-Earth''), he, too, was taken aloft to be taught secret knowledge. His sponsors and teachers were the gods Utu/Shamash and Ishkur/Adad:

> *Shamash and Adad [clothed? anointed?] him,*
> *Shamash and Adad set him on a large golden throne.*
> *They showed him how to observe oil and water,*
> *a secret of Anu, Enlil and Ea.*
>
> *They gave him a divine tablet,*
> *the* Kibbu, *a secret of Heaven and Earth.*
> *They placed in his hand a cedar instrument,*
> *a favorite of the great gods.*
> *They taught him to make calculations with numbers.*

Though the *Tale of Adapa* does not say so explicitly, it appears that he was allowed, if not actually required, to share some of his secret knowledge with his fellow humans, for else why would he compose the renowned book? In the case of Enmeduranki the transmission of the learned secrets was also mandated—but with the stricture that it must be limited to the line of priests, from father to son, begun with Enmeduranki:

The learned savant
who guards the secrets of the great gods
will bind his favored son with an oath
before Shamash and Adad.
By the Divine Tablet, with a stylus,
he will instruct him in the secrets of the gods.

The tablet on which this text has been inscribed (now kept in the British Museum) has a postscript: "Thus was the line of priests created, those who are allowed to approach Shamash and Adad."

The Bible also recorded the heavenward ascent of the pre-Diluvial patriarch Enoch—the seventh of the ten listed, as was Enmeduranki in the Sumerian King List. Of that extraordinary experience the Bible only says that, at age 365, Enoch was taken aloft to be with God. Fortunately, the extrabiblical *Book of Enoch*, handed down through the millennia and surviving in two versions, provide much greater detail; how much is originally ancient, and how much was fancy and speculation when the "books" were compiled close to the beginning of the Christian era, one cannot say. But the contents are worth summarizing, if for no other reason than for the affinity to the Enmeduranki tale, and because of a briefer but still much more extensive narrative in another extrabiblical book, the *Book of Jubilees*.

From these sources it emerges that Enoch made not one but two celestial journeys. On the first one he was taught the Secrets of Heaven, and was instructed to impart the knowledge on his return to Earth to his sons. Ascending toward the Divine Abode, he was lofted through a series of heavenly spheres. From the place of the Seventh Heaven he could see the shape of the planets; in the Eighth Heaven he could discern constellations. The Ninth Heaven was the "home of the twelve signs of the zodiac." And in the Tenth Heaven was the Divine Throne of God.

(It should be noted here that the abode of Anu, according to Sumerian texts, was on Nibiru, which we have identified as a tenth planet of our Solar System. In *Kabbalah* beliefs,

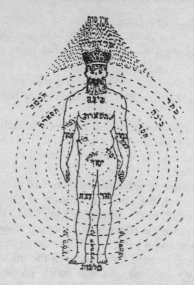

Figure 46

the way to the abode of God Almighty led through ten *Sefirot*, translated "brilliances" but actually depicted as ten concentric spheres—Fig. 46—in which the central one is named *Yessod* ("Foundation"), the eighth and the ninth *Binah* and *Hokhmah*, and the tenth *Ketter*, the "Crown" of the God Most High. Beyond that stretches *Ein Soff*, "Infinity").

Accompanied by two angels, Enoch arrived at his final destination, God's Abode. There his earthly garments were removed; he was clothed in divine garments and anointed by the angels (as was done to Adapa). On the Lord's command, the archangel Pravuel brought out "the books from the sacred storehouse" and gave him a reed stylus with which to write down what the archangel would dictate to him. For thirty days and thirty nights Pravuel dictated and Enoch wrote down "the secrets of the workings of heaven, of the Earth and of the seas; and of all the elements, their passages and goings, and the thunderings of the thunder; and [the secrets] of the Sun and the Moon, and the goings and changings of the planets; the seasons and the years and the days and the hours . . . and all the things of men, the tongues of of every human song . . . and all the things fit to learn.''

According to the *Book of Enoch*, all that vast knowledge, ''secrets of the Angels and God,'' was written down in 360 sacred books, which Enoch took back with him to Earth. Summoning his sons, he showed them the books and explained their contents to them. He was still talking and instructing when a sudden darkness fell and the two angels who had brought Enoch back lifted him and returned him to the heavens; it was precisely the day and hour of his 365th birthday. The Bible (Genesis 5:23–24) simply states: ''And all the days of Enoch were three hundred and sixty and five years; and Enoch walked with God, and he was no more, for he was taken by *Elohim*.''

A prominent similarity between all three tales (Adapa, Enmeduranki, and Enoch) is the involvement of two divine beings in the celestial experience. Adapa was met at the Gate of Anu, and accompanied in and out, by the two young gods Dumuzi and Gizidda; Enmeduranki's sponsors/teachers were Shamash and Adad; and Enoch's, two archangels. The tales undoubtedly were the inspiration for an Assyrian depiction of Anu's heavenly gate, in which it is guarded by two Eaglemen. The gate bears the symbol of Nibiru, the Winged Disc, and the heavenly location is indicated by the celestial symbols of the Earth (as the seventh planet), the Moon, and the complete Solar System (Fig. 47).

Another aspect that stands out—though not explicitly so in the case of Enoch—is the tradition that the granting of the Wisdom and Understanding made the chosen individual not just a scientist but also a priest, and moreover the progenitor of a priestly line. We find this principle employed in the Sinai wilderness during the Exodus, when Yahweh, the biblical Lord, chose Aaron (the brother of Moses) and his sons to be the Lord's priests (Exodus 28:1). Already distinguished by belonging to the tribe of Levi—both on the father's *and*

Figure 47

the mother's sides (Exodus 2:1)—Moses and Aaron were initiated into magical powers that enabled them to perform miracles as well as trigger the calamities that were meant to convince the Pharaoh to let the Israelites leave. Aaron and his sons were then sanctified—"upgraded" in current parlance—to become priests endowed with considerable Wisdom and Understanding. The Book of Leviticus sheds light on some of the knowledge that was granted to Aaron and his sons; it included secrets of the calendar (quite complex, since it was a lunar-solar calendar), of human maladies and healing, and veterinary knowledge. Considerable anatomical information is included in the relevant chapters of Leviticus, and the possibility that the Israelite priests were given "hands-on" lessons cannot be ruled out in view of the fact that clay models of anatomical parts, inscribed with medical instructions, were current in Babylon even before the time of the Exodus—Fig. 48.

(The Bible described King Solomon as the "wisest of men" who could discourse on the biodiversity of all the plants, "from cedars of Lebanon to the hyssop that grows out of a wall, and animals, and birds, and creeping things, and fishes." He could do so because in addition to the Wisdom and the Understanding (intelligence) that were God-given, he also acquired *Da'ath*—learned knowledge).

The priestly line begun with Aaron was subjected to rig-

Figure 48

orous laws imposing marital and procreation constraints. Whom they could have conjugal relations with and especially whom they could marry required that "the priestly seed shall not be profaned," and if one's seed shall be imperfect— "shall have a blemish," a mutation, a genetic defect—that man was prohibited through all generations to perform priestly duties, "for I Yahweh hath sanctified the priestly line" of Aaron.

These strictures intrigued generations of biblical scholars; but their true significance became evident only with the advent of DNA researches. It was only in January 1997, in the journal *Nature*, that an international group of scientists reported the existence of a "Priestly Gene" among Jews whose lineage can be traced back to Aaron. Unchanged Jewish traditions require that certain rituals and blessings called for on the Sabbath and High Holidays services must be performed only by a *Cohen*. The term, meaning "priest," was first used in the Bible to describe Aaron and his sons. Ever since then, the designation has been passed down through the generations from fathers to sons, and the only way to become a Cohen is to be born as a son of one. This privileged status has been as often as not identified by using "Cohen" as a family name (transmuted into Kahn, Kahane, Kuhn) or as an adjective added after a person's name, so and so *Ha-Cohen*, "the priest."

It was this aspect of the patrilineal nature of the Jewish *Cohen* tradition that intrigued a research team from Israel, England, Canada, and the USA. Focusing on the male (''Y'') chromosome that is passed from father to son, they tested hundreds of "Cohens" in different countries and found that by and large they had two unique "markers" on the chromosome. This proved to be the case both for *Ashkenazi* (East European) and *Sephardi* (Near Eastern/African) Jews who had branched out after the destruction of the Jerusalem Temple in A.D. 70, indicating the antiquity of the genetic markers.

"The simplest and most straightforward explanation is that these men have the Y chromosome of Aaron," explained Dr. Karl Skorecki of the Israel Institute of Technology in Haifa.

The tales of those who were initiated into the secret knowledge assert that the information was written down in "books." These, for sure, were not what we now call "books"—inscribed pages bound together. The many texts discovered in caves near the Dead Sea in Israel are referred to as the Dead Sea scrolls, for they were texts inscribed on sheets of parchment (made mostly of goat skins) sewn together and rolled to form scrolls, the way the *Scrolls of the Law* (the first five books of the Hebrew Bible) are inscribed and rolled to this day. The biblical Prophets (especially Ezekiel) featured scrolls as part of the divinely given messages. Ancient Egyptian texts were written on papyrus—sheets made from reeds growing in the Nile River. And the earliest known texts, from Sumer, were inscribed on clay tablets;

using a reed stylus, the scribe would make markings on a piece of wet clay that, after it dried, would become a hard inscribed tablet.

In which form were the "books" written by Adapa, Enmeduranki, and Enoch (360 of them by the latter!)? Bearing in mind that they are attributed to a time before the Deluge—thousands of years even before the Sumerian civilization—probably in none of the post-Diluvial forms, although the Assyrian king Ashurbanipal did boast that he could read "writing from before the Flood." Since in each instance what was written down was dictated by the divine Lord, it would be logical to wonder whether the writing was done in what some Sumerian and Akkadian texts call *Kitab Ilani*—"writing of the gods." References to such writings by the Anunnaki may be found, for example, in inscriptions dealing with the rebuilding of run-down temples, in which the claim was made that the reconstruction followed "the drawings from olden times and *the writing of the Upper Heaven.*" The Sumerians listed a goddess, Nisaba (sometimes spelled Nidaba), as the patron goddess of scribes and the one who kept the records for the gods; her symbol was the Holy Stylus.

One of the references to writings of the gods in the earliest times is found in a Hittite text dubbed by scholars *The Song of Ullikummis*. Written on clay tablets that have been discovered in the ancient Hittite capital Hattushas (near the present-day village of Boghaskoy in central Turkey), it relates a puzzling tale of a "vigorous god made of diorite stone" that an ancient god whom the Hittite named Kumarbis had fashioned in order to challenge the other gods. The challenged gods, unable to withstand or counter the challenger Ullikummis, rushed to Enki's abode in the Lower World to obtain from him the hidden "old tablets with the words of fate." But after the "ancient storehouse" was opened, and the "olden seals" with which the tablets were secured were removed, it was discovered that the writing was in "the olden words," requiring the Olden Gods to understand them.

In Egypt it was Thoth who was venerated as the Divine

Scribe. It was he who, after the Council of the Gods resolved to recognize Horus as the legitimate heir, inscribed on a metal tablet the Decree of the Gods, and the tablet was then lodged in the "divine Chamber of Records." In addition to records for divine use, Thoth was also credited by the Egyptians with writing books for the guidance of mortals. The *Book of the Dead*, they held, was a composition "written by Thoth with his own fingers" as a guide to the Journey in the Afterlife. A shorter work called by the Egyptians the *Book of Breathings* also contained the statement that it was Thoth who "had written this book with his own fingers." And in the *Tales of the Magicians*, to which we have already referred, it was said that the living but inanimate king and queen whom Thoth had punished guarded, in the subterranean chamber, "the book that the god Thoth has written with his own hand" and in which secret knowledge concerning the Solar System, astronomy, and the calendar was revealed. When the seeker of such "ancient books of sacred writings" penetrated the subterranean chamber, he saw the book "giving off a light as if the Sun shone there."

What were those divine "books" and what kind of writing was on them?

The epithet-name of Enmeduranna, "Master of the Divine Tablets Concerning Heaven," draws attention to the term ME in his name, translated here as "Divine Tablets." In truth no one can be sure what the ME's were, whether tablets or something more akin to computer-memory chips or discs. They were objects small enough to be held in one hand, for it was told that Inanna/Ishtar, seeking to elevate her city Uruk to capital status, connivingly obtained from Enki scores of the ME's that were encoded with the secrets of Supreme Lordship, Kingship, Priesthood, and other aspects of a high civilization. And we recall that the evil Zu stole from Enlil's Duranki the Tablets of Destinies and the ME's which were encoded with the Divine Formulas. Perhaps we will grasp what they were if we look to technology millennia ahead.

Putting aside the question of the gods' own writings and data-keeping for their own purposes, the issue of what language and what writing system were used when secret knowledge was dictated to Earthlings for use by Earthlings becomes a matter of great significance when it comes to the Bible—and especially so in regard to the events on Mount Sinai.

Paralleling the tale of Enoch staying in the heavenly abode "thirty days and thirty nights" taking dictation, is the biblical report of Moses, having ascended toward the Lord God atop Mount Sinai, "stayed there with Yahweh forty days and forty nights—bread he did not eat and water he did not drink—and he wrote upon the tablets the words of the Covenant and the Ten Commandments" as God dictated (Exodus 34:28).

Those, however, were the second set of tablets, replacing the first set that Moses smashed in anger when he had come down from Mount Sinai a previous time. The Bible provides greater—and mind-boggling—details regarding that first instance of sacred writings; then, the Bible explicitly states, *God himself did the inscribing!*

The tale begins in chapter 24 of the book of Exodus, when Moses and Aaron and two of his sons, and seventy of the Elders of Israel, were invited to approach Mount Sinai on the peak of which the Lord had landed in his *Kabod*. There the dignitaries could glimpse the divine presence through a thick cloud, blazing as a "devouring fire." Then Moses alone was summoned to the mountaintop, to receive the *Torah* ("Teachings") and the Commandments *that the Lord God had already written down*:

> *And Yahweh said unto Moses:*
> *Come up to me upon the Mount*
> *and remain there,*
> *and I will give thee the stone tablets—*
> *the Teachings and the Commandments—*
> *that I had written,*
> *so that you may teach them.*
>
> *Exodus 24:12*

"And Moses went into the midst of the cloud, and ascended the Mount; and he stayed there forty days and forty nights." Then Yahweh

> *Gave to Moses,*
> *when He had finished speaking with him,*
> *the two Tablets of Testimony—*
> *stone tablets,*
> *inscribed with the finger of* Elohim.

> *Exodus 31:17*

Additional astounding information regarding the tablets and the manner in which they were inscribed is provided in Exodus 32:16–17 that describe the events that took place as Moses was coming down the Mount after a long and (to the people) inexplicable absence:

> *And Moses turned to come down from the Mount,*
> *and the two Tablets of the Testimony in his hand—*
> *tablets inscribed on both their sides,*
> *inscribed on the one side and on the other side.*
> *And the Tablets were the handiwork of* Elohim,
> *and the writing was the writing of* Elohim,
> *and it was engraved upon the tablets*

Two tablets made of stone, divinely handcrafted. Inscribed front and back in the "writing of the *Elohim*"— which must mean both language and script; and so engraved into the stone by God himself!

And all that in a language and in a script that Moses could read and understand, for he was to teach all that to the Israelites . . .

As we know from the rest of the biblical record, Moses smashed the two tablets when, reaching the encampment, he saw that in his absence the people made a golden calf to be worshiped in imitation of Egyptian customs. When the crisis was over,

Yahweh said unto Moses:
Hew thyself two tablets of stone
like the first two ones,
and I shall write upon these tablets
the words which were on the first tablets
that thou hast broken.

Exodus 34:1

And Moses did so and went up the Mount again. There Yahweh came toward him, and Moses bowed and repeated his pleas for forgiveness. In response, the Lord God dictated to him additional commandments, saying: "Write thee these words down, for in accordance with them did I make a Covenant with thee and with the people of Israel." And Moses stayed on the Mount forty days and forty nights, recording on the tablets "the words of the Covenant and the Ten Commandments" (Exodus 35:27–28). This time, *Moses was taking down dictation*.

Not only the sections in Exodus, Leviticus, and Deuteronomy recording the Teachings and Commandments, but all of the first five books of the Hebrew Bible (the above plus Genesis and Numbers) have been deemed, from the very beginning, to be sacred writings. Embraced by the general term *Torah*, they are also known as the *Five Books of Moses*, because of the tradition that Moses himself wrote or authored all five of them as a divine revelation to him. Therefore, the *Torah* scrolls that are taken out of their ark in synagogues and read on the Sabbath and High Holidays must be copied (by special scribes) precisely the way they have come down through the ages—book by book, chapter by chapter, verse by verse, word by word, *letter by letter*. An error of one letter disqualifies the whole five-book scroll.

While this letter-by-letter precision has been studied by Jewish sages and biblical scholars throughout the ages (long before the latest interest in "secret codes" in the *Torah*), an even more challenging aspect of the long and extensive dictation and the required letter-by-letter accuracy has been completely ignored:

And that is, that such a method of writing upon Mount Sinai could not have been the slow cuneiform script of Mesopotamia that was usually written with a stylus on wet clay, nor the monumental hieroglyphic picturelike script of Egypt. The volume and speed and the letter-by-letter accuracy required an *alphabetic script*!

The problem is that at the time of the Exodus, circa 1450 B.C., nowhere in the ancient world did an alphabetic script yet exist.

The concept of an alphabet is the work of genius; and whoever the genius was, he based it on existing foundations. Egyptian hieroglyphic writing advanced from picture-signs depicting objects to signs standing for syllables or even consonants; but it has remained a complex writing system of countless picture-signs (see Fig. 24b). Sumerian writing advanced from its original pictographs to cuneiform (Fig. 49) and the signs acquired a syllabic sound; but to form from them a vocabulary required hundreds of different signs. The genius combined cuneiform ease with Egyptian advances to consonants, and *achieved it with just twenty-two signs*!

Starting with that, the ingenious inventor asked himself as well as his disciple: What is the word for what you see? The answer—*in the language of the Semitic Israelites*—was *Aluf*. Fine, said the inventor: Let us call this symbol *Aleph* and simply pronounce it "A." He then drew the pictograph for house. What do you call that? he asked, and the disciple answered: *Bayit*. Fine, said the inventor, from now on we will call this sign "*Beth*" and pronounce it simply as "B."

We cannot vouch that such a conversation actually took place, but we are certain that this was the process of creating and inventing the Alpha-Bet. The third letter, *Gimel* (pronounced "G") was the image of a camel (*Gamal* in Hebrew); the next one, *Daleth* for "D," represented *Deleth*, "door" (on its hinges); and so on through the twenty-two letters of the Semitic alphabet (Fig. 50), all of which serve as consonants and three of which can double up as vowels.

Who was the ingenious innovator?

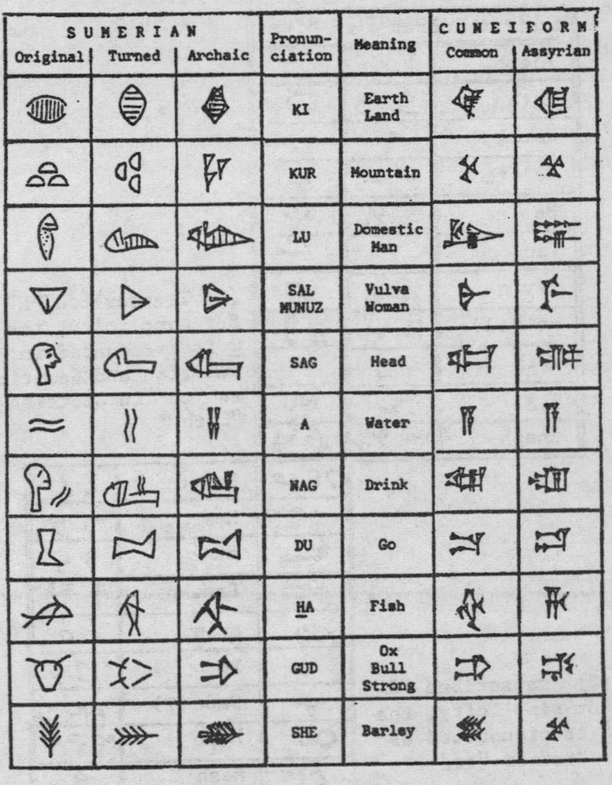

| SUMERIAN | | | Pronun- | Meaning | CUNEIFORM | |
Original	Turned	Archaic	ciation		Common	Assyrian
			KI	Earth Land		
			KUR	Mountain		
			LU	Domestic Man		
			SAL MUNUZ	Vulva Woman		
			SAG	Head		
			A	Water		
			NAG	Drink		
			DU	Go		
			HA	Fish		
			GUD	Ox Bull Strong		
			SHE	Barley		

Figure 49

If one is to accept the learned opinion, it was some manual laborer, a slave in the Egyptian turquoise mines in the western Sinai, near the Red Sea, because it was there that Sir Flinders Petrie found in 1905 signs carved on walls that, a decade later, Sir Alan Gardiner deciphered as "acrophonic"—spelling out L-B-A-L-T (Fig. 51); it meant Dedicated "To the Mistress" (presumably the goddess Hathor)—but in Semitic, not Egyptian! Further similar writings discovered in that area left no doubt that the alphabet originated there; from

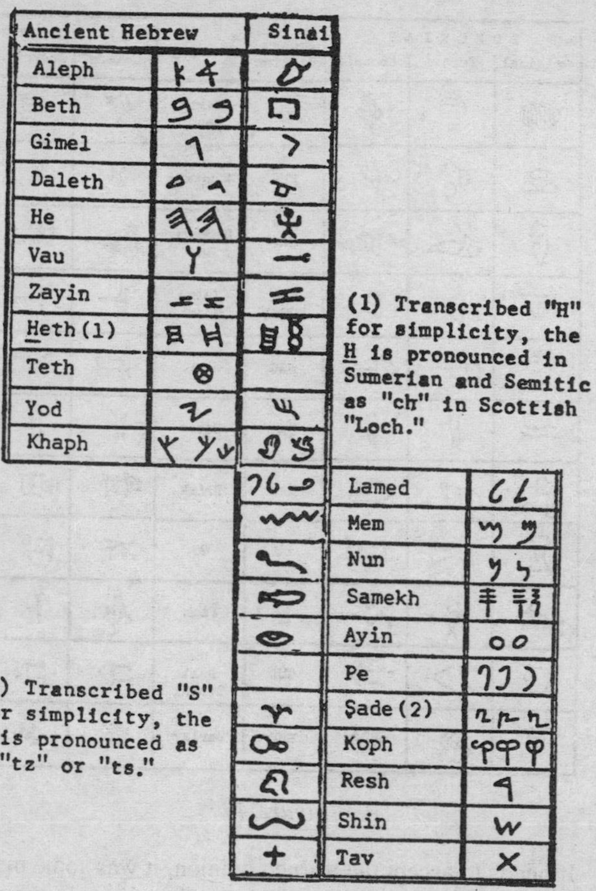

Ancient Hebrew			Sinai	
Aleph				
Beth				
Gimel				
Daleth				
He				
Vau				
Zayin				
Heth (1)				
Teth				
Yod				
Khaph				

(1) Transcribed "H" for simplicity, the H̲ is pronounced in Sumerian and Semitic as "ch" in Scottish "Loch."

(2) Transcribed "S" for simplicity, the Ṣ is pronounced as "tz" or "ts."

	Lamed	
	Mem	
	Nun	
	Samekh	
	Ayin	
	Pe	
	Ṣade (2)	
	Koph	
	Resh	
	Shin	
	Tav	

Figure 50

there it spread to Canaan and then to Phoenicia (where an attempt to express the ingenious idea with cuneiform signs—Fig. 52—was short-lived). Beautifully executed, the original "Sinaitic script" served as the Temple script in Jerusalem and as the royal script of Judean kings (Fig. 53a) until it

Figure 51

was replaced, during the time of the Second Temple, with a square script borrowed from the Aramaeans (the script used in the Dead Sea scrolls unto modern times, Fig. 53b).

No one has really been comfortable with the attribution of the revolutionary innovation, at the end of the Bronze Age, to a slave in turquoise mines. It required an outstanding knowledge of speech and writing and linguistics, apart from outstanding Wisdom and Understanding, that could hardly have been possessed by a mere slave. And what was the purpose of inventing a new script when, in the very same mining areas, monuments and walls were filled with *Egyptian* hieroglyphic inscriptions (Fig. 54)? How could an obscure innovation in a restricted area spread to Canaan and beyond and replace there a writing method that had existed and served well for more than two millennia? It just does not make sense; but in the absence of another solution, that theory still stands.

But, if we have imagined right the conversation that

Figure 52

had led to this alphabet, then it was Moses to whom the first lesson was given. He was in the Sinai; he was there at the right time; he engaged in extensive writings; and he had the supreme teacher—God himself.

Little noticed in the biblical tales of Exodus is the fact that Moses was instructed by Yahweh to write things down even before the ascent upon Mount Sinai to receive the tablets. The first time was after the war with the Amalekites, a tribe that instead of acting as an ally betrayed the Israelites and attacked them. The betrayal, God said, should be remembered by all future generations: "And Yahweh said unto Moses: *Write this down in a book* for a remembrance" (Exodus 17:14). The second mention of a book of writings occurs in Exodus 24:4 and 24:7, in which it is reported that after the Lord God, speaking in a booming voice from atop the Mount, listed the conditions for an everlasting Covenant between Him and the Children of Israel, "Moses *wrote down* all the words of Yahweh, and built an altar at the foot of the Mount and erected twelve stone pillars according to the number of the tribes of Israel." And then "he took the covenant *book* and read from it to the people to hear."

The dictating and writing down had thus begun before the ascents of Moses to the mountaintop and the two separate writings on the stone tablets. One has to look to the earlier chapters of Exodus to find out when and where the alphabetic innovation—the language and writing employed in the Lord's communications with Moses—could have taken place. There we read that Moses, adopted as a son by the

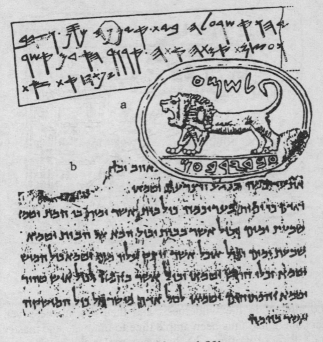

Figures 53a and 53b

Pharaoh's daughter, fled for his life after he had killed an Egyptian official. His destination was the Sinai peninsula, where he ended up dwelling with the Midianite high priest (and marrying his daughter). And one day, shepherding the flocks, he wandered into the wilderness where the "Mount of the *Elohim*" was, and there he was summoned by God out of the burning bush and given the task of leading his people, the Children of Israel, out of Egypt.

Moses returned to Egypt only after the death of the Pharaoh who had sentenced him (Thothmes III, by our calculations), in 1450 B.C., and struggled with the next Pharaoh (Amenophis II in our opinion) for seven years until the Exodus was permitted. Having started to hear from the Lord

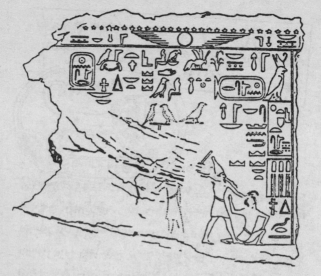

Figure 54

God already in the wilderness, and then during the seven years, there had thus been ample time to innovate and master a new form of writing, one that was simpler and much faster than those of the great empires of the time—Mesopotamian, Egyptian, Hittite.

The Bible relates extensive communications between Yahweh and Moses and Aaron from the moment Moses had been summoned to the burning bush onward. Whether the divine messages, sometimes involving detailed instructions, were ever in writing the Bible does not say; but it might be significant that the "magicians" in the Pharaoh's court thought that they had been written instructions: "And the Pharaoh's magicians said to him: This is the finger of god" (Exodus 8:15). "The *finger of God*," it will be recalled, was the term used in Egyptian texts regarding the god Thoth, to indicate a writing by the god himself.

If all this leads to the suggestion that alphabetic writing

began in the Sinai Peninsula—it should not be surprising that archaeologists have reached that same conclusion, but without being able to explain how such a tremendous and ingenious innovation could have originated in a wilderness.

Did the conversation that we have imagined actually take place, or did Moses invent the alphabet by himself? After all, he was in the Sinai peninsula at the very same time, he was highly educated in the Egyptian court (where correspondence with both the Mesopotamians and Hittites had been going on), and he undoubtedly learned the Semitic language from the Midianites (if not knowing it already from his Israelite brethren in Egypt). Did he, in his wanderings in the Sinai wilderness, see the Semitic slaves (Israelites who had by then been enslaved in Egypt), crudely etch on the mines' walls his idea of a new way of writing?

One would have liked to be able to attribute the brilliant innovation to Moses, acting alone; it would have been gratifying to credit the biblical leader of the Exodus, the only one who had conversed with God person-to-person according to the Bible, with the invention of the alphabet and the cultural revolution it had triggered. But the repeated references to Divine Writing, writing by God himself, and Moses only taking dictation, suggest that the alphabetic writing and language system were one of the "secrets of the gods." Indeed, it was to the same Yahweh that the Bible attributed the invention/innovation of other diverse languages and scripts on a previous occasion—in the aftermath of the incident of the Tower of Babel.

One way or another, we feel that Moses was the initiate through whom the innovation was revealed to Mankind. And thus we can rightly call it *The Mosaic Alphabet.*

There is more to the first alphabet as a "secret of the gods." It is based, in our opinion, on the most sophisticated and ultimate knowledge—that of the genetic code.

When the Greeks adopted the Mosaic alphabet a thousand years later (though reversing it as a mirror image, Fig. 55), they found it necessary to add more letters in order to allow

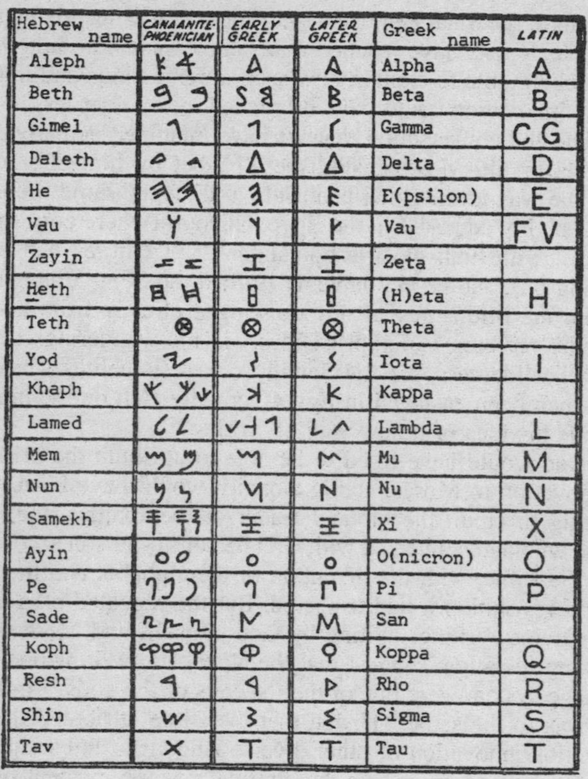

Hebrew name	CANAANITE-PHOENICIAN	EARLY GREEK	LATER GREEK	Greek name	LATIN
Aleph	ḳ ϥ	A	A	Alpha	A
Beth	ϑ ϑ	ϟ ϑ	B	Beta	B
Gimel	˥	˥	˥	Gamma	C G
Daleth	◿ ◺	Δ	Δ	Delta	D
He	⅃ ⅃	ⅎ	E	E(psilon)	E
Vau	Y	Y	ϒ	Vau	F V
Zayin	⊏ ⊏	I	I	Zeta	
Ḥeth	⊟ H	B	B	(H)eta	H
Teth	⊗	⊗	⊗	Theta	
Yod	⁊	ϟ	Ϛ	Iota	I
Khaph	⅄ ⅄	⋊	K	Kappa	
Lamed	⌐ ⌐	⌄⌐⌐	L ∧	Lambda	L
Mem	⌐ᶮ ⌐ᶮ	ᶭ	ᶭ	Mu	M
Nun	⅄ ⅃	Ⅵ	N	Nu	N
Samekh	⊤ ⅋⊤	Ξ	Ξ	Xi	X
Ayin	o o	o	o	O(nicron)	O
Pe	⁊ ⁊ ⁊	⌐	Γ	Pi	P
Sade	⌐ ⌐ ⌐	Ⅳ	M	San	
Koph	ϙϙϙ	Φ	ϙ	Koppa	Q
Resh	⅃	⅃	⌐	Rho	R
Shin	w	ϟ	∋	Sigma	S
Tav	×	T	T	Tau	T

Figure 55

for all the pronunciation needs. In fact, within the confines of the twenty-two letters of the Mosaic-Semitic alphabet, some letters can be pronounced as "soft" (V, Kh, S, Th) or hard (B, K, SH, T); and other letters had to double up as vowels.

Indeed, as we contemplate this limitation to *twenty-two*— no more, no less—we cannot help recalling the constrictions applied to the sacred number *twelve* (requiring the addition or dropping of deities in order to keep the "Olympian Circle" to precisely twelve). Did such a hidden principle—divinely inspired—apply to the restriction of the original alphabet to twenty-two letters?

The number ought to be familiar in this day and age. It is the number of human chromosomes when The Adam was created, before the second genetic manipulation had added the sex chromosomes "Y" and "X"!

Did the Almighty who had revealed to Moses the secret of the alphabet, then, use the genetic code as the secret code of the alphabet?

The answer seems to be Yes.

If this conclusion seems outlandish, let us read the Lord's statement in Isaiah 45:11: "It is I who created the Letters . . . It is I who made the Earth and created the Adam upon it," thus sayeth Yahweh, the Holy One of Israel. Whoever was involved in the creation of Man was involved in the creation of the letters that make up the alphabet.

Present-day computer systems construct words and numbers from just two "letters," a Yes-No system of ones and zeroes matching an On-Off flow of electrons (and thus called binary). But attention has already shifted to the four-letter genetic code and the much greater speed with which the transactions take place within the living cell. Conceptually, the present computer language that is expressed in a sequence such as 010011001111001100001 0100 etc. (and in countless variations using "0" and "1") can be envisaged as the genetic language of a DNA fragment expressed as the nucleotides CGTAGAATTCTGCGAACCTT and so on in a chain of DNA letters (that are always arranged in *three letter "words"*) bound as base-pairs in which the A binds with T, C with G. The problem and the challenge is how to create and read computer chips that are coated not with "0" and "1" electrons but with bits of genetic material. Advances since 1991 at various academic institutions as well as at commercial enterprises involved in genetic treatments have succeded in creating silicon chips coated with nucleotides. Comparing the speed and the capabilities of DNA Comput-

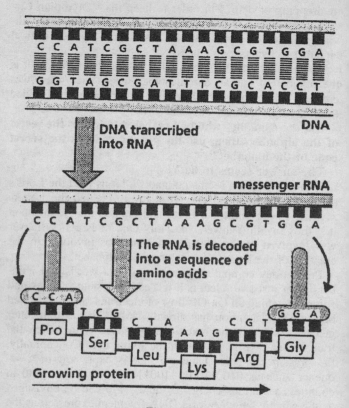

Figure 56

ing, as the new science is called, "the information storage capacity of DNA is huge," a research paper published in *Science* (October 1997) stated.

In nature, the genetic information encoded in the DNA is decoded, at lightning speed, by a messenger called RNA that transcribes and recombines the DNA "letters" into "words" consisting of three letters. These three-letter groupings, it has been established, lie at the core of all life forms on Earth because they spell out chemically and biologically the twenty amino acids whose chains form the proteins of which all life on Earth—and probably elsewhere in the cosmos—consists. Figure 56 illustrates schematically, and in a simplified manner, how a given DNA sequence is decoded and recombined into the amino acids Propraline ("Pro"), Serine ("Ser"), etc., by means of the three-letter word code to build a protein.

The rich and precise Hebrew language is based on "root" words from which verbs, nouns, adverbs, adjectives, pronouns, tenses, conjugations and all other grammatical variants derive. For reasons that no one has been able to explain, these root words are made up of *three letters*. This is quite a departure from the Akkadian, the mother-language of all Semitic languages, which was formed from syllables—sometimes just one, sometimes two or three or more.

Could the reason for the three-letter Hebrew root words be the three letter DNA-language—the very source, as we have concluded, of the alphabet itself? If so, then the three letter root words corroborate this conclusion.

"Death and life are in the language," the Bible states in Proverbs (18:21). The statement has been treated allegorically. It is time, perhaps, to take it literally: *the language of the Hebrew Bible and the DNA genetic code of life (and death) are but two sides of the same coin.*

The mysteries that are encoded therein are vaster than one can imagine; they include among other wondrous discoveries the secrets of healing.

8

HIDDEN CODES, MYSTIC NUMBERS

It was probably inevitable that with the advent of the modern computer age, some masters of the craft would turn their capabilities to a novel and new goal: the search for a "secret code" in the Bible.

While this is presented in scientific papers and even books as the epitome of modern sophistication, the fact is that this search is actually a *renewed*, not a new, search, albeit with new and more advanced tools.

The Hebrew Bible consists of three parts, the *Torah* ("Teachings"), which comprises the Pentateuch (the *Five Books of Moses*) and, historically and chronologically, covers the time from Creation through the wanderings of the Exodus and the death of Moses; *Neviyim* ("Prophets"), encompassing the books of Joshua and the Judges, Samuel and the Kings, and then the major and minor Prophets, the Psalms and Proverbs and Job—historically from the Israelite settlement in Canaan through the destruction of the First Temple of Jerusalem; and *Ketuvim* ("Writings"), starting with the Song of Songs through the books attributed to the two leaders who led the exiles back to Judea to rebuild the Temple (Ezra and Nehemiah) and (in the arrangement of the Hebrew Bible's canon) ending with 1 and 2 Chronicles. All together the three parts are called by the acronym *TaNaKh*; and it was already in the time of the Prophets that interpretive references to the first part, the Torah, were made.

Discussions by Jewish sages and religious leaders intended to "read between the lines" of the words of the Torah, then of the Prophets, intensified during the exile after the destruction (by the Babylonian king Nebuchadnezzar) of the First Temple, and even more so after the destruction of the Second Temple (by the Romans). The record of those deliberations is the *Talmud* ("The Study"). Jewish mysticism, known as the *Kaballah*, took over and built upon those earlier searches for hidden meanings.

That such hidden meanings did exist, the Bible itself attests. The key was the alphabet, the twenty-two letters.

A simple encoding device, which even schoolchildren often play, is the serial substitution of letters. Kabbalist sages in the Middle Ages used as a search tool a system known as ATBSh, in which the last letter of the Hebrew alphabet, Tav ("T") is substituted for the first letter Aleph ("A"); the last but one, Shin ("Sh") for the second Beth ("B"), and so on. The Kabbalist Abraham ben Jechiel Hacohen illustrated the system and provided the key to it in a book published in A.D. 1788.

But in fact such a coding system was used by the Prophet Jeremiah (7th century B.C.) who, prophesying the fall of mighty Babylon, substituted the spelling B-B-L (Babel) with the letters Sh-Sh-Kh to avoid imprisonment (Jeremiah 25:26 and 51:42). The Book of Lamentations, attributed to the Prophet Jeremiah, in which the fall and destruction of Jerusalem are bewailed, employed another hidden code, called Acrostics, in which the first (or sometimes last) letter of a verse make up a word or a name, or (as in the case of Jeremiah) reveal the identity of the sacred alphabetical letters. The first word in the first verse (translated "alas") begins with an Aleph, the second verse begins with a Beth and so on through the twenty-second verse. The same acrostics is repeated by the Prophet in the second chapter; then each letter starts two verses in the third chapter, reverting to one per verse in the fourth. Psalm 119 is constructed with eightfold acrostics!

The authenticity of certain verses in Psalms could be verified by noticing that each verse has two parts, each of which starts alphabetically (e.g., Psalm 145); the same clue is hidden in the verse arrangement of Proverbs 31. In Psalm 145, moreover, the three verses (11, 12, 13) that extol the kingship of Yahweh begin with the letters Kh-L-M, which read backward spell *MeLeKh*, "King."

The use of acrostics as a hidden code, evident in other books of the Bible as well, is also found in post-biblical books (some of which are included in the Christian arrangement of the Old Testament). A prominent example comes from the time of the revolt against Greek rule in the second century B.C. The revolt bears the name of its leaders, the Maccabees—a name which was in fact an acronym based on the verse in the Song of Moses (Exodus 15:11)—"Who is like thee among the gods, oh Yahweh"—the first letters of the four Hebrew words forming the acronym M-K-B-I, pronounced "Maccabee."

After the destruction of the Second Temple by the Romans in A.D. 70, the spiritual and religious mainstay for the Jews were the Holy Scriptures—the treasure of divine and prophetic words. Was it all fated, was it all predicted? And what is still destined, what is yet to come? The keys to the past and to the future had to be hidden in the sacred writings, by then canonized not only as to content but also as to every word and every letter. That search for hidden meanings obscured by secret codes became known after the Temple's destruction as "entering the forbidden grove," the word for "grove"—*PaRDeS*—in itself being an acronym created from the first letters of four methods of extracting the scriptures' message: *Peshat* (literal meaning), *Remez* (hint), *Drash* (interpretation) and *Sod* (secret). A Talmudic tale intended to illustrate the risks of dealing prematurely with what has been meant to remain unrevealed relates how four rabbinic sages entered the Pardes; one "gazed and died," another lost his mind, a third went wild and began to "uproot the plants"; only one, Rabbi Akiba, came out whole.

The search for hidden meanings was resumed in Medieval times by the Kabbalists and their forerunners. What would an examination of the Bible by the ATBSh code reveal? What if another letter rearrangement is used? What if a word is deemed inserted just to hide the real meaning, and thus should be skipped to read the intended text? By such methods, for example, one could prove that Psalm 92 ("A Song for the Sabbath Day") was actually composed by Moses in the Sinai, and not by King David. In another instance it was asserted that the great Jewish savant Maimonides (Spain and Egypt, twelfth century A.D.) was named in the Book of Exodus, where the first letters of the last four words in verse 11:9 create the acronym R-M-B-M—matching the acronym resulting from the full name of Maimonides, *Rabbi Moshe Ben Maimon* (explaining the prevalent reference to him as *Rambam*).

But, Medieval savants wondered, had the search to be limited to only first or last letters of words, the beginning or end of verses? What happens if one searches for hidden meanings by skipping letters? Every second, every fourth, every fortysecond? It was perhaps inevitable that with the advent of computers, someone would apply this tool to an expedited search for a "code" based on letter spacing. The latest spate of interest in the subject indeed resulted from such an application of computer techniques by a number of Israeli scientists; it was launched by the publication in August 1994 of a paper titled "Equidistant Letter Sequences in the Book of Genesis" in the prestigious journal *Statistical Science* by Doron Witzum, Eliyahu Rips and Yoav Rosenberg.

Subsequent reviews, analyses, and books (*The Bible Code* by Michael Drosnin and *The Truth Behind the Bible Code* by Jeffrey Satinover) deal, in essence, with one basic premise: If you list all of the 304,805 letters in the Pentateuch in sequence, and arrange them in "blocs" that segment those letters into sections consisting of a certain number of lines, and each line a certain number of letters, then choose a skipping method—certain letters will form words that, unbelievable as it sounds, spell out predictions for our time and for all time, such as the assassination of Prime Minister Rabin of Israel or the discovery of the Theory of Relativity by Albert Einstein.

However, in order to achieve such alleged "predictions" of future events in texts written thousands of years ago, the searchers had to devise arbitrary and changeable rules for how to read the "code words." The letters forming the predictory words end up sometimes lying next to each other, sometimes spaced out (with the spacing varied and flexible), sometimes read vertically, sometimes horizontally or diagonally, sometimes backward, sometimes from down up . . .

Such arbitrariness in selecting the length and number of lines, the direction of reading, the skipping or nonskipping of letters and so on must rob the uninitiated of the uncritical acceptance of the code claims that are based exclusively on letters in the Bible; and to do that without belaboring the issue of whether the current text of the Pentateuch is precisely the original, divinely endowed, letter-by-letter arrangement. We say that not only because minor deviations (example: writing certain words with a vowel-letter or without one) had apparently occurred, but also because of our belief (expounded in *Divine Encounters*) that there was one more letter, an Aleph, at the beginning of Genesis. Apart from the theological implications, the immediate issue is a distortion of the letter count.

Nevertheless, the encryption of hidden words or meanings into the biblical text must be accepted as a serious possibility, not only because of the examples cited above, but for two other very important reasons.

The first of them is that instances of encoding and encryption have been found in non-Hebrew texts from Mesopotamia, both from Babylonia and from Assyria. They include texts that begin or end with the warning that they are secret, to be shown only to the initiated (or, conversely, not to be revealed to the uninitiated), under penalty of death in the hands of the gods. Such texts sometimes employed decipherable encoding methods (such as acronyms), and sometimes encrypting methods that remain an enigma. Among the former is a hymn by the Assyrian king Ashurbanipal in praise of the god Marduk and Marduk's spouse Zarpanit. It uses the cuneiform syllabic signs at the beginning of lines to spell out a hidden message to the god Marduk. Apart from the acronymic encoding the king employed a second method of encryption: The syllables that formed the secret message began on line 1, skipped line 2, used line 3, skipped line 4 and so on, skipping one line through line 9. Then the coded message skipped two lines at a time, returning to a single line skip on line 26, returning to a two-line skip from line 36, and then back to a one-line skip through the rest of the tablet (including its reverse side).

In this double-encoding, the Assyrian king spelled out the following secret message to the god (we provide the translation horizontally, though the message in the tablet is read vertically, from top to bottom):

A-na-ku Ah-shur-ba-an-ni-ap-li
I am Ashurbanipal
Sha il-shu bu-ul-li-ta ni-shu-ma Ma-ru-du-uk
Who to his god called give me life Marduk *[and]*
Da-li-le-ka lu-ud-lu
I will praise thee

The discovery of an acrostic inscription by one Shaggil-kinam-ubbib, a priest in the temple of Marduk in Babylon, indicates not only the priesthood's accessibility to such encoding, but also raises questions regarding its antiquity. In that acronym (in which there is an eleven-line skip between the coded syllables) the encoder's name is clearly stated. As far as is known, a priest by that name did serve in the Esagil temple in Babylon circa 1400 B.C. That would date the concept of encoding to about the time of the Exodus. Since most scholars find this early date too much to swallow, they prefer to date it to the eighth century B.C. after all.

A somewhat different encoding method was used by the Assyrian king Esarhaddon, Ashurbanipal's father. On a stela that commemorated a historic invasion by him of Egypt (known to scholars as the Black Stone of Esarhaddon, now in the British Museum—Fig. 57) he claimed that he had launched the military campaign not only with the blessing of the gods, but also under the celestial aegis of seven constellations that "determine the fates"—a certain

Figure 57

reference to zodiacal constellations. In the inscription (on the stela's back side) he claimed that the cuneiform signs naming the constellations "are in the likeness of the writing of my name, *Asshur-Ah-Iddin*" (Asarhaddon or Esarhaddon in English).

Exactly how this code or encryption worked is unclear; but one can figure out another hidden meaning claimed by this king in the same inscription. Dealing with the restoration of Marduk's temple in Babylon, which the Assyrian king undertook as a way to be accepted also as a ruler of Babylonia, he recalled that Marduk, having become angry at the Babylonians, had decreed that the city and its temple shall remain in ruins for seventy years. That was, Esarhaddon wrote, what "Marduk wrote down in the Book of Fates." However, responding to Esarhaddon's appeals,

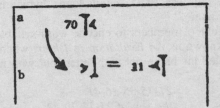

Figure 58

The merciful Marduk,
in a moment when his heart was appeased,
turned the tablet upside down
and, in the eleventh year,
approved the restoration.

What can be figured out regarding this hidden oracle is that the god's act represented a sleight of hand with figures—with the symbols (also in cuneiform) that stood for numbers. In the Sumerian sexagesimal (meaning "base sixty") system, the sign for "one" could mean both 1 and 60, depending on position. The sign for 10 was a chevronlike symbol. What Esarhaddon asserted was that the god took the Book of Fates, on which the decreed period of desolation was "70" years (Fig. 58a) and turned it upside down, so that the cuneiform signs represented "11" (Fig. 58b).

The association of hidden messages and secret meanings not with words alone but with *numerals and numbers* was even more prominent in the writings of Sargon II, the grandfather of Ashurbanipal. During his reign (721–705 B.C.) he established a new administrative-military capital on the site of a village some twelve miles northeast of the ancient royal capital and religious center Nineveh. His Assyrian name was

Sharru-kin ("Righteous King") and he named the new city Dur Sharrukin ("Fort Sargon"—an archaeological site now known as Khorsabad). In the inscription commemorating this achievement, he wrote that the mighty wall he had built around the city was 16,283 cubits long, "which is the number of my name."

Such a use of numbers to encode word-syllables appears in a text known as *An Exaltation to Ishtar*, where the worshiper signed his name not with letters but with numbers:

> 21-35-35-26-41
> the son of 21-11-20-42

The key to such numerical encodings remains undeciphered. But we have reason to believe that such Mesopotamian encoding methods were known to the Hebrew Prophets.

One of the most difficult passages in the Bible is the prophecy of Isaiah about the time of Retribution, when "it shall come to pass that a great trumpet shall be blown, and they shall return those who were lost in the land of Assyria and those who were cast out to the land of Egypt, and they shall bow down to Yahweh on the Holy Mount in Jerusalem." At that time, Isaiah prophesied, confusion shall reign and people will ask each other, "Who shall be given the understanding" of the message which has somehow been altered to hide its meaning:

> *For precept is upon precept,*
> *precept is within precept;*
> *Line is upon line,*
> *line is with line—*
> *A little here, somewhat there;*
> *For with a confused*
> *   language*
> *and in a strange tongue*
> *will He address this people.*

> Isaiah 28:10–11

No one has really understood how a "precept upon precept" and "line with line" will result in a "confused language" and a "strange tongue." The Hebrew words are *Tzav* ("order") and *Kav* ("line"), and have been rendered in more modern English translations as "command" and "rule" respectively (*The New American Bible*), "mutter" and "murmur" (*Tanakh, the Holy Scriptures*), or even "harsh cries" and "raucous shouts" (!) (*The New English Bible*).

What language could be confused, or its written signs given a strange meaning, by changing the "order" and a "line" here and there? It is our suggestion that what the Prophet Isaiah—a contemporary of Sargon II and Sennacherib—was talking about is the *cuneiform script* of the Assyrians and the Babylonians!

It was of course not an unknown language; but as the verse quoted above states, the message delivered in that language could not be understood because it had been encoded by *Kav* to *Kav*, by changing a "line" here and a "line" there, thereby changing the "precept" of what the message was saying. The changed *Tzav* ("order") hints at encryption methods (like the A/T-B/Sh) using the changed order of the letters.

This suggested solution to the enigma of verses 28:10–11 can serve to explain the subsequent description by the Prophet (29:10–12) of the inability of anyone to understand the envisioned writings because "the words of the book have become unto you as a book that has been sealed." The last word, *hatoom*, is usually translated "sealed," but in the biblical usage it had the connotation of "hidden," made a secret. It was a term employed in the same sense as the Mesopotamian encoded writings that were sealed from the eyes of the uninitiated. It was so employed in the prophetic Song of Moses (Deuteronomy 32:34) where God is quoted as stating that the predetermined things to come are "a secret with me hidden, stored and sealed within my treasures." The term is also used in the sense of "hidden away" or "made a secret" in Isaiah 8:17; and even more so in the Book of

Daniel and its vision and symbolisms of things to come at the End of Things.

Isaiah, whose prophecies were attuned to the international arena and the encryption of royal messages of his time, may have given away the very clue to the existence of a "Bible Code." Three times he revised the word *Ototh* ("signs") that is used in the Bible to denote divine or celestial signs to read *Otioth*—a plural of *Oth* that means both "sign" and "letter," conveying the meaning of *letters* in his prophecy.

We have already mentioned the reference by Isaiah to Yahweh as the creator of the Letters (of the alphabet). In verse 45:11 the Prophet, extolling the uniqueness of Yahweh, states that it was Yahweh who "hath arrayed by letters that which shall come to pass." And that such an arrayment was encoded ought to be the way to understand the enigmatic verse 41:23. Describing how the bewildered people of the Earth seek to divine the future from the past, Isaiah quotes them as begging God:

Tell us the letters backward!

Were the word the usual *Ototh*, it would have meant, "tell us the signs back from the beginning of things." But the Prophet has chosen—three times—to write *Otioth*, "letters." And the clear request is to be enabled to understand the divine plan by being shown the letters *backward*, as in a code, in which the letters have been scrambled.

But as the Mesopotamian examples indicate, acrostics was too simple a device, and the real encodement—still undeciphered in the case of Sargon II—relied on the *numerical values* of cuneiform signs. We have already mentioned the "secret of the gods" concerning their rank numbers—numbers which sometimes were written or invoked instead of the gods' names. Other tablets in which Sumerian terminology was retained even in Akkadian texts (many remaining obscure because of breaks in the tablets) point to the early use

א	1	ל	30
ב	2	ם	40
ג	3	נ	50
ד	4	ס	60
ה	5	ע	70
ו	6	פ	80
ז	7	צ	90
ח	8	ק	100
ט	9	ר	200
י	10	ש	300
כ	20	ת	400

Figure 59

of *numerology* as a secret code, especially when the gods were involved.

It is no wonder then that the letters of the Hebrew alphabet were granted numerical values (Fig. 59) and that such values played a much greater role in the encoding and the decoding of secret knowledge than the letters by themselves. When the Greeks adopted the alphabet, they retained the practice of assigning numerical values to letters; and it is from Greek that the art of and rules for the interpretation of letters, words or groups of words by their numerical values was given the name Gematria.

Beginning in the time of the Second Temple, the numerological Gematria became a tool in the hands of scholars as well as gnostics to pry out of the biblical verses and words untold numbers of hidden meanings or bits of information, or for drawing new rules where the biblical ones were incomplete. Thus, it was held that when a man took an oath to be a Nazirite, the unspecified period of abstention should be 30 days, because the defining word *YiHYeH* ("shall be") in Numbers chapter 6 has the numerical value 30. Comparing words and their implications by their numerical equivalents opened up countless possibilities for hidden meanings. As an example, it was suggested that Moses and Jacob had a similar divine experience, because the ladder to heaven (*Sulam* in Hebrew) that Jacob saw in the nighttime vision and the mount (Sinai) on which Moses received the Tablets of the Law had both the same numerical value, 130.

The employment of numerology and especially Gematria to detect secret meanings reached a new height with the growth of Jewish mysticism known as the Kabbalah during the Middle Ages. In those searches special attention was given to divine names. Paramount was the study of the name by which the Lord God named himself to Moses, YHWH: "I am whoever I will be, Yahweh is my name" (Exodus 3: 14–15). If added simply, the four letters of the divine name (the Tetragammaton) amount to 26 (10+5+6+5); but under more complex methods advocated by the Kabbalists, in which the spelled-out names of the four letters (Yod, Hei, Wav, Hei) were added up numerically, the total comes to 72. The numerical equivalents of these numbers made up scores of insightful other words.

(At the beginning of Christianity an Alexandrian sect held that the name of the supreme and primordial creator was Abraxas, the sum of whose letters equaled 365—the number of days in a solar year. The sect's members used to wear cameos made of semiprecious stones, bearing the god's image and name—as often as not equated with YaHU (short for Yahweh)—Fig. 60. There is every reason to believe that Abraxas stemmed from *Abresheet*, "Father/Progenitor of Beginning," that we have proposed as the full first word, starting with an "A," of Genesis, rather than the current *Bresheet* which makes Genesis start with a "B." If Genesis indeed had one more letter, the code sequencing now in vogue would have to be reexamined).

Figure 60

How much value should one attach to numerical codes or meanings—a code inherent in the letters themselves and not on arbitrary spacing between them? Because such usages lead back to Sumerian times, were valid in Akkadian times, and were deemed at all times to be "secrets of the gods" not to be revealed to the uninitiated, and because of the link to DNA, we believe that numerical codes are the secret code!

In fact, one of the most obvious (and thus, as in detective tales, the most ignored) clues is the very term for "book," *SeFeR* in Hebrew. Stemming from the root SFR, its derivations were the words for writer/scribe (*Sofer*), to tell (*Lesapher*), a tale or story (*Sippur*), and so on.

But the very same root SFR also denoted everything connected with numbers! To count was *Lisfor*, numeral is *Sifrah*, number is *Mispar*, counting is *Sephirah*. In other words, from the very moment that the three-letter root words of the Hebrew emerged, to write with letters and to count with numbers were considered one and the same.

Indeed, there are instances in the Hebrew Bible where the meanings "book" and "number" were interchangeable, as in 1 Chronicles 27:24 where, reporting a census conducted by King David, the word "number" was used twice in the same sentence, once to denote the number (of the people counted) and then to mean David's book of records.

Such a double meaning, and perhaps a triple meaning, has challenged translators of verse 15 in Psalm 71. Seeking God's help though he knows not all of God's miracles, the Psalmist vowed to recount God's deeds of salvation and justice "although I know not *Sefuroth*." The King James version translates the word as "numbers"; more modern translations prefer the connotation of "to tell,"—"tellings." But in this unusual form, the Psalmist has included a third meaning, that of "mysteries."

As times became more turbulent in Judea, with one revolt (that of the Maccabees against Greek rule) followed by another (against Roman oppression), the search for messages of hope—Messianic bodings—intensified. The scanning of earlier texts for coded numbers evolved into the use of numbers as secret codes. One of the most enigmatic and best encrypted instances found its way into the New Testament: The number of a "beast" encoded as "666" in the Book of Revelation,

> Here is Wisdom;
> Let him that hath Understanding
> count the number of the beast,
> for it is the Number of a Man;
> And his number is six hundred and three score and six.
>
> *Revelation 13:18*

The passage deals with Messianic expectations, the downfall of evil, and in its aftermath a Second Coming, the return of the Kingdom of Heaven to Earth. Countless attempts have been made over the millennia to decipher the numerical code of "666" and thus understand the prophecy. The number clearly appears in the early (Greek) manuscript of the book whose full title is The Gospel According to St. John, which begins with the statement "In the beginning was the Word, and the Word was with God, and the Word was God" and which is filled with numerical references. Using the numerical values of the Greek letters (which follow closely the

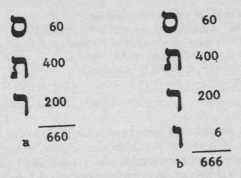

Figures 61a and 61b

Hebrew arrangement) and the methods of Gematria, it has been suggested that the "beast" was the evil Roman empire because the numerical value of *LATEINOS* was 666. Others have suggested that the numerical code meant the evil emperor himself (Trajan) whose middle name, ULPIOS, also added up numerically rendered to 666. Still another suggestion was that the code was in Hebrew, standing for *Neron Qesar* ("Nero the Emperor"), whose Hebrew spelling N-R-W-N + Q-S-R also added up to 666; and so on, in a variety of Gematria approaches both using straight addition as well as triangulation methods.

The possibility that the encoded secret of "666" is to be uncovered in Hebrew rather than Greek or Roman word meanings might well be the key to finally resolving the enigma. We find that 660 in Hebrew is the numerical equivalent of *SeTeR* (Fig. 61a)—a hidden thing, an occult mystery; it was employed in the Bible in connection with divine Wisdom and Understanding that were hidden and occulted from Man. To make it 666, the letter *Wav* (= 6) has to be added (Fig. 61b), changing the meaning from a "secret" to "his secret," *SiTRO*, "his hidden thing." Some find this rendition of "*his* secret" to describe a "watery darkness" where the Celestial Battle with Tiamat is recalled:

The Earth shook and trembled,
the foundations of the hills were shaken . . .
There went up smoke from his nostrils,
a devouring fire out of his mouth . . .
He made darkness his secret,
by a watery darkness and celestial clouds covered.

Psalms 18:8–12

There are repeated references in the Bible to that Celestial Battle, which in the Mesopotamian *Epic of Creation* took place between Nibiru/Marduk and Tiamat, and in the Bible between Yahweh as the Primeval Creator and *Tehom*, a "watery deep." Tehom/Tiamat was sometimes spoken of as *Rahab*, the "haughty one," or rendered with an inversion of letters *RaBaH* ("the great one") instead of RaHaB. The wording in Psalm 18 echoes a much earlier statement in Deuteronomy 29:19, in which the judgments of Yahweh "on the last generation" are prophesied and described as a time when "smoke shall go up from the nostrils" of God. That time of final accounting is often referred to in the Bible by the adverb *Az*—"then," at that particular future time.

If the author of Revelation, as is evident, also had in mind that *Az*, that "then" at the time of the Last Generation, when the Lord shall reappear as He had when Heaven and Earth were created at the time of the battle with *Tehom Rabah* (a term used in combination in Amos 7:4, Psalms 36:7, Isaiah 5:10), then a numerical approach to the enigma of the "666" would suggest that the Book of Revelation was speaking of the Return of the Celestial Lord in a reenactment of the Celestial Battle; *for the sum total of the numerical value of Az + Tehom + Rabah is 666* (Fig. 62).

Such an attempt by us to decode the number "666" by reconverting it into letters and then search for words containing those letters in the Old Testament does not exhaust the possibilities. The transmutation of *Abresheet* into *Abraxas* (with its numerical value 365) as a gentile deity, and the biblical references (earlier quoted) to encodements in cuneiform writings by changing the lines in the cuneiform

אז 8

תהום 451

רבה 207

666

Figure 62

signs, as well as the reference to backward reading as well as the A-T-B-Sh employment to hide identities of foreign gods, raise the question: To what extent, especially as the destiny of the Hebrews became entangled in the fate of other nations and their gods, did biblical encodements actually hide secret data from foreign writings and pantheons? If the creation tales of Genesis were actually shorter versions of the creation secrets recorded in *Enuma elish*, what about those secret portions that had been revealed to Enmeduranki and Adapa (and Enoch)?

We read in Genesis that when the Pharaoh elevated Joseph, who interpreted dreams, to high office, he gave him as was appropriate to an Egyptian official a new, Egyptian name: Zophnat-Pa'aneach. While scholars have attempted to reconstruct the hieroglyphic writing and Egyptian meaning of the epithet-name, what is obvious is that it was in reality a name whose meaning was encoded in *Hebrew*, for in Hebrew it clearly meant "Solver" (*Pa'aneach*) of "Secret/Hidden Things" (*Zophnot*).

Such language/letter/number transfigurations reinforce the question (and the possibility)—and not only in regard to the reason for "666"—of whether the codes might have included allusions to other deities of pantheons known in antiquity.

One of the unexplained aspects of the Hebrew alphabet is

Figures 63a, 63b and 63c

that five letters are written differently when their place is at
the end of a word (Fig. 63a). If we are to do our own ven-
turing into the Pardes, the "forbidden grove," and adopting
the premise of a combination letter+number code, we could
say that read in reverse (from left to right) the encoded reason for these odd five letters is a "secret code" (*Zophen*) of
"60" (*M+Kh*), which is the secret number of Anu! (Fig.
63b).

If so, was it just a coincidence that the first letter in the
Hebrew word for "secret"—SOD—("S") has the numerical value "60," and even more so that the numerical value
of the full word is "70"—the secret number of the desola-

tion decreed by Marduk (and then reversed by him) for the city of Babylon? And for that matter, was the statement (in Jeremiah and elsewhere) that the desolation of Jerusalem and its Temple would also last the exact same 70 years—a prophecy that, when announced, was presented as a revelation of a secret, a *Sod*, of God? (Fig. 63c).

An approach that accepts the possibility that the Old Testament as well as the New Testament borrowed for their encodings from earlier Mesopotamian secret writings and divine rankings leads to another possible solution of the "666" enigma.

One of the rare (discovered) instances where the number "6" was revealed as a divine rank was in a tablet that was put together by Alasdair Livingstone in *Mystical and Mythological Explanatory Works of Assyrian and Babylonian Scholars*. The reconstructed tablet—which bears the admonition regarding the undisclosable secrets it contains—begins with 60 as the rank of "the preeminent god, father of the gods" and then, in a separate column, reveals his identity: Anu. Followed by Enlil (50), Ea/Enki (40), Sin (30) and Shamash (20), it lists *Adad*, the "god of rain and thunders," as "6." As the listing continues on the obverse as well as the reverse sides, it lists *"600" as the secret number of the Anunnaki.*

What emerges from that Mesopotamian tablet regarding the secret numbers of the gods may well have the key to finally solving the mystery of "666" by looking at it as a Sumerian-based encoding:

$$600 = \text{The Anunnaki, "Those Who From Heaven to Earth Came"}$$
$$60 = \text{Anu, their supreme ruler}$$
$$6 = \text{Adad, one of the gods who teaches Initiates}$$
$$\overline{666} = \text{"Here is Wisdom," "Counted by him who has Understanding"}$$

(The proximity of Anu and Adad beginning in the second millennium B.C. found not only textual expressions but also in their having joint temples. Incredible as it may sound, the Bible, too, lists Anu and Adad next to each other in a list of gods of "other nations"—2 Kings 17:31).

The secret numbers of the gods can serve as clues to the deciphering of secret meanings in other divine names. Thus, when the alphabet was conceived, the letter "M"—*Mem*, from *Ma'yim*, water, paralleled the Egyptian and Akkadian pictorial depictions of water (a pictograph of waves) as well as the pronunciation of the term in those languages for "water." Was it then just a coincidence that the numerical value of "M" in the Hebrew alphabet was "40"—the secret numerical rank of Ea/Enki, "whose home is water," the prototype Aquarius?

Was there an equally secret numerical code that has originated in Sumer for YaHU—the shortened form for the Tetragammaton YaHWeH? Were one a Sumerian initiate seeking to apply the secret numbers code to this theophoric name (as used in prefixes and suffixes to personal names), one could say that YHU is a secret code for "50" (IA = 10, U = 5, IA.U = 10×5 = 50), with all the theological implications thereof.

While attention has been focused on the *meaning* of "666," we find in the cryptic verse in Revelation a statement of utmost significance. The secret code, it states, is what *Wisdom* is all about, and it can be deciphered only by those who have *Understanding*.

These are precisely the two terms used by the Sumerians, and those who came after them, to denote the secret knowledge that only privileged initiates had been taught by the Anunnaki.

At the foundation of the incredible and encompassing Sumerian knowledge lay an equally amazing knowledge of numbers. As the Assyriologist-mathematician Herman V. Hilprecht observed earlier this century after the discovery of numerous Mesopotamian mathematical tablets (*The Babylonian Expedition of the University of Pennsylvania*), "all the multiplication and division tables from the temple libraries of Nippur and Sippar, and from the library of Ashurbanipal in Nineveh, are based upon the number 12960000''—a virtual astronomical number, a number that required astounding sophistication to be comprehended, and whose utility to humans in the fourth millennium B.C. seemed completely questionable.

But analyzing this number—with which some mathematical tablets started—Professor Hilprecht concluded that it could only be related to the phenomenon of Precession—the retardation of the Earth in its orbit around the Sun that takes 25,920 years to complete (until the Earth returns to the exact same spot). That complete circling of the twelve houses of the zodiac has been named a Great Year; the astronomical number 12,960,000 represented 500 such Great Years. But who, except for the Anunnaki, could grasp or have use for such a vast span of time?

In considering numerical and counting systems, the decimal system (''base ten'') is the most obviously ''man-friendly,'' resulting from counting on the fingers of our hands. Even the perplexing Mayan calendar system called *Haab*, which divided the solar year into 18 months of 20 days each (plus 5 special days at year's end) can be assumed to have resulted from counting all 20 human digits, fingers and toes combined. But from where did the Sumerians take the sexagesimal (''base 60'') system whose lasting expression is still extant in time reckoning (60 minutes, 60 seconds), astronomy (a celestial circle of 360 degrees), and geometry?

In our book *When Time Began* we have suggested that the Anunnaki, coming from a planet whose orbital period (one year on Nibiru) equaled 3,600 orbits of the planet Earth, needed some kind of a common denominator for such diverse periods—and have found one in the phenomenon of Precession (which only they, not men with the shorter life spans dictated by Earth's cycles, could have discovered). When they divided the celestial circle into twelve parts, the preces-

Figure 64

sional retardation—that could be easily observed by them—
was 2,160 years per "house." That, we have suggested, led
to the ratio of 3,600:2,160 or 10:6 (the eventual Golden Ratio
of the Greeks), and to the sexagesimal system that ran 6 ×
10 × 6 × 10 and so on (resulting in 60, 360, 3600 and so
on to the immense number 12,960,000).

In this system, several numbers of celestial or sacred im-
port seem to be out of place. One is the number seven, whose
significance in the story of Creation, as the seventh or Sabbath day, in the name of Abraham's abode *Beer-Sheba*
("The Well of Seven") and so on is easily recognized. In
Mesopotamia it was applied to the Seven Who Judge, the
Seven Sages, the seven gates of the Lower World, the seven
tablets of *Enuma elish*. It was an epithet of Enlil ("Enlil is
Seven," the Sumerians stated); and—undoubtedly the origin
of the number's significance—it was the planetary number
of Earth. "Earth (KI) is the seventh," all Sumerian astronomical texts asserted. This, as we have explained, made
sense only to someone coming into the center of our Solar
System from the outside. To him (or them) coming from the
far-out Nibiru, Pluto would be the first planet, Neptune and
Uranus the second and third, Saturn and Jupiter the fourth
and fifth, Mars would be the sixth and Earth the seventh (and
then Venus the eighth—as indeed these planets were depicted on monuments and cylinder seals, Fig. 64).

(In Sumerian hymns to Enlil, "the all-beneficent," he was
credited with seeing to it that there was food and well-being
in the land; he was also invoked as the guarantor of treaties

and oaths. No wonder, then, that in Hebrew the root from which seven stems—Sh-V-A—is the same root from which the meanings "to be satiated" *and* "to swear, to take an oath" derive).

The number "7" is a key number in Revelation (7 angels, 7 seals, and so on); so was the next extraordinary number—12—or multiples thereof, 144,000 in Revelation 7:3–5, 14:1 etc. We have already recounted its applications and its significance, as stemming from the number of the members of our Solar System (Sun, Moon, and 10 planets—the 9 we know of plus Nibiru).

And then—hardly realized—was the peculiar number 72. To say, as has been done, that it is simply a multiple of 12 by 6, or that when multiplied by 5 it results in 360 (as the number of degrees in a circle), is merely to state the obvious. But *why* 72 to begin with?

We have already observed that the mystics of the Kaballah arrived through Gematria methods at the number *72 as the numerical secret of Yahweh*. Although obscured in the biblical report of the time when God instructed Moses and Aaron to approach the Holy Mount and to take along 70 of the elders of Israel, the fact is that Moses and Aaron had 72 companions: In addition to the 70 elders, God instructed that 2 sons of Aaron also be invited (although Aaron had 4 sons)—making the total 72.

Of all places we also find this odd number 72 in the Egyptian tale dealing with the contending of Horus and Seth. Relating the tale from its hieroglyphic sources, Plutarch (in *De Iside et Osiride*, wherein he equated Seth with Typhon of Greek myths) said that when Seth tricked Osiris into the doomed chest, he did so in the presence of 72 "divine comrades."

Why then 72 in these various instances? The only plausible answer, we believe, is to be found in the phenomenon of Precession, for it is there that the crucial number 72 is to be found, as the number of years it takes to retard the Earth by one degree.

To this day it is not certain how the concept of a Jubilee

had come about, the 50-year period decreed in the Bible and used as the time unit in the *Book of Jubilees*. Here is the answer: to the Anunnaki, whose one orbit around the Sun equaled 3,600 Earth years, the orbit passed through 50 precessional degrees $(50 \times 72 = 3,600)$!

It was perhaps more than a coincidence that Enlil's secret rank number—and the number sought by Marduk—was also 50. For it was one of the numbers that expressed the relationships between Divine Time (stemming from Nibiru's motions), Earthly Time (relating to the motions of the Earth and its Moon), and Celestial Time (or zodiacal time, resulting from Precession). The numbers 3,600, 2,160, 72, and 50 were numbers that belonged to the Tablets of Destinies in the heart of Nippur's DUR.AN.KI; they were truly numbers expressing the "Bond Heaven-Earth."

The Sumerian King List asserts that 432,000 years (120 orbits of Nibiru) had passed from the arrival of the Anunnaki on Earth until the Deluge. The number 432,000 is also key in the Hindu and other concepts of Ages and the periodic catastrophies that befall the Earth.

The number 432,000 also embraces 72 precisely 6,000 times. And it is perhaps worth keeping in mind that according to Jewish sages the count of years in the Jewish calendar—5,758 in A.D. 1998—will come to a completion, a terminus, when it reaches 6,000; it is then that it will all come full cycle.

As is evident from the ancient records concerning such initiates—Adapa, Enmeduranna, Enoch—the core of the knowledge and understanding revealed to them, no matter what else, was astronomy, the calendar, and mathematics (the "secret of numbers"). Indeed, as a review of the encoding and encrypting practices in antiquity has shown, the common thread between them, no matter what language used, was numbers. If there was once a single universal language on Earth (as the Sumerian texts and the Bible assert), it had to be mathematically based; and if—or rather, when—we communicate with extraterrestrials, as had once been done with the Anunnaki on their visits here, and as we shall do when we venture into space—the cosmic language will be one of numbers.

In fact, current computing systems have already adopted a universal numbers language. When in typewriters the key for "A" was pressed, a lever holding this letter was activated and it struck the paper with an "A." In the computers, when the key for "A" is pressed, an electronic signal is activated that expresses the "A" as a series of "0" or "1" numbers— the letters have been digitized. Modern computers have, in other words, converted letters into numbers; and one can say that they have *Gematriatized* writing.

And if one takes seriously the Sumerian and biblical statements about the inclusion of medical knowledge in the Knowledge and Understanding passed on to us—is there somewhere in all the ancient texts, so meticulously copied with precision because they had been "canonized," the key to sharing with us the genetic knowledge that went into our creation, and thus still accompanies us in health and in sickness and in death?

We have reached the point where our scientists have identified a specific gene—calling it, say, P51—at a specific site on chromosome number 1 or 13 or 22, that is responsible for a trait or malady. It is a gene and a location that can be expressed on computers—now as numbers, or wholly in letters, or in combinations thereof.

Is there already in those ancient texts, and especially the Hebrew Bible, such coded genetic information? If we could only decipher such a code, we could become beings like the "Perfect Model" that Enki and Ninharsag had intended to create.

9

PROPHECY: WRITINGS FROM THE PAST

Mankind's enduring belief that someone in the past could foresee the future—that, in Sumerian parlance, someone had known Destiny and could determine Fate—was founded upon the Written Word. Revealed or secret, straightforward or encrypted, the information had to be recorded, written down. A covenant, a treaty, a *prophecy*—what value to those then present or to those who will inhabit the future unless the words be written down?

When archaeologists excavate an ancient site, nothing is deemed more exciting and significant than "something" with writing on it—an object, a brick, a stone slab, pottery shards, and needless to say a text or part thereof inscribed on a clay tablet or a papyrus sheet. What was the place, what was its ancient name, to what culture did it belong, who were its rulers? A few scribbled letters, a couple of words offer answers; and so much more, of course, fuller texts.

One of the earliest antiquarians, if not a full-fledged archaeologist, was the Assyrian king Ashurbanipal. Believing that his own fate and the land's Destiny were determined way back in the past, he made written records from the past the prime prize or booty of his conquests; and the library of his palace in Nineveh was at the time (seventh century B.C.) perhaps the greatest collection of clay tablets of countless ancient texts of "myths" and epics, royal annals, and what was then the "books" (on clay tablets) of astronomy, mathematics, medicine, and other invaluable texts. The tablets were carefully arranged on wooden shelves, and each shelf began with a catalogue tablet listing what was on that shelf.

178

In all a tremendous treasure of ancient knowledge, records, and prophecy was assembled there. A great many of the texts now known come from the tablets, or fragments thereof, found in Nineveh. At the same time, the catalogue tablets at the start of each shelf also reveal how much is still missing and undiscovered.

Certainly missing—for none has been duplicated elsewhere—are what Ashurbanipal himself identified as "writings from before the Deluge"; we know that they had existed because Ashurbanipal had boasted that he could read that writing.

The king's assertion, one might note here, has not been taken seriously by modern Assyriologists. Some have amended the king's statement to read "writings in Sumerian," for it seems incredible not only to claim that there had been writing millennia before Mesopotamian tablets, but that such writing (on whatever tablets) had survived the global catastrophe.

Yet other texts and sources, unrelated to Ashurbanipal or his time, make those very assertions. Adapa—a pre-Diluvial initiate—wrote a book whose title, rendered in Sumerian, was *U. SAR Dingir ANUM Dingir ENLILA* (*Writings Regarding Time [from] divine Anu and divine Enlil*).

Enoch, another pre-Diluvial ancestor, returned from heaven with 360 "books"—a number not only with a celestial/mathematical allusion, but one, let us point out, which when converted into letters spells out *SeQeR* (60+100+200)—"that which is hidden." The name-place *Saqqarah* in Egypt, the "hidden place" of early royal pyramids and burials, stems from the same root.

The *Book of Enoch* (known as 1 Enoch) purports to have been written by Enoch himself as a first-person report. Although by all scholarly opinions it was compiled shortly before the Christian era, citations from it in other early works and parallels with other extrabiblical writings (as well as the fact that it was canonized in early Christian times), attest to its being based on truly ancient texts. In the book itself, after a brief introduction that explains who the *Nefilim* (of Genesis

6 renown) were, Enoch states that what follows is "the book of the words of righteousness and of the reprimand of the eternal *Nefilim*" that were heard by him during a vision and which he now proceeds to put down "in a human language"—a language "which the Great One has given to men to converse therewith."

Having been given knowledge of the heavens and the Earth and their mysteries, Enoch was told to write down prophecies of future events (according to the *Book of Jubilees*, Enoch was shown "what was and what will be"). Although scholars assume that the "prophecies" were really hindsight, the incorporation in *1 Enoch* of earlier texts and its subseqent canonization attest that at the time of the Second Temple it was firmly believed that the future could be and was foretold in the past by divine inspiration—even dictated by the Lord himself or his Angels to humans, to be recorded and written down and passed to future generations.

Even more emphatic in asserting that Enoch brought down with him books that contained not only scientific knowledge but also prophecies of the future is the version known as 2 Enoch or by the full title *The Book of the Secrets of Enoch*. It states that God instructed Enoch to "give the handwritten books to his children" so that they may be handed down "from generation to generation and from nation to nation." Then God disclosed to him the "secrets of Creation" and the cycles of the events on Earth. "At the beginning of the eighth thousand of years there will be a time of Not-Counting, [a time] with neither years nor months or weeks, nor days or hours" (2 Enoch 33:1–2).

A reference is then made to even earlier writings that belonged to Enoch's ancestors Adam and Seth—"handwriting that should not be destroyed till the end of time." There is also reference to a "chart" that God has "put on Earth" and "ordered that it be preserved, and that the handwriting of thy fathers be preserved, and that it *perish not in the Deluge* which I shall bring upon thy race."

The reference to a future Deluge, included in 2 Enoch as a prophetic revelation by God to Enoch, thus speaks of "handwritings" by both Adam and his son Seth and a divine "chart" that were deposited on Earth and were to survive the Deluge. If such "handwritings" ever existed, they must be counted among the missing pre-Diluvial writings. At the time of the Second Temple it was held that among such pre-Diluvial writings were the *Books of Adam and Eve*, in which many details were provided, augmenting the biblical tale.

Scholars agree that *1 Enoch* has clearly incorporated, verbatim, sections from a much earlier manuscript called the *Book of Noah*, a work that was mentioned in other writings besides the *Book of Enoch*. It could well have been the source of the very enigmatic eight verses in Genesis chapter 6; preceding the biblical version of the Deluge and its hero Noah, those verses speak of the *Nefilim*, the "sons of the *Elohim*" who had married the Daughters of The Adam as the background for God's decision to wipe mankind off the face of the Earth. In it, the tale is fully told, the Nefilim are identified, the nature of the divine wrath is explained. Harking back in all probability to Sumerian times and sources, it includes some details otherwise known only from the Mesopotamian *Atra Hasis* text.

It is more than likely that the two books mentioned above—the *Books of Adam and Eve* and the *Book of Noah*—did in fact exist, in one form or another, and were actually known to the compilers of the Old Testament. After having described the creation of The Adam and of Eve, and the incident in the Garden of Eden and the birth of Cain and Abel and then of Enosh, Genesis restarts (in chapter 5) the genealogical record by saying, "This is the book of the generations of Adam" and recounts the creation tale. The Hebrew word translated "generations" (*Toledoth*) connotes more than "generations"—it bespeaks "the histories of"; and the ensuing text gives the impression of a summary based on some longer prior text.

The same term, *Toledoth*, starts the story of Noah and the Deluge. Again translated "These are the generations of Noah," the words really begin the story not so much of Noah as of the Deluge—a story based, without question, on earlier Sumerian (and then Akkadian) texts.

Interesting and intriguing light on what the *Book of Noah* might have contained is to be found in the *Book of Jubilees*, another one of the Apocrypha (extrabiblical) books from the time of the Second Temple (or earlier). It states that the Angels "explained to Noah all the medicines, all the diseases and how he might heal them with herbs of the earth; and Noah wrote down all things in a book, concerning every kind of medicine." And after the Deluge, Noah "gave all that he had written to his son Shem."

Starting a new chapter not only in the Bible but in human affairs again with the word *Toledoth* is next found in Genesis chapter 10. Dealing with the post-Diluvial times, it begins, "Now these are the 'generations' of the sons of Noah: Shem, Ham and Japhet; and unto them were born sons after the Deluge." The general list, nicknamed by biblical scholars the Table of Nations, reverts to Shem and his descendants and pays special attention to the line of his middle son Arpackhshad both in this chapter and by returning to the subject in chapter 11 with the opening "These are the 'generations' of Shem." The significance, we soon gather, is that it was the direct ancestral line of Abraham's family.

The existence of a book that we might arbitrarily title *The Book of Shem* or, more specifically, the *Book of Arpakhshad*, is suggested by yet another tradition concerning writings from before the Deluge. The reference is found in the *Book of Jubilees*; it informs us that Arpackhshad, a grandson of Noah, was taught by his father Shem to write and read; and seeking a place where to settle, "he found a writing which former generations had carved on a rock, and he read what was thereon, and he transcribed it." Among other information "it included the teachings of the Nefilim concerning how to observe the omens of the sun and the moon and the stars and the signs of heaven." This description of the contents of the writings by the Nefilim—and thus from before the Deluge—parallels the wording in the *Book of Enoch* about the knowledge of the Sun and the Moon and the stars/

planets that he was taught from "the heavenly tablets, and all that was written thereon." All that Enoch passed on to his son Metuselah, saying to him:

> All these things I am recounting to thee
> and writing down for thee;
> I have revealed to thee everything
> and given thee books concerning all this.
> So preserve, my son Metuselah,
> the books from thy father's hand
> and deliver them to the generations of the world.

An unambiguous reference to pre-Diluvial writings and what had happened to them as far as the destruction by the avalanche of waters was concerned is found in the writings of Berossus. A Babylonian historian-priest who compiled a history of Mankind for the Greek rulers of the Near East after the death of Alexander, he clearly had access to a library of ancient writings in Akkadian (and possibly in Sumerian, too: In the first volume of his writings, describing events from the splash landing of Ea to the Deluge, he called the hero of the Great Flood by his Sumerian name, Ziusudra). In the fragments of Berossus's writings that are available from Greek historians, it is stated that after Ea/Enki had revealed to Sisithros (= Ziusudra) that there would be a Deluge, "he ordered him to conceal every available writing in Sippar, the city of Shamash. Sisithros accomplished all these things, sailed immediately to Armenia, and thereupon what the god had announced did happen." Those writings were about "beginnings, middles, and ends."

Berossus continued to relate that among those who were in the ark and survived the Deluge was *Sambethe*, the wife of one of the sons of Ziusudra/Noah—her name probably a corruption of the Sumerian or Akkadian *Sabitu* ("The Seventh"). According to Berossus "she was the first of the Sybils, and she had prophesied concerning the building of the Tower of Babylon and all that happened to the enterprises of its planners; this was before the division of the languages.''

To this first of a line of oracle prophetesses (the most renowned of which was the Sybil in Delphi) was attributed the role of intermediary between the gods and the survivors of the Deluge. She uttered to them the words that were ''a voice from the air,'' which directed them how to survive after the Deluge and ''how to recover from Sippar the books that described the future of Mankind.''

The ubiquitous traditions and recollections regarding writings from before the Flood clearly persist in asserting that apart from all manner of scientific knowledge they also included prophecies concerning the future. As often as not, such prophecies concerned not only fateful events that would befall individuals or nations, but also humanity's and Earth's ultimate destiny.

Enoch was shown ''what was and what will be,'' and wrote down for future generations the secrets of creation and the cycles of events on Earth. God had placed a ''chart'' on Earth, determining the destiny of the planet and all that is upon it. The writings from before the Deluge were about ''beginnings, middles and ends.''

Indeed, as one reviews the beliefs underlying all these diverse statements, one begins to understand why the editors of Genesis in its Hebrew version had omitted the Aleph to make the beginning start with Beginning, with a ''B'' (*Beth*). For the very notion of a beginning incorporates within it a notion of an end. The very admonition that the ancient writings, containing all that there is to be known—those ancient ''data banks,'' to use computer lingo—must be preserved until the ''end of times'' or ''end of days'' implies that such an end had been destined. By starting with *B*eginning, the Bible's editors subscribed to that belief.

These concepts permeate the Bible, from the very start in Genesis through the books of the Prophets to the final books (of the Hebrew Bible). ''And Jacob called unto his sons, and said: Come, gather, and I shall tell you that which shall befall you at the end of days" (Genesis 49:1). Fearing that the Israelites would abandon the commandments after his death, Moses alerted them to the "evils that will befall you in the last days" (Deuteronomy 31:29). Coupled with that admonition was a prediction—a prophecy—of the Fate and future of each one of the tribes of Israel. The prophetic visions of Isaiah open with the statement, "And it shall be at the end of days" (2:2); and the Prophet Jeremiah clearly explained that what shall be "at the end of days" had been planned "in Yahweh's heart" from the very beginning (23:20). "He tells the End at the Beginning," Isaiah extolled the Lord God (46:10).

God was the ultimate prophet and the source of all prophecy. That biblical view found expression even where the text seems just to report events. The punishment imposed on Adam and Eve after they had eaten the forbidden fruit in the Garden of Eden foresaw the future ways of human beings. Cain was given a protective mark, for otherwise he and his descendants would be avenged for seventy and seven generations. In a covenant made by God with Noah and his sons, He promised that there would never again be a Deluge. In a covenant with Abraham, God foretold his future as the father of multitudes of nations; but predicted that a time would come when his offspring would be enslaved in a foreign land—a bitter experience that would last 400 years (as the Israelite sojourn in Egypt eventually did). And regarding the barren Sarah, God predicted that she would have a son and that out of her womb there would come nations and kings thereof.

Encompassing the human story from Adam and Eve through the destruction of the First Temple of Jerusalem and its rebuilding by returning exiles in the sixth century B.C., the Old Testament also tells, indirectly and almost unperceptibly, the shift of prophecy from a direct communication from God to one through Angels (literally: Emissaries) and then through Prophets. Though Moses was designated a Prophet of God, the universality of the phenomenon is revealed by the biblical tale of Bile'am or Balaam. He was a renowned seer at the time of the Exodus, and was retained by the Moabite king to curse the advancing Israelites; but each time a place for the cursing and the rituals therefore were prepared, Yahweh appeared to him and warned him not to put a curse on His chosen people. After several attempts he was persuaded by the Moabite king to try once more; but then, in a divine vision, he could "hear the sayings of God and discern the knowledge of the One who is Most High." "Though not nigh, I can see it," Bala'am announced of the Star of Jacob; "though not now, it steppeth forth." And that is what the divine message is, he said: the Sons of Israel shall defeat and conquer the nations standing in their way. Incredibly, the list of those doomed nations included Assyria—a nation not at all present in Canaan at the time of the Exodus and whose kings assaulted only many centuries later the Israelite kingdoms that were yet to be formed.

A case of prophecy based on past prophecies was the future great battle of Gog and Magog that was revealed to the Prophet Ezekiel (chapters 38 and 39)—a battle that in the apocalyptic literature of the time assumed the role of the final battle in the last millennium, the Armageddon of the New Testament. Though in later writings Gog and Magog were treated as two different persons or nations, Ezekiel speaks of Gog as the ruler of the land Magog, and predicts that the end of his domination shall come when he will attack the land of Jerusalem, "the navel of the Earth." Predicting that this shall take place at, and be a sign of, "the End of Days," Yahweh declared through Ezekiel: Though thou shalt come only at the end of days, Gog—

> It is thou
> of whom I had spoken
> in the olden days
> through the Prophets of Israel
> who had prophesied in those days.

In those final times, Yahweh announced through Ezekiel, there shall be a great earthquake and great destruction, and plagues and bloodshed, and torrents of rains, and fire and brimstones from the skies.

Another Prophet who recalled earlier prophets—the "First Prophets"—was Zechariah (1:4, 7:7, 7:12), who also saw the future in terms of the past, the so-called "First Days." This was in line with all the biblical prophecies: in foretelling the future, the Prophets asserted that the End was anchored in the Beginning. Foreseeing the world's nations gathered together to find out what is in store, the Prophet Isaiah envisioned them asking each other, "Who among us can tell the future by letting us hear the First Things?" Mocking that quest among the nations who ask about the past and the future not God but each other, Isaiah declared that only Yahweh, the Lord of Hosts, has that knowledge (Isaiah chapter 43). That is further enlarged upon in Isaiah chapter 48, wherein Yahweh announced:

> *It is I who had told the first things,*
> *out of my mouth were they uttered.*
> *And I shall announce them suddenly;*
> *And when I shall do so, it shall happen.*

The quest for the hidden past in order to divine the future permeates not only the books of the Prophets but also the biblical books of Psalms, Proverbs, and Job. "Give ear, my people, to my teachings, incline your ears to the words of my mouth; I will open my mouth with parables and will utter riddles from olden times," the Psalmist (78:2–3) said of the remembrances passed from generation to generation. Asserting that he was qualified to address those riddles, he explained: "For I have taken count of the days of old and the years of ancient times" (77:6).

This approach, of "Let's find out what has happened in the past so that we might know what's coming," was based on Mankind's experience throughout the millennia of human memory—"myths" to most, recollections of actual events to us. To anyone aware of the ancient tales—anyone not only now but also in biblical times—it had to be obvious that at every twist and turn Mankind depended on the plans and whims of its creators, the *Elohim*.

In the Beginning, we today and people (and certainly Prophets) millennia ago have been informed that we have come into being as a result of discussions in a council of the gods, meeting to resolve a mutiny in the gold mines. Our genetic makeup was determined as two Anunnaki—Enki and Ninmah—acted both seriously and frivolously. It was at the Council of the Great Gods that they voted and swore to bring the creative experiment to an end and let Mankind perish in the Deluge. And it was that, meeting in council, the Anunnaki gods decided after the Deluge to give Mankind "Kingship" in the three regions—the civilizations of Mesopotamia, of the Nile Valley, and of the Indus Valley.

Curious about the records of the Beginnings, the human story from Creation through the Deluge and the rise of nations, the people of the last millennium B.C.—the time of the biblical Prophets—also wondered about the Olden Days, the events in the previous millennium or two—the time when the Bible switched to Ur of the Chaldees in Sumer, and Abraham, and the War of the Kings, and the upheaval of Sodom and Gomorrah. Tell us of those Olden Days so that we would know what to expect, the people demanded of those entrusted with prophecy and knowledge.

The Bible mentions several such records—"books"—that may have held the answers but that have completely vanished. One is the *Book of Jashar*, the *Book of Straightness* if literally translated but probably meaning the record of the Right Things. The other and probably much more important was the *Book of the Wars of Yahweh*, implying by its enigmatic title that it dealt with wars and conflicts among the *Elohim*.

Such conflicts, flaring at times into open warfare, were recorded in Sumerian writings; and such writings from the past were truly Divine Words, for the texts were either written down by the Divine Scribes or dictated by the gods to human scribes. Originally recorded by the gods themselves were the events on Nibiru that involved the seizing of the throne there by Anu and the continuation of the struggle for succession to another planet, Earth; the tale of Zu; the contending between Horus and Seth (which led to the first-ever enlisting of Mankind in a war between the gods). And in that category, of writings by the gods themselves, belonged a "Prophecy Text" that has come to us in the Akkadian version and which was nothing short of an *autobiography by Marduk*. In the other category, that of books directly dictated by a deity, was a text known as the *Erra Epos*, a record of events as told by Nergal. Both those texts were attempts by the gods to explain to Mankind how two millennia of civilization—the Olden Days—had come abruptly to an end.

It was more than ironic that the events that had triggered the end of the great Sumerian civilization coincided with its most glorious epoch. An "olden book"—a Sumerian text—recorded the Council of the Great Gods at which the grant of Kingship (civilization) to Mankind was decided upon:

> *The great Anunnaki who decree Fates*
> *sat exchanging their counsels regarding the land.*
> *They who created the four regions,*
> *who set up the settlements, who oversaw the land,*
> *were too lofty for Mankind.*

And so they decided that the institution of Kingship should be created, both as a buffer as well as a link between the Lofty Ones and the mass of humanity. Up to then, the Earthlings were allowed to live beside the sacred precincts in the cities of the Gods; thereafter, they were to have their own cities, ruled by LU.GALs, "Great Men"—kings—who were to act as surrogates for the divine lords.

When the Anunnaki returned to the Edin, the plain between the Tigris and Euphrates after the plain had dried enough after the Deluge, they reestablished the Cities of the Gods exactly in accordance with the pre-Diluvial plan. The first one to be rebuilt was Eridu, Enki's city; and it was there, we believe, that the momentous decision to grant Mankind

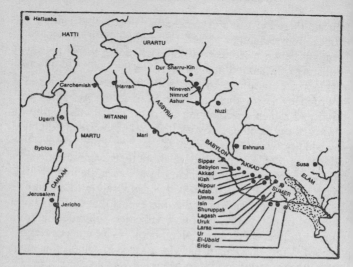

civilization was made; the time, archaeological evidence shows, was circa 3800 B.C.

But in compliance with the gods' decision, Kingship of Men had to begin at a City of Men, and that one was a new settlement called Kish. The date was marked by the grant of a calendar to Mankind, a calendar designed at Enlil's "cult center," Nippur. It began to tick in 3760 B.C.

The *Sumerian King List* recorded the recurring transfer of the land's capital city from one City of Men to another in Sumer. Such shifts were not unrelated to the fortunes and shifts of authority between the gods themselves, or even the rivalries between them—both in the First Region (Mesopotamia and neighboring lands), the Second Region (the Nile Valley) and the Third Region (the Indus Valley) (where civilizations followed circa 3100 B.C. and 2900 B.C.). Rumbling below the surface and from time to time violently erupting was the conflict between Marduk and Ninurta—the heirs apparent of Enki and Enlil respectively, who took over as their own the erstwhile rivalry between their fathers. There was indeed no Peace on Earth until Marduk—having caused the death of Dumuzi—had his sentence to be buried alive inside the sealed Great Pyramid commuted to exile. It was the same punishment—banishment to a distant land—that Marduk had imposed on his half brother Ningishzidda/Thoth, who had gone across the oceans to become the Plumed Serpent god (Quetzalcoatl) of Mesoamerica.

It was during that relative period of peace that began with the start of the third millennium B.C. that the Sumerian civilization expanded to neighboring lands and flourished under great kings, such as Gilgamesh. Within a few centuries, the northward expansion incorporated Semitic tribes; and circa 2400 B.C. a greater dominion under a Righteous King (*Sharru-kin*)—Sargon I—was formed with a capital in the new city of Agade. It was henceforth known as the unified kingdom of Sumer and Akkad.

Numerous texts, mostly fragmented, have been found that record the course of events—the affairs of both gods and men—in the ensuing centuries. The empire's center kept changing. Finally, in 2113 B.C., the most glorious chapter in the history of Sumer and Akkad began. Historians refer to the era as the Ur III period, for it was the third time that Ur had become the empire's capital. It was the "cult center" of Nannar/Sin, who resided in its sacred precinct (Fig. 65) with his spouse Ningal. Their lordship was enlightened and benevolent. The king they had anointed to start the new dynasty, Ur-Nammu ("The Joy of Ur") was wise, righteous, and a master of international trade in which Sumer exchanged grains and woolen products for metals and timbers; its colorful coats were prized, according to the Bible, even in distant Jericho. The "merchants of Ur" were internationally known and respected; through them Sumerian civilization, in all of its aspects, spread far and wide. In need of more wool, the Sumerians tapped into the grazing plains in the northern regions, where a major trading outpost was established at the gateway to Asia Minor, the land of the Hittites. It was named Harran—"The Caravanry." Intended to

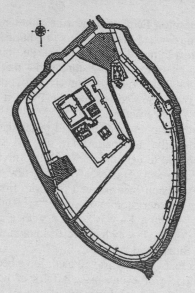

Figure 65

serve as a mini-Ur, an Ur-away-from-Ur, it emulated in layout and in its temple Ur itself.

All the while, from his exile, Marduk was watching these developments with a growing sense of frustration and anger. In his autobiography (a copy of which was discovered in the library of Ashurbanipal) Marduk recalled how, after having wandered in many lands, "from where the sun rises to where it sets," he had arrived in Hatti Land (the land of the Hittites). "Twenty-four years in its midst I nested," he wrote. And all during these years he kept asking the council of the gods: "Until when?"

In the absence of a clear or satisfactory answer, Marduk looked to the heavens. Fate, we have said, has twelve stations; the Fate-Station (zodiacal house) of Marduk was the constellation of the Ram (Aries); and as Precession kept shifting the first day of spring away from the constellation of the Bull (Taurus)—Enlil's zodiacal house—it came ever closer to "entering" the Fate-Station of Marduk's Ram. Sure that the time has come for his Destiny to be fulfilled, Marduk envisioned himself returning to Babylon with pomp and circumstance, appointing a worthy king, watching the nations at peace and the peoples prosper—a prophetic vision of what shall come to pass at the Latter Days when Babylon shall live up to its name: *Bab-ili*, "Gateway of the Gods."

Other texts from that time, that scholars consider part of the collection of *Akkadian Prophecies*, recorded reports of astronomers who watched the heavens for planetary omens connected with the constellation of the Ram. The omens, however, were mostly ones of warfare, slaughter, plunder, destruction; and it was those prophecies, rather than Marduk's rosy ones, that have come to pass. The other gods, led by Ninurta and by Marduk's own brother Nergal, using scientific tools "from the Olden Days," "artifacts of Heaven and Earth," claimed that the shift to the Age of the Ram had not yet occurred. Impatient, Marduk sent his son Nabu to raise a human army from among their followers in the Lands of the West—the lands west of the Euphrates River. In 2024 B.C. Nabu launched a successful invasion of Mesopotamia and opened the gates of Babylon to his father Marduk.

The *Erra Epos* relates those momentous events from the viewpoint of Nergal (nicknamed *Erra*, The Annihilator) and Ninurta (nicknamed *Ishum*, The Scorcher). It details frantic negotiations to settle the dispute peacefully, calls on Marduk to be patient; endless debates at the Council of the Anunnaki that in the end was meeting in continuous session; alarm at the true intentions of Nabu and his human army; and finally suspicions that while Marduk speaks of Babylon as the Gateway of the Gods, his son—with followers in the areas bordering on the spaceport in the Sinai—was really intending to capture the *spaceport* and thus control contact with the home planet Nibiru.

Seeing no other way to stop Marduk and Nabu, the Council of the Great Gods authorized Nergal and Ninurta to unlock the "Seven Awesome Weapons" that had been hidden under lock and seal in the Abzu (Enki's abode in southeastern Africa). A nuclear holocaust was unleashed; it vaporized the spaceport, leaving a huge gash in the peninsula's face and a vast blackened area all around it. The "sinning cities" that sided with Nabu in what was then a fertile valley south of the Dead Sea were likewise obliterated—an upheaval that Abraham could see from his abode in the south of Canaan.

But as Fate would have it, the nuclear "cloud of death," carried by the prevailing Mediterranean winds, drifted east-ward toward Mesopotamia; in its path, all that was alive—people, animals, plants—died a horrible death. As the deathly cloud neared Sumer, the Anunnaki gods began to abandon their cities. But Nannar/Sin would not accept the doom of his splendid city Ur. His appeals to Anu and Enlil to find a way to spare Ur were of no avail; and as the helpless Enlil bluntly told him, "Ur was granted kingship—an ev-erlasting reign it was not granted . . . Its kingship, its reign, has been *cut*"—not to everlast was its NAM.TAR, a Destiny that can be cut and broken, Fate.

But as fate would have it, the winds, as they reached Mes-opotamia, changed course to the southeast. And while Sumer and its great olden cities lay prostrate and desolate, the city of Babylon to the north was completely spared.

Until then Marduk had looked to the heavens to divine his Fate. The miraculous sparing of Babylon from the nuclear death and desolation led him to wonder whether his now unobstructed way to supremacy was more than Fate—whether it was his Destiny.

Were Marduk not a deity already, one could have said that what ensued was his deification. In the circumstances, let us call it his *Celestialization*. The vehicle for that was an alter-ation ("falsification" is equally applicable) of the hallowed text of *Enuma elish*: to call Nibiru "Marduk" and thereby make the supreme planetary god and the supreme god on Earth one and the same. After so substituting "Marduk" for Nibiru in the tale of the Celestial Battle, the crucial words were then applied to him: Obtaining a Tablet of Destinies from Kingu, the chief of Tiamat's host,

The Tablet of Destinies he took from him,
Sealed it with a seal,
To his [own] breast fastened it.

His was now a Destiny. And the gods, in their Assembly, to "this utterance paid heed." They bowed and shouted: "Marduk is king!" Accepting the inevitable, Anu and Enlil (in the words of an inscription by the Babylonian king Hammurabi),

Determined for Marduk, the firstborn of Enki,
the Enlil-functions over all mankind,
Made him great among the gods who watch and see,
Called Babylon by name to be exalted,
made it supreme in the world;
And established for Marduk, in its midst,
an everlasting Lordship.

The coronation—to use an understandable term—of Marduk as "king of the gods" took place in a solemn ceremony, at an assembly of the Fifty Great Gods and the "Seven Gods of Destiny," and with hundreds of rank and file Anunnaki present. Symbolically, Enlil laid before Marduk his divine weapon, the Bow (which in the heavens had the Bow-star as its counterpart). Then the transfer of the Enlil-powers to Marduk was further celebrated by the transfer to Marduk of the secret numerical rank of 50. That was done by a recitation, one by one, of the "fifty names." They start with Marduk's proper name, asserting that it was Anu himself who had so named Marduk when he was born, and, running through the rest of the epithet-names, ends with Nibiru—the transformation of the god on Earth into the supreme planetary god.

The fifty names are made up from *Sumerian* words or syllable combinations—epithets of whoever had possessed the fifty names before the *Epic of Creation* was falsified to accommodate Marduk; and although the Babylonian editors of the text (written in the Akkadian language) attempted to explain to their contemporaries the enigmatic Sumerian syllabic words, it is evident that even they could not fully grasp what secret message each name had conveyed. That such secret meanings or encodings underlay the fifty names was recognized by the renowned Assyriologist and biblical scholar E. A. Speiser; rendering *Enuma elish* in English for *Ancient Near Eastern Texts Relating to the Old Testament*, he observed that "the text etymologizes the names in a manner made familiar by the Bible; the etymologies, which accompany virtually every name on the long list, are meant to be cabalistic and symbolic rather than strictly linguistic."

There is more in the Fifty Names of a "Kabbalistic" nature than the above observation allows. The first nine names are listed at the end of the sixth tablet of *Enuma elish*, and are accompanied by several accolade verses. As had been noted by Franz M. Th. Böhl in his *Die fünfzig Namen des Marduk*, the utterance of those first nine names was attributed to forefathers not only of Marduk but even of Anu himself; three of them contained triple meanings each; and in one such meaning-within-meaning, the unique (and otherwise unreported) ability to "revive the dead gods" was attributed to Marduk. That, Franz Böhl suggested, could be a reference to the death and resurrection of Osiris (of Egyptian lore), because the ensuing three names (numbers 10, 11, 12) are variants of the epithet-name ASAR (*Asaru* in Akkadian) and, according to Böhl, three epithets that paralleled three epithets of the Egyptian god.

With those three epithet-names *Enuma elish* moves on to the seventh tablet—not without implications for the seven days of Creation in Genesis (of which the first six were periods of activity and the seventh a day of rest and divine contemplation); and seven was, we will recall, the planetary designation of Earth and of Enlil as Earth's Commander.

The three ASAR epithets, after which the epithet-names become varied and diverse, bring the total of names to twelve. They are additionally explained in four verses giving the fourfold meaning of the three ASAR names, suggesting again an attempt to incorporate twelve into the text. The recitation of the fifty names thus incorporates the divine rank number of Enlil and his planetary number, the number of the members of the Solar System, and of the constellations.

"All of my instructions are embodied in the fifty names," Enki announced at the conclusion of the ceremony. In those names, "all the rites have been combined." In his own hand "he wrote it down, preserved for the future," and ordered that the writing be lodged in the Esagil temple that the gods shall build for Marduk in Babylon. There the secret knowledge shall be safeguarded by a line of priestly initiates, passed from father to son: "Let them be kept [there], let the elder explain them; let the wise and knowing father impart to the son."

What deeper meanings, what secret knowledge do the fifty names hold that, according to Enki, combine in them all that there was to know?

Perhaps one day, when a new discovery will enable us to decode the numerical encryptions of Assyrian and Babylonian kings, we too will know.

10

NAVEL OF THE EARTH

Twenty-four years before the nuclear calamity two paths crossed, and not by accident. One was that of a god who was certain that his Fate had become a Destiny; the other was of a man whose Destiny became his Fate. The god was Marduk; the man was Abraham; the place where their paths crossed was Harran.

And an outcome of that was to last to our very own times, when Babylon (now Iraq) rained deathly missiles on the land of Jerusalem (now Israel).

That Abraham had sojourned in Harran is known from the Bible. That Marduk had wanderings in faraway lands, and that he ended up in the land of the Hittites, we know from his autobiography. That the specific place where he had spent twenty-four years was Harran is surmised by us from the very opening words of Marduk's "autobiography": He begins his query, "Until when?" by addressing it to *ilu Haranim*, the "gods of Harran" (Fig. 66), as the immediately present gods, and only then goes on to the distant Great Gods Who Judge.

Indeed, to be in Harran was a logical choice, for it was a major urban and religious center—lying at the crossroads of trade routes—and a hub of communications, at the border of Sumer and Akkad but not yet within Sumer proper, Harran was a perfect headquarters for the god whose son was raising an invasion army.

A sojourn of twenty-four years before the invasion and the nuclear holocaust that occurred in 2024 B.C. means that Marduk arrived in Harran in 2048 B.C. That, by our calculations

Figure 66

(based on a careful synchronization of biblical, Mesopotamian, and Egyptian data) was on the very footsteps of Abram/Abraham. He was born, by our calculations, in 2123 B.C. Every move of Terah and his family, we have shown in *The Wars of Gods and Men*, was linked to the fast-developing events in Ur and the Sumerian empire. The Bible informs us that Abram/Abraham left Harran, on God's instructions, at age 75. The year, then, was 2048 B.C.—the very year in which Marduk had arrived in Harran! And it was then that *Yahweh*—not just "the Lord God"—"said unto Abram: Get thee out of thy country, and out of thy birthplace, and from thy father's dwelling place, unto the land which I will show thee." It was a triple departure—from Abram's *country* (Sumer), and from his *birthplace* (Nippur), and from his father's *dwelling place* (Harran); and it was to a new and unfamiliar destination, for Yahweh had to show it to Abram.

Taking his wife Sarai and his nephew Lot with him, Abram went to "the land of Canaan." Arriving from the north (crossing over perhaps where his grandson Jacob would later cross), he moved fast southward, reaching a place called Alon-Moreh—a name literally meaning "The oak tree which points," apparently a well-known landmark that a traveler could not miss. To be certain that he was traveling correctly, Abram awaited further instructions; and "Yahweh appeared there unto Abram," confirming that he was in the right place. Moving on, Abram reached Beth-El ("God's Abode") and again "called out the name of Yahweh," continuing thereafter without stopping to the Negev ("The Dryness"), the southernmost part of Canaan bordering on the Sinai peninsula.

He did not linger there long. Food was short there. So Abram moved on, all the way to Egypt. It is customary to depict Abraham as a nomadic Bedouin chieftain, spending his days tending his flocks or lolling in his tent. In fact he had to be much more than that, for otherwise why was he chosen by Yahweh to be sent on the divinely ordained mission? He was descended from a line of priests; and the names of his and his brother's wives, Sarai ("princess") and Milcah ("queenly") indicate a connection with Sumer's royal line. No sooner did Abram reach the Egyptian border than he coached his wife on how to behave when they would be received at the Pharaoh's court (and later on, back in Canaan, he dealt with its kings as an equal). After a sojourn of five years in Egypt, when Abram was ordered back to the Negev, he was provided by the Pharaoh with a great number of men and women to be in his service, and with flocks of sheep and herds of oxen and she-asses and he-asses—as well as with a flock of highly prized camels. The inclusion of camels is significant, for they were suited for military purposes in desert conditions.

That a military conflict was brewing we learn in the chapter immediately following in Genesis (chapter 14), dealing with the invasion of southern Canaan by a coalition of Kings of the East—from Sumer and its protectorates (such as Elam, in the Zagros Mountains, which was renowned for its fighting men). Capturing city after city as they followed the King's Highway, they detoured around the Dead Sea and headed straight for the Sinai peninsula (see map p. 26). But there Abram and his armed men blocked the invaders' way. Disappointed, the invaders satisfied themselves by looting the five cities (that included Sodom and Gomorrah) in the fertile plain south of the Dead Sea; among the prisoners they took was Lot, Abram's nephew.

When word reached Abram that his nephew had been taken captive, he pursued the invaders with 318 select men all the way to Damascus. Since some time had passed until a refugee from Sodom told Abram about his nephew's capture, it was quite a feat for Abram to catch up with the invaders, who were already at Dan, in the north of Canaan. It is our suggestion that the "trained young men" as they are called in Genesis were camel-riding cavalrymen (Fig. 67), from a Mesopotamian sculpture.

"It was after those events," the Bible states (Genesis 15), "that Yahweh spoke to Abram in a vision, saying: Fear not, Abram; I am thy shielder; thy reward shall be exceedingly great."

It is time to review the Abram saga up to this point and to ask some questions. Why was Abram told to forsake everything and go to a completely strange place? What was special about Canaan? Why the rush to reach the Negev, on the border of the Sinai peninsula? Why the royal reception in Egypt and the return with an army and a camel-cavalry? What was the target of the invaders from the East? And why was their defeat at the hands of Abram deserving of a promise of a "great reward" from God?

Far from the customary picture painted of Abram as a nomadic sheepherder, he turns out to be a superb military leader and a major actor on the international scene. It can all be explained, we suggest, only if one accepts the reality of the Anunnaki presence and takes into consideration the other major events occurring at the same time. The only prize worth an international war—at the very time that Nabu was

Figure 67

organizing fighters in the lands west of the Euphrates—was the spaceport in the Sinai. It was that which Abram—allied with the Hittites and trained by them in martial arts—was hurriedly sent to protect. It was to that purpose that an Egyptian Pharaoh in Memphis, himself facing an invasion by followers of Ra/Marduk based in Thebes in the south, provided Abram with a camel-riding cavalry and a large number of other men and women servants. And it was because Abram successfully protected the gateway to the spaceport that Yahweh assured him of a great reward—as well as promised him protection from future retribution by the losing side.

The War of the Kings took place, by our calculations, in 2041 B.C. The year after that the princes of the south captured Memphis in Egypt and dethroned Abram's ally, declaring allegiance to Amon-Ra, the "hidden" or "unseen" Ra/Marduk, who was then still in exile. (After Marduk's rise to

Figure 68

supremacy, the new rulers of Egypt began building in Karnak, a suburb of the capital Thebes, Egypt's greatest temple in honor of Amon-Ra; they lined the majestic avenue leading to it with ram-headed sphinxes—Fig. 68—honoring the god whose age, the Age of the Ram, had arrived).

Things were no less hectic in Sumer and its empire. Celestial omens, including a total lunar eclipse in 2031 B.C., predicted coming doom. Under the pressure of Nabu's warriors, the last kings of Sumer drew back their forces and protective outposts ever closer to the capital Ur. There was little comfort to be found in appeals to the gods, for the gods themselves were engulfed in the sharpening confrontation with Marduk. Gods as well as men looked to the heavens for signs. A human, even one as qualified or chosen as Abram, could no longer protect the essential facility of the Anunnaki, the spaceport. And so, in 2024 B.C., with the consent of the Council of the Great Gods, Nergal and Ninurta used nuclear weapons to keep the prize from Marduk. It is all described vividly and in detail in the *Erra Epos*; it is there also that a sideshow, the upheaval of the "sinning cities" that included Sodom and Gomorrah, is recounted.

Abram was forewarned about what was to happen; at his request, two Angels of the Lord went to Sodom the day before the nuking of the spaceport and the cities to save Lot and his family. Asking for time to gather his family, Lot prevailed on the two divine beings to postpone the upheaval until he and his family could reach a safe haven in the mountains. The event was thus not a natural calamity—it was predictable and postponable.

"And in the morning Abraham got up early and went to the place where he had stood before Yahweh" the day before; "and he looked toward Sodom and Gomorrah, and toward all the land of the plain; and he beheld and saw a smoky steam rising from the earth, as the steamy smoke of a furnace."

On God's orders, Abraham moved away from the place, getting closer to the seashore. In the mountains in southeastern Jordan, Lot and his daughters huddled in fear; their mother, having lingered behind as they were escaping from Sodom, was vaporized by the nuclear explosion. (The usual translation of the words, that she was turned into a pillar of salt, stems from a misreading of the Sumerian word that could mean both "salt" and "vapor"). Convinced that they had just witnessed the end of the world, the two daughters of Lot decided that the only way to enable the human race to survive was to have them sleep with their own father. Each one had a son that way; they were, according to the Bible, the progenitors of two tribes east of the Jordan River: the Moabites and the Amonites.

And as for Abraham: "God remembered Sarah as he had promised" (when He appeared to them with the two Angels the year before), "and Sarah conceived and bore Abraham a son in his old age," and they named the son Isaac. Abraham was 100 years old at the time; Sarah was 90.

With the spaceport gone, Abraham's mission had come to an end. Now it was up to God to keep His end of the bargain. He had "cut a covenant" with Abraham to give him and his descendants as an everlasting legacy the lands between the Brook of Egypt and the Euphrates River. And now, through Isaac, the promise had to be kept.

And there was also the question of what to do with the other space facilities.

There were, to be sure, two such facilities in addition to the spaceport itself. One was the Landing Place, to which Gilgamesh had set his course. The other was the Mission Control Center—no longer needed, but still intact; a post-Diluvial "Navel of the Earth," serving the same function as the pre-Diluvial "Navel of the Earth" that Nippur had been.

To understand the similar functions and consequently similar layouts, one should compare our sketches of the pre- and post-Diluvial space facilities. Before the Deluge (Fig. 69) Nippur, designated the "Navel of the Earth" because it was at the center of concentric circles delineating the Landing Corridor, served as Mission Control Center. Cities of the Gods whose names meant "Seeing the Red Light" (Larsa), "Seeing the Halo at Six" (Lagash) and "Seeing the Bright Halo" (Laraak) marked out both the equidistant spacing and the landing path toward Sippar ("Bird City"), the site of the spaceport. The landing path, within an elongated Landing Corridor, was based at its point on the twin peaks of Mount Ararat—the most prominent topographic feature in the Near East. Where that line intersected the precise line northward, the spaceport was to be built. Thus, the Landing Path formed a precise 45° angle with the geographic parallel.

After the Deluge, when humanity was granted the three Regions, the Anunnaki retained for themselves the Fourth Region—the Sinai peninsula. There, in the central plain, the ground was both flat and hard (perfect tank terrain, as modern armies have concluded), unlike the mud-buried and water-clogged post-Diluvial plain in Mesopotamia. Choosing again the twin peaks of Ararat as the anchor point, the Anunnaki drew a landing path at the same 45° angle to the geographic parallel—the 30th parallel north (Fig. 70).

There in the central plain of the Sinai peninsula, where the diagonal line intersected the 30th parallel, was to be the spaceport. To complete the layout, two more components were required: To establish a new Mission Control Center, and to delineate (and anchor) the Landing Corridor.

We believe that the outlining of the Landing Corridor preceded the choosing of the site for Mission Control Center.

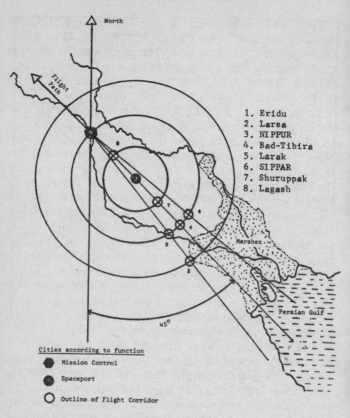

1. Eridu
2. Larsa
3. NIPPUR
4. Bad-Tibira
5. Larak
6. SIPPAR
7. Shuruppak
8. Lagash

Figure 69

The reason? *The existence of the Landing Place*, in the Cedar Mountains in Lebanon.

Every folklore, every legend connected with the place repeats the same assertion, that the place existed before the Flood. As soon as the Anunnaki landed back on Earth after the Deluge on the peaks of Ararat, they had at their disposal a real, functioning Landing Place—not a full-fledged space-

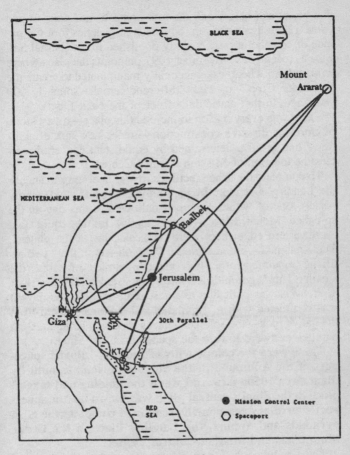

Figure 70

port, but a place to land on. All the Sumerian texts dealing
with the grant to Mankind of "domesticated" (i.e. genetically altered) plants and animals describe a biogenetic laboratory in the Cedar Mountains, with Enlil now cooperating
with Enki to restore life on Earth. All the modern scientific
evidence corroborates that it was from that particular area

that wheat and barley and the first domesticated animals had come. (Here again modern advances in genetics join the parade of corroborations: A study published in the journal *Science* as recently as November 1997 pinpoints the place where wild einkorn wheat was genetically manipulated to create the "Founder Crop" of eight different cereals: some 11,000 years ago, in that particular corner of the Near East!)

There was every reason to include this place—a vast stone platform of massive construction—in the new space facilities. That, in turn, determined by equidistant concentric circles the location of Mission Control Center.

To complete the space facilities, it was necessary to anchor the Landing Corridor. In its southeastern end, two nearby peaks—one of which remained hallowed to this day as the so-called Mount Moses—were handy. In the equidistant northwestern edge there were no peaks, just a flat plateau. The Anunnaki—not any mortal Pharaoh—built there two artificial mountains, the two great pyramids of Giza (the smaller Third Pyramid, we have suggested in *The Stairway to Heaven*, was built first as a test scale model). The layout was completed with a "mythological" animal carved from the native rock—the sphinx. It gazes precisely along the 30th parallel, eastward toward the spaceport in the Sinai.

These were the components of the post-Diluvial spaceport of the Anunnaki in the Sinai peninsula, as built by them circa 10500 B.C. And when the landing and takeoff place in the Sinai's central plain was blown up, the spaceport's auxiliary components remained standing: the Giza pyramids and Sphinx, the Landing Place in the Cedar Mountains, and Mission Control Center.

The Landing Place, as we know from the adventures of Gilgamesh, was there circa 2900 B.C. Gilgamesh witnessed there, the night before he had attempted entry, a rocketship rising. The place remained extant after the Deluge—a Phoenician coin depicted vividly what had stood atop the stone platform (Fig. 71). *The vast stone platform still exists.* The place is called Baalbek—for it was the "Secret Place of the North" of the Canaanite god Ba'al. The Bible knew the place

Figure 71

as *Beth-Shemesh*, "House/Abode of Shamash" (the Sun God) and it was within the domains of King Solomon. The Greeks after Alexander called the place *Heliopolis*, meaning "City of Helios," the Sun God, and built there temples to Zeus, his sister Aphrodite, and his son Hermes. The Romans after them erected temples to Jupiter, Venus, and Mercury. The temple to Jupiter was the largest temple ever built by the Romans anywhere in the empire, for they believed that the place was the most important oracle place in the world, one that would foretell the fate of Rome and its empire.

The remains of the Roman temples still stand atop the vast stone platform; so does, undisturbed by the passage of time and the ravages of nature and men, the platform itself. Its flat top rests on layer upon layer ("courses") of large stone blocks, some weighing hundreds of tons. Of great renown from antiquity is the *Trilithon*—a group of three colossal stone blocks, lying side by side and forming a middle course where the platform had sustained its greatest load-impact (Fig. 72, with a passing man for size comparison). Each of these colossal megaliths weighs about 1,100—one thousand one hundred—tons; it is a weight that no modern piece of equipment can even come close to lifting and moving.

But who could have done that in antiquity? The local leg-

Figure 72

end says: the Giants. They not only placed those stone blocks where they are, they also quarried and shaped and carried them over a distance of almost a mile; that is certain, for the quarry has been found. There, one of the colossal stone blocks protrudes from the mountainside half-quarried (Fig. 73); a man sitting on it looks like a fly on a block of ice.

Down at the southern end of the Landing Corridor, the Giza pyramids still stand, defying all traditional explanations, challenging Egyptologists to accept that they had been built millennia before the Pharaohs and not by any one of them. The sphinx still gazes precisely eastward along the 30th par-

Figure 73

allel, keeping to itself its secrets—perhaps even the secrets of the *Book of Thoth*.

And what about Mission Control Center?

That, too, exists; it is a place called *Jerusalem*.

And there, too, a great and sacred platform rests atop colossal stone blocks that no man or ancient machine could have moved, raised, and put in place.

The biblical record of Abraham's comings and goings in Canaan includes two instances of seemingly unnecessary digression; in both instances, the place digressed to was the site of the future Jerusalem.

The first time the digression is reported as an epilogue to the story of the War of the Kings. Having caught up with and defeated the invaders all the way north near Damascus, Abraham returned to Canaan with the captives and the booty;

> *And the king of Sodom went forth toward him—*
> *after he was returning from smiting Khedorlaomer*
> *and the kings who were with him—*
> *to the Valley of Shaveh, which is the king's valley.*
>
> *And Melchizedek, the king of Shalem—*
> *and he was a priest unto the God Most High—*

brought forth bread and wine,
and he blessed him, saying:

"Blessed be Abram unto God Most High,
Creator of Heaven and Earth;
And blessed be the God Most High,
who hath delivered thy enemies unto thy hands."

Melchizedek (whose name has meant in Hebrew exactly what the Akkadian Sharru-kin, "Righteous King," has meant) offered Abram to keep a tenth of all of the booty that he had retrieved. The king of Sodom was more generous: Keep all the wealth, he said, just return to me the captives. But Abram would have none of that; swearing by "Yahweh, the God Most High, Creator of Heaven and Earth," he said he would not keep even a shoelace (Genesis chapter 14).

(Scholars have long debated, and will undoubtedly continue to debate, whether Abraham swore by the "God Most High" of Melchizedek, or meant to say: No, *Yahweh* is the God Most High by whom I will swear.)

This is the first time that an allusion is made in the Bible to Jerusalem, here called *Shalem*. That this was a reference to what was later known as Jerusalem is based not only on long-standing traditions, but also on the clear identification in Psalm 76:3. It is generally accepted that the full name, *Yeru-Shalem* in Hebrew, meant "The city of Shalem," Shalem being a deity's name. Some suggest, however, that the name could also mean "Founded by Shalem." And it could also be argued that the word *Shalem* was not a name or even a noun, but an adjective, meaning "complete," "without defect." That would make the place's name mean "the Perfect Place." Or, if Shalem be a deity's name, it could mean the place of the "One who is perfect."

Whether honoring a god, established by a god, or the Perfect Place, Shalem/Jerusalem was located in the most unlikely place as far as Cities of Man were concerned. It was located amidst barren mountains, neither at any trade or military crossroads, nor near any food or water sources. Indeed, it was a place almost completely bereft of water, and the proper supply of drinking water was constantly to be a principal problem and vulnerability of Jerusalem. Shalem/Jerusalem featured neither in Abraham's migrations nor in the route of the invasion from the east, nor in his pursuit of the invaders. Why then a detour for a victory celebration—a detour, one is inclined to say, to a "godforsaken place"—except that the place was definitely not God-forsaken. It was a place—the only place in Canaan—where a priest serving the God Most High was located. And the question is, Why there? What was special about the place?

The second seemingly unnecessary digression had to do with the testing by God of Abraham's devotion. Abram had already carried out his mission to Canaan. God had already promised him that his reward would be great, that God himself should protect him. The miracle of a son and Legal Heir at extreme old age had happened; Abram's name was changed to Abraham, "Father of a multitude of nations." The land was promised to him and his descendants; the promise was incorporated in a covenant that involved a magical ritual. Sodom and Gomorrah had been destroyed and all was ready to let Abraham and his son enjoy the peace and quiet to which they were surely entitled.

Then, all of a sudden, "it was after all those things," the Bible says (Genesis chapter 22), "that God tested Abraham," telling him to go to a certain place and there sacrifice his own beloved son:

> *Take now thou thy son Isaac,*
> *thy only one whom thy lovest,*
> *and get thee unto the Land of Moriah;*
> *and offer him there as a sacrifice*
> *on one of the mounts*
> *which I shall point out to thee.*

Why God decided to test Abraham in that excruciating way, the Bible does not explain. Abraham, ready to carry out the divine order, found out in the nick of time that it was only a test of his devotion: An Angel of the Lord pointed out to him a ram caught in the bushes, and told him that it was the ram that was to be sacrificed, not Isaac. But why was the test, if it was needed at all, not conducted just where Abraham and Isaac dwelt, near Beersheba? Why the need to undertake a journey of three days? Why go to the part of Canaan that God identified as the Land of Moriah, and there to locate a specific mount—which God himself pointed out—to conduct there the test?

As in the first instance, there had to be something special about the chosen place. We read (Genesis 22:4) that, "On the third day Abraham lifted his eyes and saw the place from a distance." The area was rich, if with anything, with barren mounts; from nearby, and certainly from a distance, they all look alike. Yet Abraham *recognized* the particular mount "from a distance." There had to be something there that distinguished it from all the other mounts. So much so that when the ordeal was over he gave the place a long-remembered name: The Mount Where Yahweh Is Seen. As 2 Chronicles 3:1 makes clear, Mount Moriah was the Jerusalem peak on which the Temple was eventually built.

From the time Jerusalem became a city, it encompassed three mounts. Listed from the northeast to the southwest, they have been Mount *Zophim* ("Mount of Observers," now called Mount Scopus in English), Mount *Moriah* ("Mount of Directing, of Pointing Out") in the center, and Mount *Zion* ("Mount of the Signal"); these are designations of functions that bring to mind the function-names of the Beacon Cities of the Anunnaki marking out Nippur and the Landing Path when the spaceport had been in Mesopotamia.

Jewish legends relate that Abraham recognized Mount Moriah from a distance because he saw upon it "a pillar of fire reaching from the Earth to Heaven, and a heavy cloud in which the Glory of God was visible." This language is almost identical to the biblical description of the presence of the Lord upon Mount Sinai during the Exodus. But putting such lore aside, what we believe Abraham saw that identified the mount as different, that distinguished it from all others there, was the *great platform upon it.*

A platform which, though smaller than at Baalbek's Landing Place, was also part of the space facilities of the Anunnaki. For Jerusalem (before it became Jerusalem), we suggest, was the post-Diluvial Mission Control Center.

And, as at Baalbek, that platform, too, still exists.

The reason (for the first) and purpose (of the second) digressions thus come into focus. The fulfillment of his mission was marked by a formal celebration, including a priestly blessing of Abraham with the ceremonial bread and wine, at a site—the only site in Canaan—directly connected to the presence of the *Elohim.* The second diversion was meant to test Abraham's qualifications for a chosen status *after* the destruction of the spaceport and the resulting dismantling of the accoutrements of Mission Control Center; and to renew there the covenant in the presence of Abraham's successor, Isaac. Such a renewal of the divine vow indeed followed right away after the test:

> *And the Angel of Yahweh*
> *called out to Abraham for a second time*
> *from the skies, saying, this is Yahweh's word:*
> *"This is my oath:*
> *Because thou hast done this thing,*
> *and hast not withheld thy son, the unique one,*
> *I will greatly bless thee*
> *and I will exceedingly multiply thy seed . . .*
> *And in thy seed shall the nations of the Earth*
> *be blessed."*

By renewing the divine vow at this particular site, the site itself—hallowed ground ever since—became part and parcel of the heritage of Abraham the Hebrew and his descendants. The Divine Promise to Abraham, he had already been told by God, was to come true only after a passage of time and a servitude in a foreign land for four hundred years. All told it was a thousand years later when the descendants of Abraham took possession of the sacred mount, Mount Moriah. When the Israelites arrived in Canaan after the Exodus, they found that a tribe of Jebusites had settled south of the sacred mount, and let them be, for the time to take possession of that most hallowed ground had not yet come. The singular prize went to King David, who circa 1000 B.C.—a thousand years after the testing of Abraham—captured the Jebusite settlement and moved the capital from Hebron to what has been called in the Bible the City of David.

It is important to realize that the Jebusite settlement that David captured, and his new capital, were not at all ''Jerusalem'' as it is now envisioned, not even the walled ''Old City.'' The area captured by David and thereafter known as the City of David was on Mount Zion, not Mount Moriah. Even when David's successor Solomon extended the city northward to a section called Ophel (Fig. 74), it still stopped short of encroaching on the unique area to the north. It indicates, we suggest, that the *sacred platform extending from there northward on Mount Moriah already existed* at the time of David and Solomon.

The Jebusite settlement was thus not on Mount Moriah and its platform, but well to its south. (Human dwellings near—but not within—a sacred precinct were common in Mesopotamian ''cult centers,'' such as at Ur (see Fig. 65) or even in Enlil's Nippur, as evidenced by an actual map of Nippur discovered drawn on a clay tablets, Fig. 75).

One of David's first actions was to transfer the Ark of the Covenant from its latest temporary location to the capital, in preparation for placing it in a proper House of Yahweh which David planned to erect. But that honor, he was told by the Prophet Nathan, was not to be his on account of all the blood that his hands had shed during the national wars and his personal conflicts; the honor, he was told, would go to his son Solomon. All he was allowed to do in the meantime was to erect an altar; the precise place for it was shown

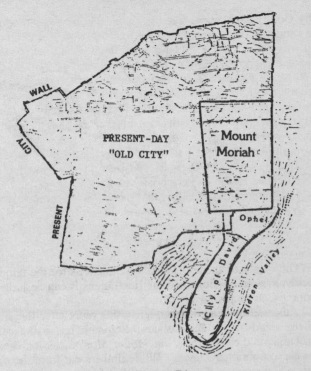

Figure 74

to David by an "Angel of Yahweh, standing between Heaven and Earth," pointing out the place with a drawn sword. He was also shown a *Tavnit*—a scale model—of the future temple and given detailed architectural instructions, which, when the time came, he handed over to Solomon in a public ceremony, saying:

> *All of this, in writing by His hand,*
> *did Yahweh make me*
> *understand—*
> *all of the workings of the* Tavnit.

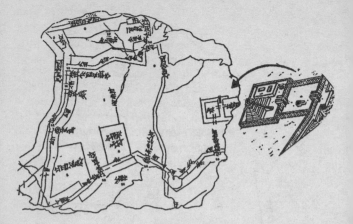

Figure 75

(The extent of those detailed specifications for the temple and its various sections and the ritual utensils can be judged from 1 Chronicles 28:11–19).

In the fourth year of his reign—480 years after the start of the Exodus, the Bible states—Solomon began the construction of the Temple, *"on Mount Moriah*, as had been shown to his father David." While timbers cut from the Cedars of Lebanon and the purest gold of Ophir were imported and copper for the specified washbasins was mined and smelted in the famed King Solomon's Mines, the structure itself had to be erected with "hewn and cut stones, large and costly stones."

The stone ashlars had to be prepared and cut to size and shape elsewhere, for the construction was subject to a strict prohibition against the use of any iron tools for the Temple. The stone blocks had to be transported, brought over to the site for assembly only. "And the House, when it was in building, was built of stone made ready before it was brought thither; so that there was neither hammer nor axe nor any tool of iron heard in the House while it was in building" (1 Kings 6:7).

It took seven years to complete the building of the Temple and to equip it with all the ritual utensils. Then, on the next New Year ("in the seventh month") celebration, the king and the priests and all the people witnessed the transfer of the Ark of the Covenant to its permanent place, in the Temple's Holy of Holies. "There was nothing in the Ark except the two stone tablets that Moses had placed therein" at Mount Sinai. No sooner was the Ark in place under the winged Cherubim, than "a cloud filled the House of Yahweh," forcing the priests to rush out. Then Solomon, standing at the altar that was in the courtyard, prayed to God "who in heaven dwells" to come and reside in his House. It was later, at night, that Yahweh appeared to Solomon in a dream and promised him a divine presence: "My eyes and my heart will be in it forever."

The Temple was divided into three parts, entered through a large gateway flanked by two specially designed pillars (Fig. 76). The front part was called the *Ulam* ("Hallway"); the largest, middle part was the *Ekhal*, a Hebrew term stemming from the Sumerian E.GAL ("Great Abode"). Screened off from that was the innermost part, the Holy of Holies. It was called the *Dvir*—literally: The Speaker—for it held the Ark of the Covenant with the two Cherubim upon it (Fig. 77), from between which God had spoken to Moses during the Exodus. The great altar and the washbasins were in the courtyard, not inside the Temple.

Biblical data and references, age-old traditions and archaeological evidence have left no doubt that the Temple that Solomon built (the First Temple) stood upon the great stone platform that still crowns Mount Moriah (also known as the Holy Mount, Mount of the Lord, or the Temple Mount). Given the dimensions of the Temple and the size of the platform, there is general agreement where the Temple stood (Fig. 78), and that the Ark of the Covenant within the Holy of Holies was emplaced upon a rock outcropping, a Sacred Rock, which according to unwavering traditions was the rock upon which Abraham was about to sacrifice Isaac. The rock has been called in Jewish scriptures *Even Sheti'yah*—"Foun-

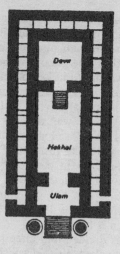

EAST

Figure 76

dation Stone''—for it was from that stone that ''the whole world was woven.'' The Prophet Ezekiel (38:12) identified it as the Navel of the Earth. The tradition was so entrenched that Christian artists in the Middle Ages depicted the place as the Navel of the Earth (Fig. 79a) and continued to do so even after the discovery of America (Fig. 79b).

The Temple that Solomon built (the First Temple) was destroyed by the Babylonian king Nebuchadnezzar in 576 B.C., and was rebuilt by Jewish exiles returning from Babylon 70 years later. That rebuilt Temple, known as the Second Temple, was later substantially enhanced and aggrandized by the Judean king Herod, during his reign from 36 to 4 B.C. But the Second Temple, in all its phases, adhered to the original layout, location, and the situating of the Holy of Holies upon the Sacred Rock. And when the Moslems captured Jerusalem in the seventh century A.D., they claimed that it was from that Sacred Rock that Mohammed ascended

Figure 77

heavenward for a nighttime visit; and they enshrined the place by building the Dome of the Rock (Fig. 80) to shelter and magnify it.

Geologically the rock is an outcropping of the underlying natural rock, protruding above the level of the stone platform some five or six feet (the face is not even). But it is a most unusual "outcropping," in more than one way. Its visible face has been cut and shaped, with an impressive degree of precision (Fig. 81a), to form rectangular, elongated, horizontal and vertical receptacles and niches of varying depths and sizes. These artificial niches and receptacles had to have some purpose known to whoever had made those incisions in the rock. What has been only surmised since long ago (e.g. Hugo Gressmann, *Altorientalische Bilder zum Alten Testament*) has been confirmed by recent researchers (such as Leen Ritmeyer, *Locating the Original Temple Mount*): the Ark of the Covenant and the walls of the Holy of Holies had been emplaced where the long straight cut and other niches in the face of the rock were made.

The implication of those findings is that the cuts and niches in the face of the rock date back at least to the time of the First Temple. There is, however, no mention whatsoever in the relevant passages in the Bible of any such cutting by Solomon; indeed, it would have been impossible—

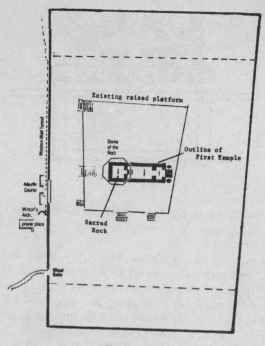

Figure 78

because of the strict prohibition against the use of metal axes and other tools on the Mount!

The enigma of the Sacred Rock and what had stood on top of it is magnified by the mystery of what might have stood under it. For the rock is not a simple outcropping. *It is hollow!*

In fact, given permission, one can descend a flight of stairs built by the Moslem authorities, and end up in a cavelike cavern the rocky roof of which is the protruding upper part of the Sacred Rock. This cavern—whether natural or not is uncertain—also features deep niches and receptacles, both in the rocky walls and (as could be seen before the floor was covered with prayer rugs) also in the floor. At one place there

Figures 79a and 79b

is what looks like an opening into a dark tunnel; but what it is and where it leads is a well-kept Moslem secret.

Nineteenth-century travelers have stated that this cavern is not the last subsurface cavity associated with the Sacred Rock; they stated that there is yet another, lower cavity beneath it (Fig. 81b). Israeli researchers, fanatically barred from the area, have determined with the aid of soil-penetrating radar and sonar technology that there is indeed another major cavity under the Sacred Rock.

These mysterious cavities have given rise to speculation not only regarding possible Temple treasures, or Temple records that might have been hidden there when the First Tem-

Figure 80

ple and then the Second Temple were about to be overrun and destroyed. There is even speculation that the Ark of the Covenant, which the Bible ceased to mention after the Egyptian Pharaoh Sheshak ransacked (but did not destroy) the Temple circa 950 B.C., might have been hidden there. That, for the time being, must remain just speculation.

What is certain, though, is that the biblical Prophets and the Psalmist referred to this Sacred Rock when they had used the term "Rock of Israel" as a euphemism for "Yahweh." And the Prophet Isaiah (30:29), speaking of the future time of universal redemption on the Day of the Lord, prophesied that the nations of the Earth shall come to Jerusalem to praise the Lord "on the Mount of Yawheh, at the Rock of Israel."

The Temple Mount is covered by a horizontal stone platform, slightly off-perfect rectangular in shape (because of the contours of the terrain), whose size is about 1,600 by 900

Figures 81a and 81b

feet, for a total stone-paved area of close to 1,500,000 square feet. Although it is believed that the present-day platform includes sections, at the extreme south and possibly also in the north, that had been added between the First Temple's building and the destruction of the Second Temple, it is certain that the bulk of the platform is original; it is certainly so regarding the slightly raised portion, where the Sacred Rock (and thus the Dome of the Rock) are located.

As the visible sides of the platform's retaining walls show, and as more recent excavations have revealed, the natural bedrock of Mount Moriah slopes considerably from north to south. Though no one can say with any certainty what the size of the platform had been in the time of Solomon, nor estimate precisely the depth of the slopes that had to be filled, an arbitrary assumption of a platform measuring only 1,000,000 square feet and an average depth of 60 feet (much less in the north, much more in the south), the result is a landfill requiring 60,000,000 cubic feet of aggregate (soil, fieldstones). This is a very major construction undertaking.

Yet nowhere in the Bible is there even a mention or a hint of such an undertaking. The instructions for the First Temple cover pages upon pages in the Bible; every small detail is given, measurements are precise to an amazing degree, where this or that utensil or artifact should be is prescribed, how long the poles that carry the Ark is specified, and so on and on. But it all applies to the *House* of Yahweh. Not a word about the platform on which it was to stand; and that could only mean that the platform has already been there; there was no need to construct it.

Standing out in complete contrast to that absence of mention are the repeated references in 2 Samuel and 1 Kings to the *Millo*, literally "the filling"—a project begun by David and enlarged by Solomon to fill up part of the slopes on the sotheastern corner of the sacred platform, so as to enable the City of David to expand northward, closer to the ancient platform. Clearly, the two kings were quite proud of that achievement and made sure it was recorded in the royal chronicles. (Recent excavations in that area indicate, however, that what was done was to raise the sloping level by constructing a series of terraces that grew smaller as they rose; that was much easier than first surrounding the expanded area with high retaining walls and filling up the gap with aggregate).

This contrast undoubtedly corroborates the conclusion that neither David nor Solomon built the vast platform on Mount Moriah, with the immense retaining walls and enormous amount of landfill required. All the evidence suggests that the platform already existed when the construction of a Temple was even contemplated.

Who then built the platform, with all the earthworks and stonework that it entailed? Our answer, of course, is: the same master builders who had built the platform at Baalbek (and, for that matter, the vast and precisely positioned platform on which the Great Pyramid of Giza stands).

The great platform that covers the Temple Mount is surrounded by walls that serve both as retaining walls and as fortifications. The Bible reports that Solomon built such walls, as did Judean kings after him. Visible sections of the walls, especially on the southern and eastern sides, display constructions from various later periods. Invariably, the lower (and thus more ancient) courses are built of larger and better-shaped stone blocks. Of these walls, only the Western Wall, by tradition and as confirmed by archaeology, has remained hallowed as an actual remnant from the time of the First Temple—at least in its lowest courses where ashlars (perfectly cut and shaped stone blocks) are the largest. For almost two millennia, since the destruction of the Second Temple, Jews held on to this remnant, worshiping there, praying to God, seeking personal succor by inserting slips of paper with a request to God between the ashlars, bewailing the Temple's destruction and the Jewish people's dispersion—so much so that, in time, the Crusaders and other conquerors of Jerusalem nicknamed the Western Wall the "Wailing Wall."

Until the reunification of Jerusalem by Israel in 1967, the Western Wall was no more than a sliver of a wall, about a hundred feet or so squeezed between residential houses. In front was left a narrow space for the prayers, and on both sides, rising house atop house, it encroached on the Holy Mount. When the houses were removed, a large plaza was formed in front of the Western Wall and its extension all the way to its southern corner was unveiled (Fig. 82). And, for the first time in almost two millennia, it was realized that the retaining walls extend downward nearly as much as they had

Figure 82

been exposed above what has been considered ground level. As suggested by the hitherto visible portion of the "Wailing Wall," the lower courses were larger, better shaped, and of course much older.

Beckoning with mystery and with a promise of ancient secrets was the extension of the Western Wall to the north.

There Captain Charles Wilson explored in the 1860s an archway (which still bears his name) that led northward to a tunnel-like passage and westward to a series of arched chambers and vaults. The removal of the encroaching dwellings revealed that the current street level lay atop several lower, now-subterranean, levels of ancient structures that included more passages and archways. How far down and how far north did all that extend? That was a puzzle that Israeli archaeologists finally began to tackle.

In the end what they discovered was mind-boggling.

Using data from the Bible, from the Book of Maccabees and from the writings of the Jewish-Roman historian Josephus (and taking into account even a medieval legend that King David knew of a way to ascend the Mount from the west), Israeli archaeologists concluded that Wilson's Arch was the entranceway to what must have been in earlier times an open-air street that ran along the Western Wall, and that the Wall itself extended northward by hundreds of feet. The laborious clearing of the rubble, confirming those assumptions, led to the opening in 1996 of the ''Archaeological Tunnel'' (an event that made headlines for more than one reason).

Extending for about 1,600 feet from its start at Wilson's Arch to its exit on Via Dolorosa (where Jesus walked carrying the cross), the Western Wall Tunnel uncovered and passes through remains of streets, water tunnels, water pools, archways, structures, and marketplaces from Byzantine, Roman, Herodian, Hasmonean, and biblical times. The thrilling and eerie experience of walking through the tunnel, deep below ground level, is akin to being transported in a time machine—backward into the past with every step.

All along the visitor can see—and touch—the actual parts of the western retaining wall from the earliest times. Courses that have been hidden for millennia have been exposed. In the northernmost section of the tunnel, the natural bedrock that slopes upward comes into view. But the greatest surprise, for the visitor as well as for the archaeologists, lies in the more southerly section of the uncovered wall:

There—at the ancient street level but not yet the lowest bottom course—there had been emplaced massive stone

Figure 83

blocks and on top of them four colossal blocks each weighing hundreds of tons!

In that portion of the Western Wall, a 120-foot section is made up of stone blocks that are an extraordinary 11 feet high, about double even the unusually large blocks that form the course below. Only 4 stone blocks make up the section; one of them is a colossal 42 feet long (Fig. 83); another is 40 feet long, and a third over 25 feet long. Soil-penetrating radar and other soundings have indicated that the depths of these stones is 14 feet. The largest of the three is thus a stone mass of about 6,500 cubic feet, weighing 1,200,000 pounds, which is about 600 tons! The somewhat smaller one weighs about 570 tons, and the third one about 355 tons.

These are colossal sizes and weights by any yardstick; the blocks used in the construction of the Great Pyramid in Giza average 2.5 tons each, with the largest weighing about 15 tons. Indeed, the only comparison that comes to mind are the three Trilithons in the great stone platform of Baalbek, that also form a course above somewhat smaller but still-colossal stone blocks (see Fig. 72).

Who could have emplaced such colossal stone blocks, and what for?

Because the stone blocks are indented at their margins, archaeologists assume that they are from the time of the Second Temple (or more specifically the Herodian period, first century B.C.). But even those who hold that the original stone platform was smaller than the present one agree that the central portion that encompasses the Sacred Stone, and to which the massive retaining wall belongs, had existed from the time of the First Temple. At that time the prohibition against using iron tools (that dates back to the time of Joshua) was strictly enforced. All the stone blocks used by Solomon, without exception, were quarried, cut, shaped, and prepared elsewhere, to be brought to the site only for assembly. That this was the case regarding the colossal stone blocks under discussion is additionally clear from the fact that they are not part of the native rock; they lie well above it, and have a somewhat different hue. (In fact, the latest discoveries west of Jerusalem suggest that they might have come from a quarry there). How they were transported and raised to the required level and then pushed into the necessary emplacement remain questions that archaeologists are unable to resolve.

An answer, however, to the question what for? has been offered. The site's chief archaeologist, Dan Bahat, writing in *Biblical Archaeology Review*, stated: "We believe that on the other (eastern) face of the western wall at this point, under the Temple Mount, is an enormous hall; our theory is that the Master Course" (as this section had come to be called) "was installed to support and serve as a counter-force to the vault inside."

The section with the enormous stone blocks lies only slightly to the south of the location of the Sacred Stone. To suggest, as we do, that this massive section was needed for heavy impacts associated with the site's function as a Mission Control Center with its equipment installed on and within the Sacred Rock, seems to be the only plausible explanation after all.

11

A TIME OF PROPHECY

Was the delay in the start of building the Jerusalem Temple due to the reason given—David's shedding of enemy blood in wars and feuds—or was that just an excuse, obscuring another more profound reason?

One finds it odd that as a result of the delay the span of time that had passed from the renewed covenant with Abraham (and on that occasion also with Isaac) on Mount Moriah until the Temple's building began was exactly a thousand years. It is odd because the exile of Marduk had also lasted a thousand years; and that seems to be more than a chance coincidence.

The Bible makes it clear that the timing of the Temple's building was determined by God himself; though the architectural details and even a scale model were ready, it was He who said, through the Prophet Nathan: Not yet, not David, but the next king, Solomon. Likewise, it is evident that it was not Marduk himself who had set the time for ending his exile. Indeed, almost in desperation he cried out: Until When? And that had to mean that the end of his days of exile was unknown to him; it was determined by what might be called Fate—or, if deliberate, by the unseen hand of the Lord of Lords, the God whom the Hebrews called Yahweh.

The notion that a millennium—a thousand years—signifies more than a calendrical event, portending apocalyptic events, is commonly held to have stemmed from a visionary account in the Book of Revelation chapter 20, in which it was prophesied that the "Dragon, that old Serpent, which is the Devil and Satan," shall be bound for a thousand years,

232

cast into a pit and shut therein for a thousand years, unable to deceive the nations "till the thousand years should be fulfilled." It will be then that Gog and Magog shall be engaged in a world war; the First Resurrection of the dead shall occur, and Messianic Times will begin.

Those visionary words, introducing in Christianity the notion (and expectation) of an apocalyptic millennium, were written in the first century A.D. So, although the book names Babylon as the "evil empire," scholars and theologians assume that this was a code name for Rome.

But even so, it is significant that the words in Revelation echo the words of the Prophet Ezekiel (sixth century B.C.) who had a vision of the resurrection of the dead on the Day of the Lord (chapter 37) and the world war of Gog and Magog (chapters 38, 39); it shall take place, Ezekiel stated, "at the End of Years." It was all, he said, foretold by the Prophets of Yahweh in the Olden Days, "who had then prophesied about the Years."

"The Years" to be fulfilled, the count till the "End of Years." It was indeed many centuries before Ezekiel's time that the Bible offered a clue:

> A thousand years,
> in thy eyes,
> are but as one day that has passed.

The statement, in Psalm 90:4, is attributed in the Bible to Moses himself; the application of a thousand years to a divine time measurement thus goes back to at least the time of the Exodus. Indeed, Deuteronomy (7:9) assigns to the duration of God's Covenant with Israel a period of "a thousand generations;" and in a Psalm of David composed when the Ark of the Covenant was brought over to the City of David, the duration of a thousand generations was recalled once more (1 Chronicles 16:15). Other Psalms repeatedly applied the number "thousand" to Yahweh and his wonders; Psalm 68:18 even gave a thousand years as the duration of the Chariot of the *Elohim*.

The Hebrew word for "thousand," *Eleph*, is spelled with the three letters *Aleph* ("A"), *Lamed* ("L") and *Peh* ("P" or "Ph"), which can be read as *Aleph*, meaning the first letter of the alphabet, and numerically "1." Added together the three letters have the numerical value 111 (1+30+80), which can be taken as a triple affirmation of the Oneness of Yahweh and of monotheism, "One" being a code word for "God." Not by chance, the same three letters rearranged (P-L-A) spell *Peleh*—a wonder of wonders, an epithet for God's handiwork, and the mysteries of Heaven and Earth that are beyond human understanding. Those wonders of wonders referred principally to the things created and foretold in the long-ago past; they were also the subject of Daniel's inquiry when he sought to divine the End of Time (12:6).

There thus appear to be wheels within wheels, meanings within meanings, codes within codes in those verses concerning a millennial period: not just the obvious numerical sequential count of passing time, but also a built-in duration of the Covenant, a coded affirmation of monotheism, and a prophecy concerning the millennium and the End of Years.

And, as the Bible makes clear, the thousand years whose count began with the building of the Temple—coinciding with what is now called the last millennium B.C.—was a time of prophecy.

To understand the events and prophecies of that last millennium, one ought to turn the clock back to the preceding millennium, to the nuclear calamity and the assumption of supremacy by Marduk.

The *Lamentation Texts* describing the havoc and desolation that engulfed Sumer and Akkad as the deathly nuclear cloud wafted toward Mesopotamia vividly describe how the Sumerian gods hurriedly abandoned their "cult centers" as the Evil Wind advanced toward them. Some "hid in the mountains," some "escaped to the distant plains." Inanna, leaving her possessions behind, sailed off to Africa in a submersible ship; Enki's spouse Ninki, "flying as a bird," went to the Abzu in Africa while he sought safe haven in the north; Enlil and Ninlil left to an unknown destination, as did the spinster Ninharsag. In Lagash the goddess Bau found herself alone, for Ninurta had been gone since the nuclear blasting; she "wept bitterly for her temple" and lingered on; the result was tragic, for "on that day the storm caught up with her; Bau, as if she were mortal, the storm caught up with her."

The list of fleeing gods goes on and on, until it gets to Ur and its deities. There, as we have already mentioned, Nannar/ Sin refused to believe that his city's fate was sealed. In the lamentation she herself wrote later, his spouse Ningal described how, in spite of the foul smell of the dead whose bodies filled the city they stayed on "and did not flee." Nor did they flee on the night that followed the awesome day. But by morning the two deities, huddled in their ziggurat's subterranean chamber, realized that the city was doomed, and they, too, left.

The nuclear cloud, shifted southward by the winds, spared Babylon; and that was taken as an omen reinforcing the grant of the fifty names to Marduk as an indication of his deserved supremacy. His first step was to carry out his father's suggestion that the Anunnaki themselves build for him his house/temple in Babylon, the E.SAG.IL ("House of Lofty Head"). To that was added in the sacred precinct another temple for the celebration of the New Year and the reading of the revised *Enuma elish*; its name, E.TEMEN.AN.KI ("House of the Foundation Heaven-Earth") was clearly intended to indicate that it had replaced Enlil's DUR.AN.KI ("Bond Heaven-Earth"), which had been at the heart of Nippur when it was Mission Control Center.

Scholars have paid scant attention to the issue of mathematics in the Bible, leaving untackled what should have been a puzzle: Why has the Hebrew Bible adopted completely the decimal system, although Abraham was an *Ibri*—a Sumerian from Nippur—and all the tales in Genesis (as echoed in the Psalms and elsewhere) were based on Sumerian texts? Why was the Sumerian sexagesimal system ("base 60") not at all echoed in the Bible's numerology—a practice that culminated in the concept of a millennium?

One wonders whether Marduk had been cognizant of this issue. He marked his assumption of supremacy by proclaiming a New Age (that of the Ram), by revising the calendar, and by building a new Gateway of the Gods. In those steps one can find evidence also for a new mathematics—a tacit shift from the sexagesimal to the decimal system.

The focal point of those changes was the temple-ziggurat honoring him, that Enki suggested be built by the Anunnaki themselves. Archaeological discoveries of its remains (after repeated rebuildings) as well as the information provided by tablets with precise architectural data, reveal that the ziggurat rose in seven stages, the topmost of which served as the actual residence of Marduk. Planned (as Marduk himself had claimed) "in accordance with the writings of the Upper Heaven," it was a square structure whose base or first stage measured 15 *gar* (about 300 feet) on each side and rising 5.5 *gar* (about 110 feet); atop that there was a second stage, smaller and shorter; and so on, until the whole temple reached a combined height of the same 300 feet as the bottom base. The result was a cube whose circumference equaled 60 *gar* in each of its three dimensions, giving the structure the celestial number 3600 when squared (60×60) and 216,000 when cubed ($60 \times 60 \times 60$). But in that number was hidden a shift to the decimal system, for it represented the zodiacal number 2,160 multiplied by 100.

The four corners of the ziggurat faced precisely to the four cardinal points of the compass. As studies by archaeoastronomers have shown, the staggered height of each of the first six stages was precisely calculated to enable celestial observations at that particular geographic location. The ziggurat was thus intended not only to surpass Enlil's onetime Ekur, but also to take over Nippur's astronomical/calendrical functions.

This was carried out in practice by the institution of a revision of the calendar—a matter of theological prestige as well as of necessity, because the zodiacal shift (from Taurus to Aries) also necessitated an adjustment of one month in the calender if *Nissan* ("The Standard Bearer") was to remain the first month and the month of the spring equinox. To achieve that, Marduk ordered that the last month of the year, Addaru, was to be doubled that year. (The device of doubling Addar seven times within a cycle of nineteen years has been adopted in the Hebrew calendar as a way to periodically realign the lunar and solar years).

As in Mesopotamia, so was the calendar revised in Egypt. Originally devised there by Thoth, whose "secret number" was 52, it divided the year into 52 weeks of 7 days each, resulting in a solar year of only 364 days (an issue prominent in the *Book of Enoch*). Marduk (as Ra) instituted instead a year based on a division into 10: he divided the year into 36 "decans" of ten days each; the resulting 360 days were then followed by five special days, to complete 365.

The New Age ushered in by Marduk was not one of monotheism. Marduk did not declare himself sole god; indeed, he needed the other gods to be present and to hail him as supreme. To that purpose he provided in the sacred precinct of Babylon shrines, small temples and residences for all the other principal gods, and invited them to make their homes therein. There is no indication in any of the texts that any accepted the invitation. In fact, at about the time that the royal dynasty that Marduk had envisioned was finally installed in Babylon circa 1890 B.C., the dispersed gods began to establish their own new domains all around Mesopotamia.

Prominent among them was Elam in the east, with Susa (later the biblical Shushan) as its capital and Ninurta as its "national god." In the west, a kingdom whose capital was called Mari (from the term *Amurru*, the Western One) blossomed out into its own on the western banks of the Euphrates River; its magnificent palaces were decorated with murals showing Ishtar investing the king (Fig. 84), attesting to the high standing of that goddess there. In the mountainous Hatti Land, where the Hittites had already worshiped Enlil's youngest son Adad by his Hittite name Teshub (the Wind/Storm God), a kingdom with imperial strength and aspirations be-

Figure 84

gan to grow. And between the Land of the Hittites and Babylonia there arose a brand-new kingdom—that of *Assyria*, with a pantheon identical to that of Sumer and Akkad, except that the national god was named *Ashur*—the "Seeing One." He combined the powers and identities of both Enlil and Anu, and his depiction as a god within a winged circular object (Fig. 85) dominated Assyrian monuments.

And, in distant Africa, there was Egypt, the Kingdom of the Nile. But there a chaotic period, called by scholars the Second Intermediate Period, removed the country from the international scene until the so-called New Kingdom began circa 1650 B.C.

Scholars are still hard put to explain why the ancient Near East came astir just at that time. The new (17th) dynasty that took control of Egypt was seized with imperial fervor, thrusting into Nubia in the south, Libya in the west, and the lands along the Mediterranean coast to the east. In the Land of the Hittites, a new king sent his army across the barrier of the Taurus Mountains, also along the Mediterranean coast; his successor overran Mari. And in Babylon, a people called Cassites, appearing out of nowhere (actually, from the northeastern mountain region bordering on the Caspian Sea) at-

Figure 85

tacked Babylon and brought the dynasty that started with Hammurabi to an abrupt end.

As each nation made the claim that they went on the warpath in the name and on the orders of their national god, the growing conflicts might well have represented a struggle between the gods through human surrogates. A clue that seems to confirm this is the fact that the theophoric names of Pharaohs of the 18th dynasty dropped the prefix or suffix Ra or Amen in favor of Thoth. The change, that began with Thothmes (sometimes rendered Tuthmosis) I in 1525 B.C., also marked the beginning of the oppression of the Israelites. The reason given by the Pharaoh is enlightening: Launching military expeditions to Naharin, on the Upper Euphrates, he feared that the Israelites would become an internal fifth column. The reason? Naharin was the very area where Harran was located, and where the people were descendants of the Patriarchal relatives.

As much as this explains the given reasons for the oppression of the Israelites, it leaves unexplained why, and what for, did the Egyptians—now venerating Thoth—send armies to conquer distant Harran. It is a puzzle that bears keeping in mind.

The military expeditions on the one hand and the concurrent oppression of the Israelites, peaking with the edict ordering the killing of all Israelite newborn males, reached a climax under Thothmes III, forcing Moses to flee after he

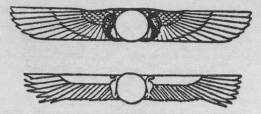

Figure 86

had stood up for his people. He could return to Egypt from the Sinai wilderness only after the death of Thothmes III in 1450 B.C. Seventeen years later, after repeated demands and a series of afflictions wrought by Yahweh upon "Egypt and its gods," the Israelites were let go, and the Exodus began.

Two incidents mentioned in the Bible, and a major change in Egypt, indicate theological repercussions among other peoples as a result of the miracles and wonders attributed to Yahweh in support of his Chosen People.

"And when Jethro, the Priest of Midian, the father-in-law of Moses, heard of all that God had done for Moses and for his people Israel," we read in Genesis chapter 18, he came to the Israelite encampment, and after getting the full story from Moses, Jethro said: "Now I know that Yahweh is greater than all the gods;" and he offered sacrifices to Yahweh. The next incident (described in Numbers chapters 22–24) occurred when the Moabite king retained the seer Bile'am (also rendered Bala'am) to put a curse on the advancing Israelites. But "the spirit of God came upon Bilam," and in a "divine vision" he saw that the House of Jacob was blessed by Yahweh, and that His word cannot be countermanded.

The recognition by a non-Hebrew priest and seer of the powers and supremacy of Yahweh had an unexpected effect on the Egyptian royal family. In 1379 B.C.—just as the Israelites were entering Canaan proper—a new Pharaoh changed his name to Akhenaten—the Aten being represented by the Winged Disc (Fig. 86), moved his capital to a new place, and began to worship one god. It was a short-lived experiment to which the priests of Amen-Ra put a quick end . . . Short-lived, too, was the concept of a universal peace that accompanied the faith in a universal God. In 1296 B.C. the Egyptian army, ever thrusting toward the Harran region, was decisively defeated by the Hittites in the Battle of Kadesh (in what is now Lebanon).

As the Hittites and Egyptians exhausted each other, there was more room for the Assyrians to assert themselves. A series of expansions virtually in all directions culminated in the recapture of Babylon by the Assyrian king Tukulti-Ninurta I—a theophoric name that indicates the religious allegiance—and the seizing of Babylon's god, Marduk. What followed is typical of the polytheism of the time: Far from denigrating the god, he was brought over to the Assyrian capital and, when the time came for the New Year ceremonies, it was Marduk, not Ashur, who featured in the age-old rituals. This "unification of the churches," to coin an expression, failed to stop the increasing exhaustion among the once-imperial kingdoms; and for several ensuing centuries, the two erstwhile powers of Mesopotamia joined Egypt and Hatti Land in a retraction and loss of conquering zeal.

It was undoubtedly that withdrawal of imperial tentacles that made possible the emergence of prosperous city-states in western Asia, especially along the Mediterranean coast, in Asia Minor, even in Arabia. Their rise, however, became a magnet attracting migrants and invaders virtually from all directions. Invaders who came in ships—the "Peoples of the Sea" as the Egyptians called them—tried to settle in Egypt and ended up occupying the coast of Canaan. In Asia Minor, the Greeks launched a thousand ships against Troy. People speaking Indo-European languages pushed their way into Asia Minor and down the Euphrates River. The forerunners of the Persians encroached on Elam. And in Arabia, tribes that became wealthy from controlling trade routes cast their eyes to the fertile lands to their north.

In Canaan, tired of constantly battling city-kings and princedoms all around them, the Israelites sent, through the

High Priest Samuel, a request to Yahweh: Make us one strong nation, give us a king!

The first one was Saul; after him came David, and then the transfer of the capital to Jerusalem.

The Bible lists Men of God during that period, even calls them "prophets" in the strictest sense of the word: "spokesmen" for God. They did deliver divine messages, but they were more in the nature of oracle priests known elsewhere in antiquity.

It was only after the Temple to Yahweh was built, that prophecy—the foretelling of things to come—came into full bloom. And there was nothing akin to the Hebrew Prophets of the Bible, who combined the preaching of justice and morality with the foreseeing of things to come, anywhere else in the ancient world.

The period that is now called in hindsight the first millennium B.C. was actually the *last millennium* in the four-thousand-year-old human story that began with the blossoming out of the Sumerian civilization. The midpoint in this human drama, whose story we have called *The Earth Chronicles*, was the nuclear holocaust, the demise of Sumer and Akkad, and the hand-over of the Sumerian baton to Abraham and his seed. That was the watershed after the first two thousand years. Now, the next half of the story, the last two millennia of what had begun in Sumer and a state visit to Earth by Anu circa 3760 B.C., was also coming to an end.

That, indeed, was the thread connecting the great biblical prophecies at that time: The cycle is coming to a closure, what had been foretold at the Beginning of Years shall be coming true at the End of Years.

Mankind has been given an opportunity to repent, to return to justice and morality, to recognize that there is only one true God, the God even of the *Elohim* themselves. With every word, vision, symbolic act the Prophets tolled the message: Time is running out; great events are about to happen. Yahweh does not seek the death of the evildoers—He seeks their return to righteousness. Man cannot control his Destiny but can control his Fate; Man, kings, nations, can choose the course to follow. But if evil shall prevail, if injustice shall rule human relations, if nation shall continue to take sword to other nations, all shall be judged and doomed on the Day of the Lord.

As the Bible itself acknowledges, it was not a message to a receptive audience. Surrounded by peoples who seemed to know whom they worshiped, the Jews were asked to adhere to strict standards demanded by an unseen God, one whose mere image was unknown. The true prophets of Yahweh had their hands full facing "false prophets" who also claimed to be delivering God's word. Sacrifices and donations to the Temple will atone all sins, the latter said; Yahweh wants not your sacrifices but that you live in justice, Isaiah said. Great calamities will befall the unrighteous, Isaiah said; No, no—Peace is coming, the false prophets said.

To be believed, the biblical Prophets resorted to miracles—just as Moses, instructed by God, had to resort to miracles to obtain the Pharaoh's release of the Israelites, and then to convince the Israelites of Yahweh's almightiness.

The Bible describes in detail the difficulties faced by the Prophet Elijah during the reign (in the northern kingdom, Israel) of Ahab and his Phoenician wife Jezebel, who brought with her the worship of the Canaanite god Ba'al. Having already established his reputation by making a poor woman's flour and oil last and last, and by reviving a boy who had died, Elijah's greatest challenge was a confrontation with the "prophets of Ba'al" on Mount Carmel. Who was a "true prophet" was to be determined, in front of an assembled multitude headed by the king, by the performance of a miracle: A sacrifice on a pile of wood was readied, but no fire was lit—the fire had to come from heaven. And the prophets of Ba'al called in the name of Ba'al from morning till noon, but there was no sound and no answer (1 Kings chapter 18). Mocking them, Elijah said: Perhaps your god is asleep—why don't you call to him much louder? And they did till evetime, but nothing happened. Then Elijah took stones and rebuilt an altar to Yahweh that was in ruins, and arranged the wood and the sacrificial ox on it, and asked the people to pour water on the altar, to make sure there was no hidden fire there. And he called the name of Yahweh, the god of Abraham and Isaac and Jacob; "and a fire of Yahweh decsended upon the sacrifice and it and the altar were burnt down." Convinced of Yahweh's supremacy, the people seized the prophets of Ba'al and killed them all.

After Elijah was taken up to heaven in a fiery chariot, his disciple and successor Elisha also performed miracles to establish his authenticity as a true Prophet of Yahweh. He turned water blood red, revived a dead boy, filled up empty vessels from a minute amount of oil, fed a hundred people with a bit of leftover food, and made a bar of iron float on water.

How believable were such miracles then? We know from the Bible—the tales from the time of Joseph and then the Exodus—as well as from Egyptian texts themselves, such as the *Tales of the Magicians*, that the royal court there had its fill of magicians and soothsayers. Mesopotamia had omen-priests and oracle priests, diviners and seers, and solvers of dreams. Nevertheless, when a scholarly discipline called Bible Criticism became fashionable in the nineteenth century A.D., such tales of miracle-making added to the insistence that everything in the Bible must be supported by independent sources to be believed. Fortunately, among the earliest finds by archaeologists in the nineteenth century was an inscribed stela of the Moabite king Mesha, in which he not only corroborated data regarding Judea in the time of Elijah, but was one of the rare extrabiblical mentions of Yahweh by His full name (Fig. 87). Though this is no corroboration of the miracles themselves, this find—as others later on—went far to authenticate events and personalities recorded in the Bible.

While the texts and artifacts discovered by archaeologists provided corroboration, they also shed light on profound differences between the biblical Prophets and those fortune-tellers of other nations. From the very beginning the Hebrew *Nebi'im*—translated "prophets" but literally meaning

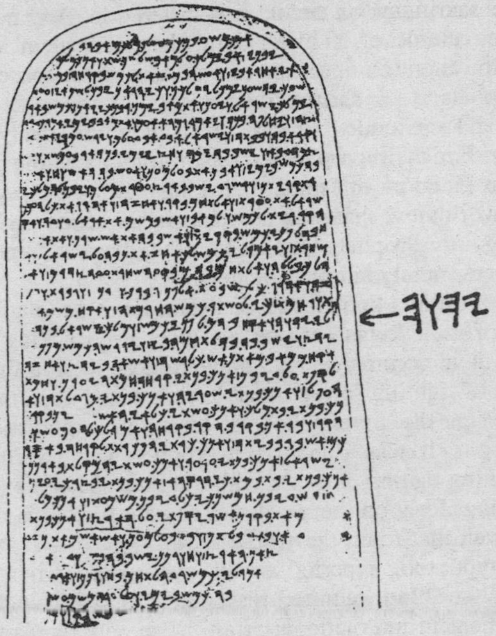

Figure 87

"spokesmen" of God—explained that the magic and foresight were not theirs but God's. The miracles were His, and what was foretold was just what God had ordained. Moreover, rather than acting as court employees, as "Yes-men prophets," they as often as not criticized and admonished the high-and-mighty for personal wrongdoing or wrong national decisions. Even King David was reprimanded for coveting the wife of Uriah the Hittite.

By an odd coincidence—if that is all it was—at the same time that David captured Jerusalem and took the initial steps to establish the House of Yahweh on the Sacred Platform, the decline and decay of what is termed Old Assyria came to an abrupt end and, under a new dynasty, what historians call the Neo-Assyrian period was ushered in. And no sooner was the Temple of Yahweh built, than Jerusalem began to attract the attention of distant rulers. As a direct consequence, its prophets, too, shifted their sights to the international arena, and embedded prophecies concerning the world at large within their prophecies regarding Judea, the split-off northern kingdom of Israel, their kings, and their peoples. It was a worldview that was amazing in its scope and understanding—by Prophets who, before they were summoned by God, were mostly simple villagers.

Such profound knowledge of distant lands and nations, the names of their kings (in one instance, even a king's nickname), their commerce and trade routes, their armies and makeup of fighting forces, must have amazed even the kings of Judea at the time. Once, at least, an explanation was spelled out. It was Hanani the Prophet who (warning the Judean king against a treaty with the Aramaeans) explained to the king: Rely on the word of Yahweh, for "it is the eyes of Yahweh that roam the whole Earth."

In Egypt, too, a period of disunity ended when a new dynasty, the 22nd, reunited the country and relaunched the involvement in international affairs. The new dynasty's first king, the Pharaoh Sheshonq, seized the historical first of being the first foreign ruler of one of the then-great powers to forcefully enter Jerusalem and seize its treasures (without, however, damaging or defiling the Temple). The event, occurring in 928 B.C., is related in 1 Kings 14 and in 2 Chronicles 12; it was all foretold by Yahweh to the Judean king and his noblemen ahead of time by the Prophet Shemaiah; it was also one of the instances where the biblical account has been corroborated by an outside, independent record—in this case by the Pharaoh himself, on the southern walls of the temple of Amen in Karnak.

Assyrian encroachments on the Jewish kingdoms, accurately recorded in the Bible, began with the northern kingdom, Israel. Here again, biblical records are fully corroborated by the annals of the Assyrian kings; Shalmaneser III (858–824 B.C.) even pictured the Israelite king Jehu

Figure 88

bowing down before him, in a scene dominated by the Winged Disc symbol of Nibiru (Fig. 88a). Some decades later another Israelite king warded off an attack by prepaying tribute to the Assyrian king Tiglat-Pileser III (745–727 B.C.). But that only gained some time: in 722 B.C. the Assyrian king Shalmaneser V marched on the northern kingdom, captured its capital Samaria (*Shomron* "Little Sumer"—in Hebrew), and exiled its king and noblemen. Two years later the next Assyrian king, Sargon II (721–705 B.C.) exiled the rest of the people—giving rise to the enigma of the Ten Lost Tribes of Israel—and ended the independent existence of that state.

The Assyrian kings began each record of their numerous military campaigns with the words "On the command of my god Ashur," giving their conquests the aura of religious wars. The conquest and subjugation of Israel was so important that Sargon, recording his victories on the walls of his palace, began the inscription by identifying himself as "Sargon, conqueror of Samaria and of the entire land of Israel." With that achievement, crowning his conquests elsewhere, he wrote, "I aggrandized the territory belonging to Ashur, the king of the gods."

*   *   *

While those calamities, according to the Bible, befell the northern state Israel because its leaders and people failed to heed the Prophets' warnings and admonitions, the kings of Judea to the south were more attentive to the prophetic guidance and, for a while, enjoyed a period of relative peace. But the Assyrians had their eye on Jerusalem and its temple; and for reasons which their annals do not explain, many of their military expeditions started in the Harran area and then extended westward to the Mediterranean coast. Significantly, the annals of the Assyrian kings, describing their conquests and domains in the Harran area, identify by name a city called Nahor and a city called Laban—cities bearing the names of the brother and brother-in-law of Abraham.

The turn of Judea and specifically Jerusalem to come under Assyrian attack was not long in coming. The task of extending the territories and the "command" of the god Ashur to the House of Yahweh fell to Sennacherib, the son of Sargon II and his successor in 704 B.C. Aiming to consolidate his father's conquests and put an end to recurring rebellions in Assyrian provinces, he devoted his third campaign (701 B.C.) to the capture of Judea and Jerusalem.

The events and circumstances of that attempt are extensively recorded both in the Assyrian's annals and in the Bible, making it one of the best documented instances of biblical veracity. It was also an occurrence that showed the veracity of the biblical prophecy, its value as a foretelling guide, and the scope of its geopolitical grasp.

Furthermore, there exists physical evidence—to this very day—corroborating and illustrating an important aspect of those events; so that one can see with one's own eyes how real and true it all was.

As we start relating those events with the words of Sennacherib himself, let it be noticed that here again the campaign against distant Jerusalem began with a detour to "Hatti Land," to the area of Harran, and only then swung all the way westward to the Mediterranean coast, where the first city attacked was Sidon:

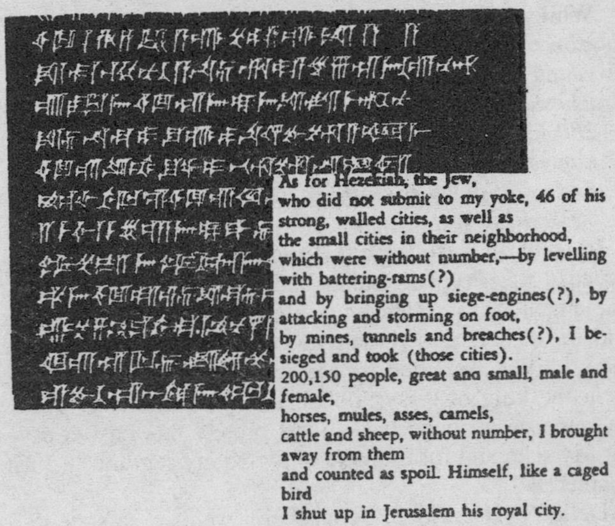

As for Hezekiah, the Jew,
who did not submit to my yoke, 46 of his
strong, walled cities, as well as
the small cities in their neighborhood,
which were without number,—by levelling
with battering-rams(?)
and by bringing up siege-engines(?), by
attacking and storming on foot,
by mines, tunnels and breaches(?), I besieged and took (those cities).
200,150 people, great and small, male and
female,
horses, mules, asses, camels,
cattle and sheep, without number, I brought
away from them
and counted as spoil. Himself, like a caged
bird
I shut up in Jerusalem his royal city.

Figure 88b

In my third campaign I marched against Hatti.
Luli, king of Sidon, whom the terror-inspiring
glamor of my lordship had overwhelmed,
fled far overseas and perished.

The awe-inspiring splendor of the Weapon of Ashur,
my lord, overwhelmed the strong cities of Greater
Sidon . . .
All the kings from Sidon to Arvad, Byblos, Ashdod,
Beth-Ammon, Moab and Adom brought sumptuous
gifts;
the king of Ashkelon I deported to Assyria . . .

The inscription (Fig. 88b) continued:

As for Hezekiah the Judean
who did not submit to my yoke

46 of his strong walled cities
as well as the small cities in their neighborhood
which were without number . . .
I besieged and took them and
200,150 people old and young male and female
horses, mules, camels, asses, cattle and sheep
I brought away from them.

In spite of these losses, Hezekiah remained unyielding—because the Prophet Isaiah had thus prophesied: Fear not the attacker, for Yahweh will impose His spirit on him, and he shall hear a rumor, and will return to his land, and there he will be felled by the sword . . . "Thus sayeth Yahweh: the king of Assyria shall not enter this city! The way he came he shall go back, for I protect this city to save it, for My sake and for the sake of David my servant." (2 Kings chapter 19).

Defied by Hezekiah, Sennacherib went on to state thus in his annals:

In Jerusalem, I made Hezekiah
a prisoner in his royal palace,
like a bird in a cage, surrounding him
with earthworks, molesting those who
left by the city gates.

"I then took away districts of Hezekiah's kingdom and gave them away to the kings of Ashdod and Ekron and Gaza—Philistine city-states—and increased the tribute on Hezekiah," Sennacherib wrote; and then he listed the tribute that Hezekiah "sent to me later in Nineveh."

Almost imperceptibly thus, the annals mention neither the capture of Jerusalem nor the seizing of its king—just the imposition of heavy tribute: gold, silver, precious stones, antimony, cut red stones, furnishings inlaid with ivory, elephant hides "and all kinds of valuable treasure."

The boasting omits telling what had really happened in Jerusalem; the source for the more complete story is the Bible. It records, in 2 Kings chapter 20 and, similarly, in the book of the Prophet Isaiah and in the Book of Chronicles, that "in the fourteenth year of Hezekiah, Sennacherib the king of Assyria came upon all of the fortified cities of Judea and captured them. Then Hezekiah the king of Judea sent word to the king of Assyria, who was in Lachish, saying: I have done wrong; turn back, and whatever you impose on me I shall endure. So the king of Assyria imposed on Hezekiah the king of Judea three hundred bars of silver and thirty bars of gold;" and Hezekiah paid it all, including as an extra tribute the bronze inlays of the temple and palace doors, and handed them over to Sennacherib.

But the king of Assyria reneged on the deal. Instead of retreating back to Assyria, he sent a large force against the Judean capital; and as the Assyrian siege tactic had been, the first thing the attackers did was to seize the city's water reservoirs. The tactic worked elsewhere, but not in Jerusalem. For, *unbeknown to the Assyrians, Hezekiah had a water tunnel dug under the city's walls, diverting the plentiful waters of the Spring of Gihon to the Pool of Silo'am inside the city.* This subterranean secret water tunnel provided the besieged city with fresh water, defying the Assyrians' plans.

Frustrated by the failure of the siege to subdue the city, the Assyrian commander turned to psychological warfare. Speaking in Hebrew so that the common defenders would understand, he pointed out the futility of resistance. None of the other nations' gods could save them; who is this "Yahweh" and why would he do better for Jerusalem? He was a god as fallible as the others . . .

Hearing all that, Hezekiah tore his clothes and put on a mourner's sackcloth, and went to the Temple of Yahweh, and prayed to "Yahweh the God of Israel, who abides upon the Cherubim, the sole God upon all the nations, the maker of the Heaven and the Earth." Assuring him that his prayer was heard, the Prophet reiterated the divine promise: The Assyrian king shall never enter the city; he will return home in failure, and there he will be assassinated.

That night a divine miracle happened, and the first part of the prophecy came true:

> *And it came to pass that night,*
> *that the Angel of Yahweh went forth*
> *and smote in the camp of the Assyrians*
> *a hundred and eighty five thousand.*
> *And at sunrise, lo and behold:*
> *they were all dead corpses.*
> *So Sennacherib, the king of Assyria, departed*
> *and journeyed back and dwelt in Nineveh.*

> *2 Kings 19:35–36*

In a postscript, the Bible made sure to record that the second part of the prophecy had also come true, adding "And Sennacherib went away, and journeyed back to Nineveh. And it was when he was bowing down in his temple to his god Nisrokh, that Adramelekh and Sharezzer struck him down with a sword; and they fled to the land of Ararat. His son Esarhaddon became king in his stead."

The biblical postscript regarding the manner in which Sennacherib died has long puzzled scholars, for the royal Assyrian annals left the king's death a mystery. Only recently did scholars, with the aid of additional archaeological finds, confirm the biblical account: Sennacherib was indeed assassinated (in the year 681 B.C.) by two of his own sons, and the heir to the throne became another, younger son called Esarhaddon.

We, too, can add a postscript to further confirm the veracity of the Bible.

Early in the nineteenth century, archaeologists exploring Jersalem discovered that *the Tunnel of Hezekiah was fact, not myth*: that a subterranean tunnel indeed served as a conduit for a secret supply of water in Jerusalem, cut through the city's native rock under the defensive walls from the time of the Judean kings!

In 1838 the explorer Edward Robinson was the first in modern times to traverse its full length, 1,750 feet. In the

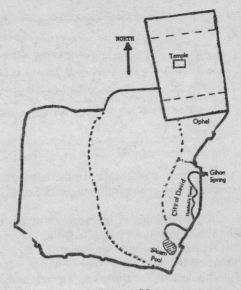

Figure 89

ensuing decades other renowned explorers of ancient Jeru-salem (Charles Warren, Charles Wilson, Claude Conder, Conrad Schick) cleared and examined the tunnel and its var-ious shafts. It indeed connected the water's source at the Spring of Gihon (outside the defensive walls) to the Pool of Silo'am inside the city (Fig. 89). Then, in 1880, playing boys discovered that about midway in the tunnel an inscription had been carved into the wall. The Turkish authorities of the time ordered that the inscribed segment of the wall be ex-cised and brought to Istanbul (the Turkish capital). It was then ascertained that the inscription (Fig. 90), in beautiful ancient Hebrew script current at the time of the Judean kings, commemorated the completion of the tunnel when the tun-nelers of Hezekiah, cutting through the rock from both ends, met at that very spot where the inscription was found.

The inscription (on the piece of rock excised from the

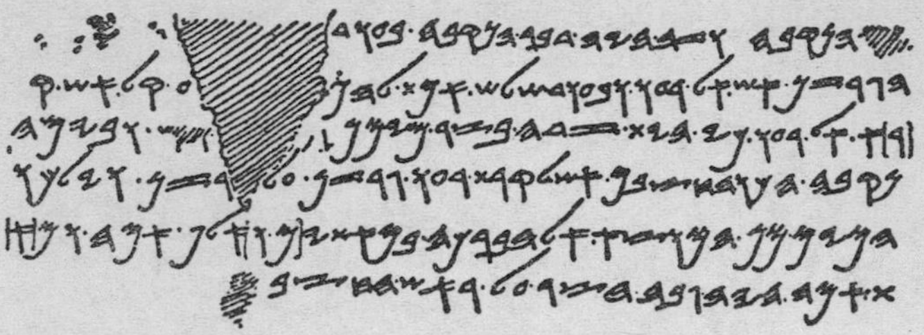

Figure 90

tunnel's wall), which is on display in the Istanbul Archaeological Museum, renders the following account:

> ... the tunnel. And this is the account of the breakthrough. When [the tunnelers lifted] the axe each toward his fellow, and while there were still three cubits to be tunneled [through], the voice of a man was heard calling to his fellow, for there was a crack in the rock on the right ... And on the day of the breakthrough the tunnelers struck each toward his comrade, axe toward axe. And the water started to flow from its source to the pool, a thousand and two hundred cubits; and the height of the rock above the heads of the tunnelers was one hundred cubits.

The accuracy and veracity of the biblical account of the events in Jerusalem extended to the events in faraway Nineveh concerning the succession on the throne of Assyria: It was indeed a bloody affair that pitted sons of Sennacherib against him and ended with the younger son, Esarhaddon (also spelled Asarhaddon), ascending the throne. The bloody events are described in the *Annals of Esarhaddon* (on the artifact known as Prism B), in which he ascribes his choice to kingship over his older brothers as the result of an oracle given to Sennacherib by the gods Shamash and Adad—a choice approved by the great gods of Assyria and Babylon "and all the other gods residing in heaven and on Earth."

The bloody end of Sennacherib was but one act in a raging drama concerning the role and standing of the god Marduk. The Assyrian attempt to bring the Babylonians to heel and in reality annex Babylon by bringing Marduk over to the Assyrian capital did not work, and within decades Marduk was returned to his honored position in Babylon. The texts suggest that a crucial aspect of the god's restoration was the need to celebrate the Akitu festival of the New Year, in which the *Enuma elish* was publicly read and the Resurrection of Marduk was reenacted in a Passion Play, in Babylon and nowhere else. By the time of Tiglat-Pileser III, the king's legitimacy required his humbling himself before Marduk until Marduk "took both my hands in his" (in the king's words).

To cement his choice of Esarhaddon as his successor, Sennacherib had appointed him as Babylon's viceroy (and named himself "King of Sumer and Akkad"). And when he ascended the throne, Esarhaddon took the solemn oath of office "in the presence of the gods of Assyria: Ashur, Sin, Shamash, Nebo, and Marduk." (Ishtar, though not present, was invoked in later annals).

But all those efforts to be religiously inclusive failed to bring stability or peace. As the seventh century B.C. began, ushering in the second half of what, counting forward from the Sumerian start, was the Last Millennium, turmoil seized the great capitals and spread throughout the ancient world.

The biblical Prophets saw it all coming; it was the beginning of the End, they announced in behalf of Yahweh.

In the prophesied scenario of events to come, Jerusalem and its Sacred Platform were to be the focal point of a global catharsis. The divine fury was to manifest itself first against the city and its people, for they had abandoned Yahweh and his commandments. The kings of the great nations were to be the instruments of Yahweh's wrath. But then they, too, each one in his turn, would be judged on the Day of Judgment. "It will be a judgment upon all flesh, for Yahweh has a quarrel with all the nations," the Prophet Jeremiah announced.

Assyria, the Prophet Isaiah quoted Yahweh as saying, was his punishing cane; he foresaw its sweeping down upon many nations, even invading Egypt (a prophecy that did come true); but then Assyria, too, would be judged for its sins. Babylon was to be next, the Prophet Jeremiah said; its king would come upon Jerusalem, but seventy years later (as indeed came to be) Babylon, too, would be brought to heel. The sins of nations great and small, from Egypt and Nubia all the way to distant China (!) were to be judged on the Day of Yahweh.

One by one, the prophecies were fulfilled. Of Egypt the Prophet Isaiah foresaw its occupation by Assyrian forces after a three-year war. The prophecy came true at the hands of Esarhaddon, Sennacherib's successor. What is remarkable, beside the fact of the prophecy's fulfillment, is that before leading his army westward then southward toward Egypt, the Assyrian king made a detour to Harran!

That was in 675 B.C. In the same century, the fate of Assyria itself was sealed. A resurgent Babylon under king Nabupolassar captured the Assyrian capital Nineveh by breaking the river dams to flood the city—just as the Prophet Nahum had foretold (1:8). The year was 612 B.C.

The remnants of the Assyrian army retreated—of all places—to Harran; but there the ultimate instrument of divine judgment made its appearance. It would be, Yahweh told Jeremiah (Jeremiah 5:15–16), "a distant nation . . . a nation whose language thou knowest not:"

> Behold,
> a people cometh from a country in the north,
> a great nation shall be roused
> from the remoteness of the Earth.
> They grasp bows and spears,
> they are cruel, they show no mercy.
> The sound of them is like the roaring sea,
> they ride upon horses,
> arrayed as men of battle.
>
> Jeremiah 6:22–23

The Mesopotamian records of the time speak of the sudden appearance, from the north, of the Umman-Manda—perhaps advance hordes of Scythians from central Asia, perhaps forerunners of the Medes from the highlands of what is now Iran, perhaps a combination of both. In 610 B.C. they captured Harran, where the remnants of the Assyrian army holed up, and gained control of the vital crossroads. In 605 B.C. an Egyptian army headed by the Pharaoh Necho thrust once again—as Thothmes III had attempted before the Exodus—to reach and capture Naharin, on the Upper Euphrates. But a combined force of Babylonians and Umman-Manda, at a crucial battle at Carcemish near Harran, gave Egypt's empire the final coup de grace. It was all as Jeremiah had prophesied concerning haughty Egypt and its king Necho:

> Like a river that riseth and as surging streams
> has been Egypt, [saying]
> I will rise, I will cover the Earth,
> I will wipe out towns and all who dwell therein . . .
>
> But that day,
> the day of Yahweh, Lord of Hosts, shall be,
> a day of retribution,
> in the land of the north, by the Euphrates River . . .
>
> Thus sayeth Yahweh, Lord God of Israel:
> "I have made commandments upon Amen of Thebes,
> and upon Pharaoh, and upon Egypt and its gods
> and its kings—on Pharaoh and all who on him rely:
> Into the hands of those who seek to kill them,
> Into the hands of Nebuchadnezzar king of Babylon
> and into the hands of his subjects
> I shall deliver them."
>
> Jeremiah chapter 46

Assyria was vanquished—the victor has become a victim. Egypt was beaten and its gods disgraced. There was no power left to stand in the way of Babylon—nor for Babylon to act out Yahweh's wrath against Judea, and then meet her own fate.

At the helm of Babylon was now a king of Caesarian ambitions. He was given the throne in recognition of the victory at Carchemish and the royal name Nebuchadnezzar (the second), a theophoric name incorporating the name of Nabu, Marduk's son and spokesman. He lost no time launching military campaigns "by the powers of my lords Nabu and Marduk." In 597 B.C. he sent his forces to Jerusalem, ostensibly only to remove its pro-Egyptian king Jeho'iakim and replace him with his son Jeho'iachin, a mere youth. It was only, it turned out, a test run; for one way or another, he was fated to play out the role Yahweh had assigned to him as the punisher of Jerusalem for the sins of its people; but ultimately, Babylon herself would be judged:

> *This is the word of Yahweh concerning Babylon—*
> *Declare it among the nations,*
> *raise a standard and proclaim,*
> *deny nothing, announce:*
> *'Captured is Babylon,*
> *its Lord is shamed, Marduk is dismayed;*
> *its idols are withered, her fetishes cowered'.*
> *For a nation from the north hath come upon her*
> *from the north;*
> *it will make her land desolate, without dwellers.*
>
> *Jeremiah 50:1–3*

It will be an Earthwide catharsis, in which not only nations but also their gods shall be called to account, Yahweh, the "Lord of Hosts," made clear. But at the end of the catharsis, after the coming of the Day of the Lord, Zion shall be rebuilt and all the nations of the world shall gather to worship Yahweh in Jerusalem.

When all is said and done, the Prophet Isaiah declared, Jerusalem and its rebuilt Temple would be the sole "Light unto the nations." *Jerusalem shall suffer its Fate, but will arise to fulfill its Destiny:*

And it shall come to pass
at the End of Days:
The Mount of the Temple of Yahweh
shall be established ahead of all mountains
and shall be exalted above all hills;
And all the nations shall throng unto it.
And many peoples shall come and say:
'Come ye, let us go up to the Mountain of Yahweh,
to the Temple of the God of Jacob,
that He may teach us of his ways and
that we may follow in His path;
for out of Zion shall come instruction
and the word of God from Jerusalem'.

Isaiah 2:2–3

In those unfolding events and prophecies concerning the great powers, Jerusalem and its Temple, and what is to come in the Last Days, the Prophets in the Holy Land were joined by the Prophet Ezekiel who was shown Divine Visions on the banks of the Khabur River in faraway Harran.

For there, in Harran, the divine and human drama that began when the paths of Marduk and Abraham crossed, was also destined to come to an end—at the very same time that Jerusalem and its Temple were facing Fate.

12

THE GOD WHO RETURNED FROM HEAVEN

Was the crossing of the paths of Marduk and Abraham in Harran just a chance coincidence, or was Harran chosen by the unseen hand of Fate?

It is a nagging question, calling for a divining answer, for the place where Yahweh had chosen Abram for a daring mission and where Marduk made his reappearance after an absence of a thousand years, was later on the place where a series of incredible events—miraculous events, one could well say—began to unfold. They were occurrences of prophetic scope, affecting the course of both human and divine affairs.

The key events, recorded for posterity by eyewitnesses, began and ended with the fulfillment of the biblical prophecies concerning Egypt, Assyria, and Babylon; and they included the departure of a god from his temple and his city, his ascent to the heavens, and his return from the heavens a half century later.

And, for a reason perhaps more metaphysical than geographic or geopolitical, so many of the crucial events of the last two millennia of the count that began when the gods, meeting in council, decided to give Mankind civilization, took place in or around Harran.

We have already mentioned in passing the detour of Esarhaddon to Harran. The details of that pilgrimage were recorded on a tablet that was part of the royal correspondence of Ashurbanipal, Esarhaddon's son and successor. It was when Esarhaddon contemplated an attack on Egypt, he turned northward instead of westward and looked for "the cedarwood temple" in Harran. There "he saw the god Sin leaning on a staff, with two crowns on his head. The god Nusku was standing before him. The father of my majesty the king entered the temple. The god placed a crown upon his head, saying: 'You will go to countries, therein you will conquer!' He departed and conquered Egypt." (Nusku, we know from Sumerian God List, was a member of Sin's entourage).

The invasion of Egypt by Esarhaddon is a historical fact, fully making true Isaiah's prophecy. The details of the detour to Harran additionally serve to confirm the presence there, in 675 B.C., of the god Sin; for it was several decades later that Sin "became angry with the city and its people" and was gone—to the heavens.

Nowadays Harran still stands where it did in the time of Abraham and his family. Outside the city's crumbling walls (walls from Islamic-conquest times) the well where Jacob met Rebecca still flows with water, and in the surrounding plain sheep still graze as they did four millennia ago. In centuries past Harran was a center of learning and literature, where the Greeks after Alexander gained access to the accumulated "Chaldean" knowledge (the writings of Berossus were one of the results) and much later the Moslems and Christians exchanged cultures. But the pride of the place (Fig. 91) was the temple dedicated to the god Sin, in whose ruins written testimony of the miraculous events concerning Nannar/Sin has survived the millennia.

The testimony was not hearsay; it consisted of eyewitness reports. They were not anonymous witnesses, but a woman named Adda-Guppi and her son Nabuna'id. They were not, as happens nowadays, a country sherrif and his mother reporting a UFO sighting in some sparsely inhabited area. She was the High Priestess of the great temple of Sin, a sacred and revered shrine since millennia before her time; her son was the last king of the mightiest empire on Earth in those days, Babylon.

The High Priestess and her son the king recorded the events on stelae—stone columns inscribed in cuneiform

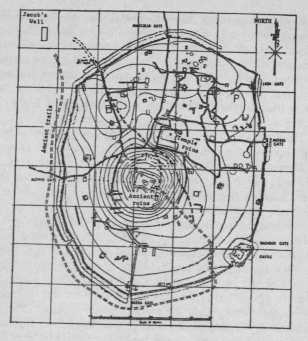

Figure 91

script, accompanied by pictorial depictions. Four of them
have been found this century by archaeologists, and it is believed that the stelae were placed by the king and his mother
each at each corner of the renowned temple to the Moon god
in Harran, the E.HUL.HUL ("Temple of Double Joy"). One
pair of stelae carried the mother's testimony, the other pair
recorded the king's words. It was on the stelae of Adda-
Guppi, the temple's High Priestess, that the departure and
heavenly ascent of the god Sin were recorded; and it was in
the inscriptions of the king, Nabuna'id, that the god's miraculous and unique return was reported. With an evident
sense of history and in the manner of a trained temple official, Adda-Guppi provided in her stelae precise dates for the

astounding events; the dates, linked as was then customary to regnal years of known kings, could thus be—and have been—verified by modern scholars.

In the better-preserved stela, cataloged by scholars as H₁B, Adda-Guppi began her written testimony (in the Akkadian language) thus:

> I am the lady Adda-Guppi,
> mother of Nabuna'id, king of Babylon,
> devotee of the gods Sin, Ningal, Nusku
> and Sadarnunna, my deities,
> to whose godliness I have been pious
> ever since my childhood.

She was born, Adda-Guppi wrote, in the twentieth year of Ashurbanipal, king of Assyria—in the middle of the seventh century B.C. Though in her inscriptions Adda-Guppi does not state her genealogy, other sources suggest that she stemmed from a distinguished lineage. She lived, according to her inscription, through the reigns of several Assyrian and Babylonian kings, reaching the ripe old age of ninety-five when the miraculous events had taken place. Scholars have found her listing of reigns to be in accord with Assyrian and Babylonian annals.

Here then is the record of the first remarkable occurrence, in Adda-Guppi's own words:

> It was in the sixteenth year of Nabupolassar,
> king of Babylon, when Sin, lord of gods,
> became angry with his city and his temple
> and went up to heaven;
> and the city and the people in it
> went to ruin.

The year bears noticing, for events—known from other sources—had taken place at that time, corroborating what Adda-Guppi had recorded. For the year was 610 B.C.—when the defeated Assyrian army retreated to Harran for a las stand.

There are quite a number of issues that call for clarificatio as a result of this statement: Was Sin "angry with the city and its people" because they let the Assyrians in? Did he decide to leave on account of the Assyrians, or the approaching Umman-Manda hordes? How, by what means, did he go up to heaven—and where did he go? To another place on Earth, or away from Earth, a celestial place? The writings of Adda-Guppi gloss over these issues, and for the moment we, too, shall leave the questions hanging.

What the High Priestess does state is that after the departure of Sin "the city and the people in it went to ruin." Some scholars prefer to translate the word in the inscription as "desolate," as better describing what had happened to the once-thriving metropolis, a city whom the Prophet Ezekiel (27:23) listed among the great international trading centers of the time, specializing "in all sorts of things, in blue clothes, and broidered work, and in chests of rich apparel, bound with cords and made of cedar." Indeed, the desolation in the abandoned Harran brings to mind the opening words of the biblical Book of Lamentations about the desolate and desecrated Jerusalem: "How solitary lies the city, once so full of people! Once great among the nations, now become a widow; once queen among the provinces, now become a tributary."

While others fled, Adda-Guppi stayed on. "Daily, without ceasing, by day and night, for months, for years," she went to the abandoned shrines. Mourning, she forsook the dresses of fine wool, took off her jewels, wore neither silver nor gold, relinquished perfumes and sweet-smelling oils. As a ghost roaming the empty shrines, "in a torn garment I was clothed, I came and went noiselessly," she wrote.

Then, in the abandoned sacred precinct, she discovered a robe that had once belonged to Sin. It must have been a magnificent garment, in the manner of robes worn at the time by various deities, as depicted on monuments from Mesopotamia (see Fig. 28). To the despondent High Priestess, the find seemed an omen from the god; it was as though he had suddenly given her a physical presence of himself. She could not take her eyes off the sacred garb, daring not to touch it except by "taking hold of its hem." As if the god himself was there to listen, she prostrated herself and "in prayer and humility" uttered the following vow:

> *If you would return to your city,*
> *all the Black-Headed people*
> *would worship your divinity!*

"Black-Headed people" was a term used by the Sumerians to describe themselves; and the employment of the term by the High Priestess in Harran was highly unusual. Sumer, as a political-religious entity, had ceased to exist almost 1,500 years before the time of Adda-Guppi, when the land and its capital, the city of Ur, fell victim to a deadly nuclear cloud in 2024 B.C. Sumer, by Adda-Guppi's time, was just a hallowed memory, its erstwhile capital Ur a place of crumbling ruins, its people (the "Black-Headed" people) dispersed to many lands. How then could a High Priestess in Harran offer to her god Sin to restore him to lordship in distant Ur, and to make him again the god of all the Sumerians, wherever they had dispersed?

It was a true vision of the Return of the Exiles and a Restoration of a god in his ancient cult center worthy of biblical prophecies. To achieve that, Adda-Guppi proposed her god a deal: If he would return and then use his authority and divine powers to make her son Nabuna'id the next imperial king, reigning in Babylon over both the Babylonian and Assyrian domains—Nabuna'id would restore the temple of Sin in Ur and would reinstate the worship of Sin in all the lands where the Black-Headed people dwelt!

The Moon god liked the idea. "Sin, lord of the gods of Heaven and Earth, for my good doings looked upon me with a smile; he heard my prayers, he accepted my vow. The wrath of his heart calmed; toward Ehulhul, the temple of Sin in Harran, the divine residence in which his heart rejoiced, he became reconciled; and he had a change of heart.''

The smiling god, Adda-Guppi wrote on in her inscription accepted the deal:

> *Sin, lord of the gods,*
> *looked with favor upon my words.*
> *Nabuna'id, my only son,*
> *issue of my womb,*
> *to the kingship he called—*
> *the kingship of Sumer and Akkad.*
> *All the lands from the border of Egypt,*
> *from the Upper Sea to the Lower Sea,*
> *in his hands he entrusted.*

Grateful and overwhelmed, Adda-Guppi raised her hands and "reverently, with imploration" thanked the god for "pronouncing the name of Nabuna'id, calling him to kingship." Then she implored the god to assure the success of Nabuna'id—to persuade the other great gods to be at Nabuna'id's side as he battled the enemies, to enable him to fulfill the vow to rebuild the Ehulhul temple and restore Harran to its greatness.

In a postscript added to the inscriptions when Adda-Guppi, aged 104, was on her deathbed (or recording her words right after she had passed on), the text reported that both sides kept their bargain: "I myself saw it fulfilled;" Sin "honored his word which he spoke to me," causing Nabuna'id to become king of a new Sumer and Akkad (in 555 B.C.); and Nabuna'id kept the vow to restore the Ehulhul temple in Harran, "perfected its structure." He renewed the worship of Sin and his spouse Ningal—"all the forgotten rites he made anew." And the divine couple, accompanied by the divine emissary Nusku and his consort (?) Sadarnunna, returned into the Ehulhul temple in a solemn and ceremonial procession.

The duplicate stela's inscription contains nineteen additional lines undoubtedly added by Adda-Guppi's son. In the ninth year of Nabuna'id—in 546 B.C.—"the Fate of herself carried her off. Nabuna'id, king of Babylon, her son, issue of her womb, entombed her corpse, wrapped in [royal] robes and pure white linen. He adorned her body with splendid ornaments of gold set with beautiful precious stones. With sweet oils he anointed her body; and laid it to rest in a secret place.''

The mourning for the king's mother was widespread. ''People from Babylon and Borsippa, dwellers of far regions, kings, princes, and governors came from the border of Egypt on the Upper Sea unto the Lower Sea''—from the Mediterranean to the Persian Gulf. The mourning, which included casting ashes upon the head, weeping, and self-inflicted cuts, lasted seven days.

Before we turn to the inscriptions of Nabuna'id and their miracle-filled tales, one must stop to wonder how—if what Adda-Guppi had recorded was true—she managed to communicate with a deity that by her own statement was no longer in the temple or in the city—gone and ascended to heaven, in fact.

The first part, that of Adda-Guppi addressing her god, is easy: she prayed, addressing her prayers to him. Prayer as a way of laying before the deity one's fears and worries, asking for health or good fortune or long life, even seeking guidance for the right choices between alternatives, is still with us. From the time when writing began in Sumer, prayers and appeals to the gods were recorded. Indeed, prayer as a means of communicating with one's deity probably preceded the written word and, according to the Bible, began when the first humans became Homo sapiens: It was when Enosh (''*Homo sapiens* Man''), the grandson of Adam and Eve, was born, ''that it was begun to call the name of God'' (Genesis 4:26).

Touching the hem of the god's robe, prostrating herself, with great humility Adda-Guppi prayed to Sin. She did so day after day, until he heard her prayers and responded.

Now comes the more tricky part—how did Sin respond, how could his words or message reach the High Priestess?

The inscription itself provides the answer: the god's response came to her in a dream. As she passed out, perhaps in a trancelike sleep, the god appeared to her in a dream:

> *In the dream*
> *Sin, lord of the gods,*
> *laid his two hands on me.*
> *He spoke to me, thus:*
> *"On account of you*
> *the gods will return to inhabit Harran.*
> *I will entrust your son, Nabuna'id,*
> *with the divine residences in Harran.*
> *He shall rebuild the Ehulhul,*
> *shall perfect its structure;*
> *he will restore Harran and make her*
> *more perfect than it was before."*

Such a manner of communication, directed from a deity to a human, was far from being unusual; indeed, it was the one mostly employed. Throughout the ancient world kings and priests, patriarchs and prophets received the divine word through the medium of dreams. They could be oracle dreams or omen ones, sometimes with words only heard, sometimes including visions. In fact, the Bible itself quotes Yahweh telling the sister and brother of Moses during the Exodus: "If there be a prophet among you, I the Lord will make myself known to him in a vision and will speak to him in a dream."

Nabuna'id also reported divine communications received by means of dreams. But his inscriptions reported much more: a unique event and an uncommon theophany. His two stelae (referred to by scholars as H_2A and H_2B) are adorned at their tops with a depiction of the king holding an unusual staff and facing the symbols of three celestial bodies, the planetary gods that he venerated (Fig. 92). The long inscription below begins right off with the great miracle and its uniqueness:

Figure 92

This is the great miracle of Sin
that has by gods and goddesses
not happened to the land,
since days of old unknown;
That the people of the Land
had neither seen nor found written
on tablets since days of old:
That divine Sin,
Lord of gods and goddesses,
residing in the heavens,
has come down from the heavens—
in full view of Nabuna'id,
king of Babylon.

The claim that this was a unique miracle was not unjustified, for the event entailed both a return of a deity and a theophany—two aspects of divine interaction with humans that, as the inscription cautiously qualifies, were not unknown in the Days of Old. Whether Nabuna'id (whom some scholars have nicknamed "the first archaeologist" on account of his penchant for uncovering and digging up the ruins of earlier sites) had qualified his statement just to be on the safe side, or whether he was actually familiar, through olden tablets, with such events that had indeed taken place far away and long ago, we do not know; but the fact is that such events did happen.

Thus, in the turbulent times that ended with the demise of the Sumerian empire circa 2000 B.C., the god Enlil, who was away somewhere else, hurried back to Sumer when he was notified that his city, Nippur, was in danger. According to an inscription by the Sumerian king Shu-Sin, Enlil returned "flying from horizon to horizon; from south to north he traveled; through the skies, over Earth, he hurried."

That Return, however, was sudden, unannounced, and not part of a theophany.

Some five hundred years later—still almost a thousand years before the return and theophany by Sin—the greatest theophany on record took place in the Sinai peninsula, during the Israelite Exodus from Egypt. Notified in advance and told how to prepare for the event, the Children of Israel—all 600,000 of them—witnessed the Lord descending upon Mount Sinai. The Bible stresses that it was done "in full sight of all the people" (Exodus 19:11). But that great theophany was not a return.

Such divine comings and goings, including the ascent and descent of Sin to and from the heavens, imply that the Great Anunnaki possessed the required flying vehicles—and indeed they did. Yahweh landed on Mount Sinai in an object that the Bible called *Kabod* that had the appearance of a "devouring fire" (Exodus 24:11); the Prophet Ezekiel described the *Kabod* (usually translated "glory" but which literally means "the heavy thing") as a luminous and radiating vehicle equipped with wheels within wheels. He might have had in mind something comparable to the circular chariot in which the Assyrian god Ashur was depicted (Fig. 85). Ninurta possessed the *Imdugud*, the "Divine Black Bird"; and Marduk had a special housing built in his sacred precinct in Babylon for his "Supreme Traveler"; it was probably the same vehicle that the Egyptian called the Celestial Boat of Ra.

What about Sin and his celestial comings and goings?

That he indeed possessed such a flying vehicle—an essential requirement for the heavenward departure and return reported in the Harran inscriptions—is attested by many hymns to him. A Sumerian one, describing Sin flying over his beloved city Ur, even referred to the god's Boat of Heaven as his "glory":

> *Father Nannar, Lord of Ur*
> *Whose glory is the sacred Boat of Heaven . . .*
> *When in the Boat of Heaven thou ascendeth,*
> *thou art glorious.*
> *Enlil hath adorned thy hand with a scepter,*
> *everlasting when over Ur*
> *in the Sacred Boat thou mountest.*

While no depiction of the Moon god's "Boat of Heaven" has so far been identified, a possible depiction does exist. Lying astride a major route linking East and West across the Jordan River was Jericho, one of the oldest known cities. The Bible (and other ancient texts) refer to it as the City of the Moon god—which is what the biblical name, *Yeriho*, means. It was there that the Prophet Elijah (9th century B.C.) was told by the biblical God to go across the Jordan River to be taken up, heavenward, in a fiery chariot. It was, as described in 2 Kings chapter 2, not a chance event, but a prearranged appointment. Starting his final journey from a place called Gilgal, the Prophet was accompanied by his aide Elisha and a group of disciples. And when they reached Jericho, the disciples inquired of Elisha: "Do you know that the Lord will take your master away today?'' And Elisha, acknowledging that, admonished them to keep quiet.

When they reached the Jordan River, Elijah insisted that the others stay behind. Fifty of the disciples advanced to the river's edge and stopped; but Elisha would not depart. So ''Elijah took his mantle and, rolling it up, struck the water, and it divided to the right and left, and the two of them crossed over on dry land.'' Then, on the other side of the Jordan,

> *A fiery chariot with fiery horses*
> *suddenly appeared*
> *and separated them one from the other;*
> *and Elijah went up to heaven*
> *in a whirlwind.*

In the 1920s an archaeological expedition sent by the Vatican began excavations at a site in Jordan called Tell Ghassul, ''Mound of the Messenger.'' Its antiquity extended back millennia, and some of the oldest dwellings in the ancient Near East were unearthed there. On some of the collapsed walls the archaeologists discovered beautiful and unusual murals painted in a variety of colors. One depicted a ''star'' that looked more like a compass pointing to the major cardinal points and their subdivisions; another showed a seated deity receiving a ritual procession. Other murals depicted black bulbous objects with eyelike openings and extended legs (Fig. 93); the latter could well have been the kind of ''fiery chariot'' that carried Elijah heavenward. Indeed, the place could well have been the very site of Elijah's ascent: standing there, atop the mound, one can see the Jordan River not far away and beyond it, shimmering in the distance, the city of Jericho.

According to Jewish tradition, the Prophet Elijah will return someday to announce the Messianic Time.

That Adda-Guppi and her son Nabuna'id thought that such a time had indeed arrived, signaled and signified by the Re-

Figure 93

turn of the Moon god, is evident. They expected their Messianic Time to usher in an era of peace and prosperity, a new era that would begin with the rebuilding and rededication of the Temple of Harran.

That similar prophetic visions had taken place at about *the same time* regarding the God and the Temple of Jerusalem is, on the other hand, hardly realized. But that, in fact, was the subject of the prophecies of Ezekiel—that began ''when the heavens opened'' and he saw the radiating celestial chariot coming in a whirlwind.

The chronology provided in the Harran inscriptions, as verified by scholars from Assyrian and Babylonian annals, indicates that Adda-Guppi was born circa 650 B.C.; that Sin departed from his temple in Harran in 610 B.C.—and returned in 556 B.C. That was the exact same period when Ezekiel, who had been a priest in Jerusalem, was called to prophecy when he was among the Judean exiles in northern Mesopotamia. We are provided by him with an exact date: It was on the fifth day of the fourth month in the fifth year of the exile of the Judean king Jeho'iachin, ''when I was among the exiles on the banks of the river Khebar that the heavens opened up and I saw divine visions,'' Ezekiel wrote right at the beginning of his prophecies. The time was 592 B.C.!

The Khebar (or Khabur, as it is now known) River is one of the tributaries of the great Euphrates River that begins its flow in the mountains of today's eastern Turkey. Not too far to the east of the Khabur River is another important tributary of the Euphrates, the River Balikh; and it is on the shores of the Balikh that Harran has been situated for millennia.

Ezekiel found himself so far away from Jerusalem, on the banks of a river in Upper Mesopotamia, at the edge of Hittite territory ("Hattiland" in cuneiform records), because he was one of several thousand noblemen, priests, and other leaders of Judea who were captured and taken into exile by Nebuchadnezzar, the Babylonian king who overran Jerusalem in 597 B.C.

Those tragic events are detailed in the second book of Kings, mainly 24:8–12. Remarkably, a Babylonian clay tablet (part of the series known as *The Babylonian Chronicles*) recorded the very same events, with matching dates.

Remarkably too, this Babylonian expedition—like the earlier one by Esarhaddon—was also launched from a starting point near Harran!

The Babylonian inscription details the capture of Jerusalem, the seizing of its king, his replacement on the throne of Judea by another king of Nebuchadnezzar's choice, and the exiling—"sending off to Babylon"—of the captured king and the land's leaders. It was thus that the priest Ezekiel found himself on the banks of the Khabur River in the province of Harran.

For a while—apparently for the first five years—the exiles believed that the calamities that had befallen their city and temple and themselves were a temporary setback. Though the Judean king Jeho'iachin was held in captivity, he was alive. Though the Temple's treasures were carried off to Babylon as booty, the Temple was still intact; and the majority of the people still remained in their land. The exiles, keeping in touch with Jerusalem by messengers, had high hopes that one day Jeho'iachin would be reinstated and the Temple restored to its sacred glory.

But no sooner had Ezekiel been called to prophecy, in the

fifth year of exile (592 B.C.), than the Lord God instructed him to announce to the people that the exile and the sacking of Jerusalem and its Temple were not the end of the ordeal. It was only meant as a warning to the people to mend their ways—behave with justice toward each other, and worship Yahweh according to the Commandments. But, said Yahweh to Ezekiel, the people did not mend their ways; rather, they turned to the worship of "alien gods." Therefore, said the Lord God, Jerusalem shall be attacked again, and this time it shall be totally destroyed, temple and all.

The instrument of his wrath, Yahweh said, would again be the king of Babylon. It is an established and known historical fact that in 587 B.C. Nebuchadnezzar, distrusting the king he himself had set on the Judean throne, again besieged Jerusalem. This time, in 586 B.C., the captured city was burned and left in ruins; so was the Temple of Yahweh that Solomon had built half a millennium earlier.

This much is indeed known. But what is hardly known is the reason why the warning was not heeded by the people and their remaining leaders in Jerusalem. It was their belief that *"Yahweh has left the Earth!"*

Accorded what would these days he deemed "remote vision," Ezekiel was shown first the Elders of Jerusalem behind their closed doors, then taken on a visionary tour of the city's streets. There was a complete breakdown of justice and religious observances, for the word that got out was

Yahweh sees us no more—
Yahweh has left the Earth!

It was in 610 B.C., according to the Harran inscriptions, that "Sin, lord of gods, became angry with his city and his temple and went up to heaven." It was in 597 B.C.—just over a decade later—that Yahweh became angry with Jerusalem his city and its people, and let the uncircumcised Nebuchadnezzar—a king by the grace of Marduk—enter, loot and destroy the Temple of Yahweh.

And the people cried out: "God has left the Earth!"

And they knew not when, or if ever, He would return.

EPILOGUE

His mother's great expectations for Nabuna'id, as a reuniter of Sumer and Akkad and restorer of the glorious Olden Days, did not prepare the new king for the turmoil that he soon faced. He might have expected military challenges; he did not anticipate the religious fervor with which his domains were seized.

No sooner was he on the royal throne in Babylon, under a deal between his mother and Sin, than he realized that Marduk—once removed and since returned to Babylon—had to be appeased and given his due. In a series of true or pretended omen-dreams, Nabuna'id reported obtaining the blessing of Marduk (and Nabu) not only to his kingship, but also to the promised rebuilding of Sin's temple in Harran.

To leave no doubt about the importance of those dream-messages, the king reported that Marduk specifically inquired of him whether he had seen the *"Great Star, the planet of Marduk"*—a direct reference to Nibiru—and what other planets were in conjunction with it. When the king reported that they were the "god 30" (the Moon, Sin's celestial counterpart) and the "god 15" (Ishtar and her counterpart Venus), he was told: "There are no evil portents in the conjunction."

But neither the people of Harran nor the people of Babylon were happy with this "co-regnum" of the gods, nor were the followers of Ishtar "and the other gods." Sin, whose temple in Harran was eventually restored, demanded that his great temple in Ur should also become again a center of worship. Ishtar complained that her golden cela in Uruk (Erech) must be reconstructed and that she be given again a chariot drawn by seven lions. And, as one reads between the lines of the king's inscription, he was getting fed up with that tug and pull by multiple gods and their priesthoods.

In a text titled by scholars *Nabuna'id and the Clergy of Babylon* (on a tablet now in the British Museum), the priests of Marduk presented a charge sheet, a list of accusations against Nabuna'id; they ran from civil matters ("law and order are not promulgated by him") through economic neglect ("the farmers are corrupted," "the trader's roads are blocked") and unsuccessful wars ("the nobles are killed in war") to the most serious charges: religious sacrilege—

> *He made an image of a god*
> *which nobody had seen before in the land;*
> *He placed it in the temple,*
> *raised it upon a pedestal . . .*
> *With lapis lazuli he adorned it,*
> *crowned it with a tiara . . .*

It was a statue of a strange deity—never seen before, the priests stressed—with "hair reaching down to the pedestal." It was so unusual or unseemly that not even Enki and Ninmah could have conceived it, so strange that "not even the learned Adapa knows his name." To make matters worse, two unusual beasts were sculpted as its guardians: one representing the Deluge-Demon and the other a Wild Bull. To add insult to sacrilege, the king placed this abomination in the Esagil temple of Marduk, and announced that the *Akitu* (New Year) festival, which was central to the equating of Marduk with the celestial Nibiru, would no longer be celebrated.

The priests announced for all to hear that "the protective deity of Nabuna'id became hostile to him," that "the former favorite of the gods was now fated to misfortune." And so Nabuna'id announced that he was leaving Babylon "on an expedition to a distant region." He named his son Bel-sharuzur ("Bel/Marduk protects the king"—the Belshazzar of the Book of Daniel) as regent.

His destination was Arabia, and his entourage included, as the various inscriptions attest, Jews from among the Judean exiles. His principal base was at a city called Teima (a name encountered in the Bible) and he established six settlements for his followers; five of them were listed, a thousand years later, by Islamic sources as Jewish towns. Some believe that Nabuna'id was seeking the seclusion of the desert to contemplate monotheism; a text fragment discovered among the Dead Sea scrolls in Qumran reports that Nabuna'id was smitten with an "unpleasant skin disease" in Teima, and was cured only after "a Jew told him to give honor to the God Most High." The bulk of the evidence suggests, however, that he was propagating the worship of Sin, the Moon god symbolized by the crescent—a symbol adopted in time by the Arabian worshipers of Allah.

Whatever the religious beliefs Nabuna'id was captivated by, they were anathema to the priests in Babylon. And so, when the Achaemenid rulers of Persia absorbed the kingdom of Medea and expanded into Mesopotamia, Cyrus the king was welcomed in Babylon not as a conqueror but as a liberator. Wisely, he rushed to the Esagil temple as soon as he entered the city and "held the hands of Marduk by both hands."

The year was 539 B.C.; it marked the prophesied end of Babylonian independent existence.

One of his first acts was to issue a proclamation permitting the Jewish exiles to return to Judea and rebuild the Temple in Jerusalem. The edict, recorded on the Cylinder of Cyrus that is now kept in the British Museum, corroborates the Biblical report, according to which Cyrus "was charged to do so by Yahweh, the God of Heaven."

The rebuilding of the Temple, under the leadership of Ezra and Nehemiah, was completed in 516 B.C.—seventy years after its destruction, as had been prophesied by Jeremiah.

*   *   *

The story of Babylon's end is told in the Bible in one of its most enigmatic books, the Book of Daniel. Introducing Daniel as one of the Judean exiles taken into Babylonian captivity, it relates how he was selected, with three other friends, to serve in the court of Nebuchadnezzar and how (as Joseph in Egypt) he was elevated to high office after solving the king's omen-dreams about future events.

The book then moves to events at the time of Belshazzar, when, during a great banquet, a hand floating by itself appeared and wrote on the wall MENE MENE TEKEL UPHARSIN. Not one of the king's seers and wizards could decipher the inscription. As a last resort, Daniel—now long retired—was called in. And Daniel explained the meaning to the Babylonian king: God has numbered the days of your kingdom; you have been weighed and found wanting; your kingdom will come to an end, divided between the Medes and the Persians.

After that Daniel himself began to have omen-dreams and see visions of the future in which the "Ancient of Days" and his archangels played key roles. Baffled by his own dreams and visions, Daniel asked the angels for explanations. In each instance they turned out to be predictions of future events that went beyond the fall of Babylon, even beyond the fulfillment of the seventy-year prophecy of the rebuilding of the Temple. The rise and fall of the Persian Empire was predicted, the coming of the Greeks under Alexander, the split of his domains after his death, and what followed.

Though many modern scholars—but not Jewish sages or the Fathers of the Christian Church—take those prophecies (only accurate in part) as hindsight, indicating a much later author (or even several authors), the central point of the dreams, visions, and omens experienced by Daniel is a preoccupation with the question: *When?* When will be the final kingdom, the only one that will survive and last?

It will be one that only the followers of the God Most High, the "Ancient of Days," will live to see (even the dead among them, who will rise). But over and over again, Daniel kept asking the angels: When?

In one instance the angel responded that a phase in the future events, a time when an unholy king shall try to "change the times and the laws," will last "a time, times, and half a time;" only after that will "the kingdoms under heaven be given to the people, the holy ones of the Most High."

Another time the revealing angel said: "Seventy weeks of years have been decreed for your people and your city until the measure of transgression is filled and prophetic vision ratified."

One more time a divine emissary was asked by Daniel: "How long until the end of these awful things?" He got again the enigmatic answer: The fulfillment of all the prophesied things shall come after "a time, times and half a time."

"I heard and did not understand," Daniel wrote. "So I said, my Lord, what will be the outcome of these things?" Speaking still in codes, the divine being answered, "From the time the regular offering is abolished and an appalling abomination is set up it will be a thousand and two hundred and ninety days. Happy is the one who waits and reaches one thousand three hundred and thirty-five days."

As Daniel stood puzzled, the Angel of God added:

> *You, Daniel, shall rest and arise*
> *to your destiny at the End of Days . . .*
> *But keep the words secret,*
> *and seal the book until the End of Time.*

At the End of Time, when the nations of Earth shall gather in Jerusalem, they shall all speak "in a clear language," stated the Prophet Zephaniah (whose very name meant "By Yahweh Encoded")—there will no longer be a need for confounded languages and letters to be read backward and hidden encodings.

And, as Daniel, we are still asking: When?

INDEX

296 Index